J.W. Gar

CW00796887

MUSIC IN THE AIR

To Jessica

whose part in this story, and
whose happy influence over the
shaping of the years is not
given due acknowledgement in
these pages.

MUSIC IN THE AIR

Clifton Helliwell

TABB HOUSE

First published 1989

Tabb House, 7 Church Street, Padstow, Cornwall, PL28 8BG

ISBN 0 907018 64 5

Typeset by St. George Typesetting, Redruth, Cornwall

Printed by Bookcraft (Bath) Ltd., Midsomer Norton, Bath

FOREWORD

TO look back over the years is for most of us a temptation hardly to be resisted. When the time comes for the past to hold so much more than can be expected of the future, that is natural enough. For some, the urge to record the events of that lifetime, to recount the joys and sorrows, its triumphs and failures, is almost equally compelling. Whether or not in my case there will be anything of significance to be discovered can only be judged when the work is done. That must be left to the reader, should he be kind enough to stay with me as far as the last page.

This attempt to capture his interest may perhaps be justified by the fact that my profession is one about which, in some quarters at least, not a great deal is known or understood. There have been occasions on which some new acquaintance has kindly enquired about my occupation. The reply, "I am a musician," has often created perplexity and, worse, has produced an embarrassed silence which has effectively brought our exchange of small talk to an end. Perhaps the questioner wondered whether such an activity could be considered entirely respectable. But things have changed, even in my lifetime. Happily, the pursuit of music has achieved a measure of recognition formerly denied to it. Hardly ever now is one met by the supplementary enquiry: "Yes, but what do you do in the daytime?"

I would like to think that this will be a true and faithful record though memory is sometimes fickle, often unreliable and always selective. That is one hazard – and there is another. It is generally supposed that advancing years bring serenity and a fresh clarity of vision. But they also bring a new sense of perspective which can deprive remembered experience of the drama with which it was once surrounded. The edges of feeling can be dulled by time and as Sir Arthur Bliss has so acutely observed: 'What is called the serenity of age is only perhaps a euphemism for the fading power to feel the sudden shock of joy and sorrow.'

Aware of the difficulties and the dangers, one can but try, if only to make some grateful acknowledgement of all the good things life has to offer.

CHAPTER 1

An upright of unfriendly aspect

THE street was short and narrow, bordered by tiny houses, their doorsteps gleaming proudly white on even the greyest day. Beyond, disappointingly visible above the chimney-pots, stood the cotton mill, ugly, graceless and impersonal, a gaunt cube of Lancashire red brick which dominated both the houses and the lives of those who lived in them. The first sound I can remember, the early morning staccato tramp of clogs over the cobblestones beneath my window, rose to its climax as the street was quickly filled by men and women answering the raucous siren-summons of the mill. For most of the year their day began and ended in darkness. The sun rarely filtered through the factory windows, nor could it penetrate the pall of smoke over the town. They were long days, hours upon hours of monotony and repetition amid the ceaseless clatter of machines which never for a moment came to rest.

But at five in the afternoon the summit of the day arrived. Once again the siren sounded, its note more welcome and more musical; work was at an end, the factory gates opened to the world and a thousand hands trooped cheerfully homeward, the men grimy in their overalls, the women clutching the inimitable Lancashire shawl over head and shoulders. Now, along the street, the clogs had a more optimistic ring. After all, work was not everything and to those who had so marked a capacity for enjoying themselves life had plenty to offer.

There were the pigeon fanciers. Just the thought of a roughly-made coop in a dingy backyard could bring to their eyes a gleam of enthusiasm and promise. The long, cold

1

wait under grey skies was a small price to pay for the thrill of excitement when a homecoming bird was sighted.

And there were many for whom the fortunes or misfortunes of a favourite football team mattered more than anything else in the world. The outcome of a Manchester United or better still, a Bolton Wanderers match, was easily enough to provide a talking point for a whole week.

No day was so rich, so full as a Saturday, the stalls set up in the market place, their hissing flares ready to be lit overhead for the evening. Here was the focal point of the town, where anything and everything could be found and bought against a background of that banter which is the distilled essence of Lancashire wit and humour. A blue serge suit? . . . A plate of tripe and onions as a change from black puddings? . . . No matter what was needed, the market was the place for it. Overall, an infinite number of pungent aromas mingled with the sweet, acrid smell of cough-drops made in the factory nearby.

Here was gaiety and laughter, warmth, kindliness, and above all, the immense vitality of Lancashire folk. For a great many, music was important. On Saturday evenings there were few empty seats for the concert in Bolton's Victoria Hall, and Sunday's music in Church or Chapel, especially the choir singing, was something to be widely shared and enjoyed. No Christmas was complete without its *Messiah*, and no Easter could be properly celebrated without a performance of Stainer's *Crucifixion*. Beyond all this, there was the Hallé Orchestra, only a few miles away in Manchester and near enough to generate inordinate pride. This was their very own orchestra and the name of Sir Hamilton Harty was revered. How they loved to tell the story, which they had surely invented as a reflection of that pride, of Sir Thomas Beecham attempting quite unsuccessfully to reserve a room at Manchester's Midland Hotel. None was available. Vigorously, Sir Thomas protested, announcing his identity, only to be told: "Sir Thomas, even if you were Sir Hamilton Harty, there still wouldn't be a room!"

Those qualities so characteristic of Lancashire people belonged in full measure to my mother, who was one of them. Warmth, kindliness and vitality were hers by nature, but her outstanding characteristic was determination and a tenacity of purpose which was quite exceptional. Strength of will was her dominant feature, and once she had decided on a certain course of action, I never knew her to falter. Her faith in the rightness of her decisions was always sufficient to justify any personal sacrifice which they might entail.

In later years she always claimed that long before I was born she had firmly decided that my life's career was to be spent in the pursuit of music. It was a resolve both inexplicable and rashly optimistic, without clear rational basis, and she saw no dangers whatever, nor any possibility that she might somehow be frustrated. Her strength and courage could never have been suspected from her appearance. She was slight in build, of medium height, and in my childhood her long hair, raven black, was piled high on the crown of her head in the fashion of the day. Later, it was parted in the middle, the long plaits coiled over the ears, creating an impression of severity which I think she rather enjoyed. It was certainly quite in keeping with her personality.

Her marriage to Thompson Helliwell was a striking example of the magnetic attraction of contradictory qualities. His nature was the antithesis of hers. Not for him an over-riding drive and constant sense of purpose. The warm and tempting satisfaction which grows out of a sense of achievement he could do without. He would probably have found it spurious and it would have been quite contrary to his nature to have subjected himself to tensions of that, or indeed, any kind. His great talent was for friendship. Beneath a quiet and usually placid exterior there lay a deep understanding of people and their ways. Perhaps it was a by-product of his reading, for with books he was happiest of all. But what did not come from his reading was his innate courtesy and kindliness of manner. His was the courtesy which could even bear with discourtesy. In this he was exceptional, even in those days when graciousness was a quality of life to a far greater extent than it is today.

He was one of a large family which a generation or so earlier had had its roots in Yorkshire, later to be more widely scattered mostly throughout Westmorland and the northern parts of Lancashire. Morecambe, where he was born, was then little more than a village by the sea and it was there that his father pursued his calling as a portrait photographer. As a boy, I saw many of his prints, typically Victorian in style, produced in a studio lit by daylight. In the fashionable setting of the time his subjects sat stiffly on a marble bench, an arm resting on a flanking column or on the edge of an ornate table which supported the inevitable pile of books and a vase of flowers. Their expressions were invariably grave; to be photographed was a very serious matter. The prints were toned in the customary rich sepia which remains unfaded to this day, and their technical quality could well be the envy of a contemporary photographer, despite his infinitely superior equipment.

For his work with a camera my grandfather was well known in the North of England and in his own field he must have been something of a pioneer. In his youth he had been one of those intrepid and enthusiastic experimenters who were willing to tramp the hills of the Lake District, burdened with the unbelievable impedimenta which was then necessary for the sensitising of a plate before it could exposed. My own lifelong preoccupation with photography surely derives from him, and in spite of the vast technological changes which have come about there are many things I should have liked to discuss with him. We would have had much in common.

My father made no great demands on life. With his friends, his books, and his flute he was content. Music was very important to him, choral singing especially, apart from his flute. There were few periods in his life when he had no active association with one choir or another, either as a singer himself or as choirmaster. For all that, he was far from ambitious in any way, and he could never have described himself as successful in a material sense. He could never agree, for example, with my mother's oft-quoted dictum that to speculate was to accumulate. His nature was too gentle and over-cautious for that. But there can be no doubt that all his activities were conditioned and hindered by the ill-health from which he suffered throughout his life. There were good times, free of such troubles, but the shadow was never very far away. I can see now that here was the reason for those prolonged bouts of depression which bore down on him from time to time. Without warning he would become withdrawn, remote and silent. The household fell quiet and tense. We would sit at meals without a spoken word whilst my mother, wise in her experience, waited for the clouds to lift. For me, these were times of acute misery. Why there had to be this unhappiness was beyond my understanding. Quite often my fear was that some misdemeanour of mine might have been the cause. On occasion, no doubt, that was true, but when my conscience was clear no explanation was possible, and I was more wretched than ever. Sooner or later the tension would ease. Gradually our normal happy family relationship would be restored and once again my father was approachable and his usual friendly self.

In 1905, the year of his marriage to my mother, he was a widower. The death of his first wife some years previously had left him with a son. Lewis, to whom I was to become half-brother, was then eleven. Between him and his stepmother there developed a tender and affectionate relationship which deepened through the years and in which I shared.

In due course we exchanged the grey skies and busy streets of industrial Lancashire for the bleak and open countryside of Cumberland, not more than a dozen miles from the Scottish border. A greater contrast was hardly possible. In those early years of the century the little town of Wigton was still untouched by the invading factories which would eventually destroy so much of its pastoral character. It was a typical, old-style market-town, the focal point of wide acres of surrounding farm land. Wigton life was leisurely, an unhurried rhythm disturbed only by the stir and bustle of the weekly market-day.

The time of which I write must be 1914, for I clearly remember a summer holiday of that year. We had gone to Heversham in Westmorland, a village where more than one of my father's sisters lived, and it was there that I met Grandmother Helliwell for the first time. Presented would be a better word for an introduction to a lady so old and

5

dignified. The moment had a distinct air of formality. Seated in her upright chair, and severe in black dress and white cap, she seemed to be holding court. For a small boy whose hands were disagreeably stained by blotches of wet tar she had only an expression of extreme disapproval.

I have only unhappy memories of that holiday. On the round table in the sitting-room of our cottage there stood a bowl of roses. I hated their musty scent; for me it was overpowering – and ominous – and, if I could, I avoided that room at all costs. That was not all. There was Heversham Head which rose steeply on the outskirts of the village. Some legend associated with it was told to me, though I have long forgotten the story. But its menace matched that of the roses, and I was afraid. Why the hill should have seemed so sinister cannot be explained but the whole area filled me with vivid and unreasonable fears. Nothing would induce me to climb to the top, even in the brilliant sunshine of those summer afternoons. We were in Heversham on that fateful day, the fourth of August, and I remember the serious faces of those around me when it was known that we were at war with Germany. To me it meant little. The dark overtones of portent were inextricably confused with the hated perfume of roses and the terrifying mysteries of Heversham Head.

Back again in Wigton, Fred Waite made his appearance. As organist of the Parish Church he commanded a good deal of respect in the town though the post laid him open to trenchant comment if his performance fell short of those standards which critical parishioners considered to be essential. Equally, on occasion, his efforts earned appreciation, as on that morning when my father sat beside him in that centre of social life, the barber's shop.

"Bah gum, Fred, tha' didn't half mek Hell's foundations quiver last neet!" an incoming farmer announced for all to hear, and beneath the concealing lather, Fred's face must have glowed with satisfaction.

He was a meek, extremely mild-mannered man with a striking propensity for innumerable cups of tea and a fatal incapacity for knowing when it was time to go home. So, at least, I gathered from scraps of my parents' small talk. But

6

his musical contribution to the town was not solely confined to his organ-playing. He was pianist, too, officiating nightly at the local cinema, and he gave piano lessons. He it was who guided me, somewhat impatiently, through the first bewildering pages of Smallwood's *Tutor*. Years earlier, my father had known William Smallwood in Kendal, but that was long before his famous *Tutor* had established itself between the candlesticks of countless pianos.

My lessons took place in the back room of the little grocery shop kept by Fred's mother. Everyone for miles around came here to buy the famous Cumberland sausages which she made from a secret recipe which was kept closely guarded. There was home-made toffee as well, a little bag of which was sent home with me at the end of every lesson.

Of the lessons themselves I remember nothing. They failed entirely to arouse any spark of interest on my part and succeeded only in creating a wholehearted dislike of practising which was to last for eight or nine years. I protested vigorously, caused a great deal of friction in our small household, and came into direct conflict with a will-power far stronger than my own. My mother was inflexible. She had made up her mind that I should play the piano and that was that! My father, always anxious to keep the peace of the house undisturbed, would have made an end of it. "There's no music in him," he would say. "He must give it up." He was firmly over-ruled and there were scenes which must have repeated themselves in thousands of homes.

Oddly enough, though the keyboard was anathema to me there were times when other kinds of music gave me the most intense pleasure. My father played the flute quite often and he had a friend, the local jeweller, who was also a flautist. Emmot Dowell must have been a musician of some standing, for on occasion he travelled to Manchester to play in the Hallé Orchestra. The repertory of music for two flutes, usually unaccompanied, was very small, and as far as I remember consisted mostly of curiously arranged selections from Handel's *Messiah*. Music-making at home drew largely on borrowed melodies arranged quite simply for a variety of instruments. Nowadays we are likely to scorn such simplicities, but it is easy to forget how much enjoyment such pieces could provide for the players and sometimes for the listeners as well. We may forget, too, that in the absence of our present-day electronic marvels, the opportunity for hearing first-class music was then hard to come by, especially for those who lived in the country.

My piano playing had had a bad start; it must surely have seemed that my mother's battle was lost, determined as she was. Perhaps it was not all that surprising. My family could claim few links with the world of music. There was one exception which I often heard mentioned. Many years earlier my father's sister, Sarah, had married J. P. Johnson, a prominent figure in the North of England who was well known not only for his promotion of concerts, bringing many of the most famous artists of the day to the district, but also for his remarkable playing of the concertina. The respect which that instrument commanded in the early years of the century is now largely forgotten. J. P. Johnson was hailed by the *Manchester Guardian* as 'the greatest living exponent of the English concertina'. Oddly enough, he was not a professional musician; officially he was a cattle dealer, a calling which he continued to combine with his ceaseless musical activity, the concert promotions, his Deputy-Conductorship of the Kendal Orchestral Society and his engagements as a soloist.

"He played often at the Free Trade Hall with the Hallé Orchestra under their conductor, the late Sir Charles, and after his day at the Brand Lane Concerts," my father told me. "And once, I remember, he came again with the Hallé; the guest conductor was Sir Frederick Cowen. Of the works he played I am sorry I have only a hazy recollection. I have heard him play the Mendelssohn Concerto with orchestra; he had quite a large repertoire. Long before he came into the family we had a walk one afternoon to Burneside near Windermere where he was to inspect some cattle. On our way back he invited me to tea and afterwards offered to play for me. I remember he opened his recital with the Bach Chaconne."

After only two or three years we moved from Wigton, southwards this time to the shores of Morecambe Bay.

I said goodbye to Fred Waite without much noticeable reluctance, and secretly cherished the hope that from now on music lessons could be forgotten.

Viewed from the railway, and that is how the majority of travellers saw it, Carnforth wore a deceptive air. The vast goods-yard with its tangle of railway lines, dominated by the dull red ugliness of the once prosperous ironworks, presented a depressing prospect. How could this little town, one might well have asked, be described as a gateway to the Lakes? Yet only a few hundred yards away, up the hill which was the main street and unseen from the railway, there were green fields. The farms were not far away, and in the distance, towards the north, the beckoning slopes of Farleton Knott held out the first promise of Lakeland. To the north-west the village of Warton, famed for its association with the family of George Washington, nestled in the shadow of Warton Crag, its outcrop of limestone gleaming in the light, and beyond stretched the dark green woods which concealed the two greystone hamlets of Yealand Conyers and Yealand Redmayne. Then, in the other direction, there was the shore, from which the sea always remained depressingly remote, but a shore all the same with firm hard sand knitted together by wiry grass – an enormous expanse, unbroken except for the scattered pools of water. Here we played cricket throughout the long hot Saturday afternoons, and here also I swung my first golf-club, patiently initiated by Lewis, the enthusiast. With the help of a few friends who shared his newly-found passion for the game, he had marked out a nine-hole course complete with flags and tee boxes. In that long grey-brown grass a lost ball was really lost, though we would spend many an hour trying to find it, and often discover the egg of a curlew instead.

So much to enjoy in this delectable spot; so much to do left little room for thoughts of anything else. But my mother had not forgotten! Before long the music lessons began again, this time more in earnest. The young lady organist of the Congregational Church took me in hand. She was not over-endowed with patience, nor, I felt, with the sweetest of dispositions. It was clear from the start that

9

stern discipline was to be the order of the day, and the lessons proceeded in an atmosphere of increasing tension. At one point we must have reached a moment of crisis for I wrote a note to her. 'Dear Miss,' it said, 'No use talking about new pieces for I shall not appear next Monday or any after. I shall neither speak to you or any of your family again. I have my reasons.' As was to be expected, that little scrap of paper was intercepted by my mother and never reached its destination. My rebellious protest had failed miserably – and the lessons continued.

It was, nevertheless, something of a turning point. From that time some positive progress began, though my dislike of practising remained. I can see now that the reason for this was that so far my tuition had included no guidance whatever on how to make the best use of my time at the piano. It was not yet appreciated that to practise in the most beneficial way was an art in itself: students of today can be grateful for a much greater understanding in this respect.

My teacher was also a singer and in due time I found myself learning to play the accompaniments of some of the ballads of the day. 'God send you back to me' and 'When you come home, dear' no doubt reflected the prevailing wartime mood. In the dark days of 1917 it needed a popular stimulus of some kind, however superficial. Another example, equally admired, of these now forgotten songs was 'Somewhere a voice is calling.' Its involved progressions of thick, chromatic chords were nothing less than terrifying. I dreaded the day of the lesson. It seemed that at least some of my work was designed as much for my teacher's convenience as it was for my progress, providing as it did an opportunity for her to sing. Only in later years did I realise how fortunate I had been to have this somewhat unusual early training which offered an introduction, far from appreciated at the age of ten, to some of the elementary principles of accompaniment.

I was playing the organ as well. There was a two-manual instrument, small but of excellent quality, in the chapel and on many a Sunday morning I was allowed to sit on the long, shiny seat, learning to follow the intricacies of the service. Not that they presented any great complication, for simplicity is the keynote of Congregational worship. For me it was a little too simple and at times I wished that the homely atmosphere, the musical content, sincere as it was, and the extempore prayers could be replaced by a more elaborate ritual, altogether grander and more majestic. I cannot think where these ideas came from. All the same, it was an excellent initiation. Before very long, I was trusted with an occasional service on my own, and then with the accompaniment of a small choir in an enthusiastic if slightly perilous performance of *Messiah*. My father, as choirmaster, stood at the end of the row of basses, sadly few in number, and I soon learned to watch out for his scowl of disapproval if I had allowed the pace to drag. It would mean an uncomfortable post-mortem on the way home to Sunday lunch.

One of our family friends in the town was Tom Rathbone, a man of many parts, and great charm. He sang, he could train a choir, he played the 'cello, he was a splendid photographer, and to everything he did he brought a rare and natural artistry. His brother, George Rathbone, was the composer of much attractive music for children's voices and a key figure in the organisation of the annual Mary Wakefield Music Festival at Kendal. We saw George only rarely though I clearly remember one of his visits when he introduced me for the first time to 'The Londonderry Air' which he played most beautifully on our ancient and rather harsh-toned grand. But Tom came every week complete with 'cello and a quantity of music for me to accompany. That I enjoyed, though once I complained that the tempo of all his pieces seemed to be very much on the slow side. Was there nothing more quickly moving? I asked. I was solemnly assured that the 'cello was not at all an instrument for frivolity. Our partnership failed to reveal the existence of Beethoven's 'Cello Sonatas, which was just as well, since I could not possibly have attempted them. But I wonder now what Tom would have thought of their technical demands and the other works of the present-day 'cellist's repertoire.

Occasionally my father could be persuaded to play the flute, but to find something which the three of us could play together presented a real difficulty. It must have been a year or so later on when I attempted, somewhat impertinently, to fill the gap by arranging one of the movements from Tchaikovsky's Suite, *The Months of the Year*. I chose 'June' and took as much care as I could to make the three parts interesting. But far more loving care was expended on the title page than on anything else. It was done in Indian ink and the letters of the arranger's name were of a size which put Tchaikovsky at a distinct disadvantage. To my great pride we played it through one evening and I looked forward eagerly to some favourable comment from my mother. Alas! She saw nothing for me to be so pleased about. After all, she said, I had only copied it out.

One feature of my father's genuine love of music was a continuing desire to share his pleasure in it with as many people as possible. To this end, and with some missionary zeal, he prepared several talks on 'The Great Composers', as they were always known. They were simple and unpretentious in character but he had an engaging style and he knew well how to capture his audience. In those far-off days country folk were quite content with an evening's entertainment no more sophisticated than this. Lectures, readings, and talks on almost any subject were widely popular; in winter time an audience of sorts could be mustered in any village, however small. What my father really wanted was to give his listeners a chance to enjoy some of his own favourite pieces of music. Once my piano playing was sufficiently advanced, those illustrations were entrusted to me. Our audiences were always very small, and always uncritical, but to play in public at that early stage was valuable experience, especially since the programme often called for pieces which had to be learned for the specific occasion.

There were a good many such evenings, one of which was so disastrous that it remains vividly in my memory. At the end of a day of continuous and torrential rain we made our way to a little village on the shores of Morecambe Bay. There, in the local Institute, my father was to address a gathering of some two or three dozen people. His subject was Mendelssohn. We arrived rather late; an expectant audience was already assembled and there was only time for my father to collect his notes and for me to confirm the presence of a piano. There it was, standing below the platform, an upright of distinctly unfriendly aspect. I would have given a great deal for a chance to make its acquaintance, but there was no time; the lecture was already under way.

I sat at the keyboard waiting for my cue to embark on the Scherzo in E minor which begins with a tiny fanfare, a single note rapidly repeated three times. The moment came, I played those three notes – and no sound emerged at all, other than a dull clatter of hammers. I caught my breath, swallowed hard and tried again, with exactly the same result. Perhaps it is just this one B natural, I thought, which is faulty, and so I started once more, but four bars later. As its name suggests, the Scherzo moves along at quite a fast pace, but of all the notes I played not one in ten produced any musical response. Even those which did proved to be entirely unpredictable in pitch and action. It was impossible to go on. I looked helplessly at my father who was as mystified as I was, and an official-looking lady rushed towards me from the audience saying, "Do, please, try again. I'm sure it will be all right." Not only was it far from being all right; it was painfully obvious that there could be no music that evening.

My father completed his talk which, in the absence of the illustrations, was all too short, and some twenty minutes later the evening's entertainment was at an end. The tea and buns appeared and helped a little to ease the general embarrassment. It was then that the reason for the deplorable state of the piano became clear. Earlier in the day the caretaker had discovered that it had been left with the lid wide open. The rain had poured through an unfortunately placed hole in the roof and the instrument had received a thorough soaking. Realising that not all was as it should be, he had helpfully removed the action and had allowed it to stand for several hours in front of a very hot stove to dry out. Nothing could have been worse. His little piece of careful forethought had caused such warping that any natural relationship between hammers and strings no longer existed. They would never meet again. It has been my misfortune to encounter a few very bad pianos in my time, but to this one belongs the distinction of being the worst of all.

CHAPTER 2

A door opens

IN 1919 a scholarship took me to the Grammar School at
Lancaster. I had waited impatiently for that day and when
at last it arrived I was thrilled beyond measure. This, I
boasted with some pardonable pride, was the 'Royal'
Grammar School, its Charter granted by Edward II more
than four hundred years ago. Now at last I was entitled
to wear that coveted schoolboy cap, to rejoice in its blue
stripes on black background, the red rose of Lancaster
emblazoned on the centre of the peak. Now I could join in
with three or four hundred other boys singing that splendid
School Song and enliven the echoes with its truly superb
tune. It was all heady and exciting; I was as happy as a
sandboy. But suddenly, I saw it all in a different light and
I became very serious. Clearly, I had turned a corner; life
was opening out, there could be no doubt of that. For the
first time I became conscious of some sense of its purpose
and direction.

At the morning assemblies I stood in the Great
Hall listening to the words of the Collect for the
Day. They were more majestic and powerful than any I
had ever known. To read them for myself in the Book
of Common Prayer was to realise, as never before, the
compelling power of the English language. Week by
week I was to hear Sir Francis Drake's incomparable
words: 'Lord God, when Thou givest to Thy servants
to endeavour any great matter, grant us also to know
that it is not the beginning but the continuing of the
same until it be thoroughly finished which yieldeth
the true glory.'

I was dreaming myself of 'great matters', though I would never have admitted it in a thousand years.

Our headmaster was the Reverend Shackleton-Bailey, Doctor of Divinity, a severe yet kindly figure of whom we went in awe. For the most part, his assistant masters were men of character – we could recognise that even then – and prominent among them were two whose names were inseparably linked. In 'Dido' and 'Vinnie' (they were never privately referred to as Mr Deeds and Mr Vincent) the whole school was embodied. As far as we knew, they could easily have already been there in 1485, getting everything started! They played an immense part in our lives.

I should have preferred to be a boarder, but my home was a mere six miles away and so I travelled backwards and forwards by train. It was exciting to have a season ticket – known in the north as a 'contract' – and I quickly discovered, as had many others before me, that the enforced inactivity of the twenty-minute journey was an admirable opportunity for homework. That it was mostly done at the last moment on the inward journey says little for the validity of my good intentions. But my enthusiasms remained, particularly in the study of French, an entirely new subject. I had eagerly anticipated it by acquiring a dictionary. My innocent theory was that for translation all I had to do was to replace an English word with its French equivalent. That illusion quickly evaporated into thin air.

Luckily, I had very little personal contact with our school music-master, whose blustering, unsympathetic personality I did not like. Through him, however, a lesson which lay beyond the official curriculum came my way. Our choral classes were held weekly in the main hall where he pounded the piano, surrounded by a couple of hundred boys using up surplus energy and singing at the top of their voices.

Once, he stopped us, to say: "There's one boy singing out of tune."

A doubt crossed my mind. Surely, I thought, he can't possibly hear one single voice in all that welter of sound. We tried again.

"Ah, he didn't sing that time," he said.

Now I knew, beyond doubt, that what he said could not be true. That afternoon, I realised for the first time in my twelve years that something said by an elder might not necessarily be the truth, and nothing but the truth. I would be on my guard from now on.

My private music lessons continued. I had said goodbye to my teacher who liked to sing, and also (I sincerely hoped) to 'Somewhere a voice is calling' which I never wanted to see again. By now, a voice was calling from another direction as I studied both piano and organ with a Miss Knowles, a lady who played a prominent part in the affairs of our town and was much respected for her musical expertise. She took me in hand very seriously and drove hard. She was a good teacher and in all she did there was a clear sense of purpose. Just occasionally, however, it struck me that there was an element of injustice in her procedures. Sitting on my left, she would complain about the lack of smoothness in my left-hand scales. Leaning over, she would demonstrate the ideal be aimed for, but with her right hand. I thought this a little unfair and made as polite a protest as I could, though not to very much avail. But I had a great deal to be grateful for. Miss Knowles made it very clear that musical education did not begin and end at the keyboard, introducing me to the study of harmony and encouraging me to read not only books on music but on many other subjects. Moreover, she did everything possible to create opportunities for me to listen to music. At home there were a few records which we played on a splendid new gramophone with a spring motor which had to be wound. Tchaikovsky's 'Pathétique' Symphony and the 'Emperor' Concerto with Backhaus as soloist introduced me for the first time to the sound of the full orchestra.

There were very few concerts within easy reach but my new tutor took me to the Mary Wakefield Festival at Kendal to hear the City of Birmingham Orchestra under Dr Boult (as he was then) with Jelly d'Aranyi as soloist in the Brahms Violin Concerto. We went to Preston to hear Alfred Cortot play the Twenty-four Preludes of Chopin, and to Morecambe where Mark Hambourg played the 'Moonlight' Sonata and Chopin's

A flat Ballade. Such events came my way as a rare treat.

At school my only troubles arose through games which, as was customary, were officially regarded as of vital importance. Without any talent for it whatever, I enjoyed cricked enormously, but rugger, the chosen game at Lancaster, was a different matter. No doubt I was very stupid about it but what I badly needed was some really clear explanation of what it was all about. Probably it never occurred to anyone that there might occasionally be an oddity such as myself to whom some enlightenment would be necessary. It never came. Could it have been my fault in some way that I could never find myself in the same part of the field as the ball? How could it be that the game invariably went its way without contribution of any kind from me? We spent many an unpleasant hour learning to keep our heads down in the scrum but why we should have to do so remained an unfathomable mystery. I dreaded Friday afternoons when the list of players required for the following day appeared on the notice board, and I was frequently dismayed to see that once again my form team was to be handicapped by having Helliwell J.C. among its forwards. My lifelong failure to identify myself (as the saying goes nowadays) with sport probably dates from this period. My view has always been that life has so much of enduring and worthwhile interest to offer, and that the vast amount of enthusiastic effort which sport engenders could be so much more valuably directed. In this respect, I am the odd man out and I can hope for few, especially in England, to agree with me.

Naturally, there was also a conflict between games and music. In due course my piano lessons with Miss Knowles came to an end but were immediately resumed on Saturday afternoons, notice board permitting, with Douglas Tayler, the organist of Lancaster's beautiful parish Church. Those lessons were now very different. Although Tayler was the mildest of men, shy, reserved and self-effacing by nature, he was a changed character when dealing with musical matters. With him I began to learn something of the inner life of music and its enormous power of expression – to

18

understand, at first in a very small way, the vital importance of every single marking on the printed page. As I played, my mentor would stride up and down the room, sometimes crouching unseen behind a chair, then leaping into the air with a roar which he intended to shock me into making the kind of sforzato which was needed and on which he insisted. I, too, suffered from a surfeit of shyness and this was a serious bar to a true, communicative musical style. Tayler worked hard to convince me that natural reserve must be surmounted if a performance was in the end to achieve full significance. First of all, he put me to work on the 'Consolations' of Liszt and then some of the earlier Beethoven sonatas. The lessons were so full of interest that I kept a notebook in which I could record as fully as possible all the many points he made. His own playing was sensitive and very beautiful. In works such as the Fantasiestücke of Schumann he could distil poetry with incredible gradations of fine tone, and achieve a range of expression wide and vivid enough to belie his own apparently diffident personality. His teaching was persuasive and inspiring. Those lessons laid an ideal foundation for a development which, by a happy and unexpected chance, was just now in the offing.

THE hamlet of Borwick lies a mile or so to the north of Carnforth. A thousand years ago it was the dairy farm of a Norse settler. Keer Holme, Mealriggs, Capenwray, Gunnerthwaite, Starrick; the place names of the district all echo the Viking invasion of long ago. In the seventeenth century Borwick became the home of the Bindloss family, wealthy traders in Kendal cloth. The young Charles II spent a night under its roof on his long journey from Scotland to his eventual defeat at Worcester. Borwick Hall was, and still is, one of the finest houses in the north-west, a gracious house planned for gracious living.

The tall, grey, clustered Tudor chimneys rising above the ancient brick can be seen from the village green, and through the narrow gate the paved courtyard with its spinning gallery and cheese press-stone offers a framed picture of Elizabethan domesticity. I was to pass through that gate many times.

In the 1920s Borwick Hall had come into the possession of John Alexander Fuller Maitland. For more than twenty years he had been music critic of *The Times*. He had published a number of books on music and edited the second edition of Grove's *Dictionary of Music and Musicians*. His many interests had embraced the revival of early English instrumental music and at the turn of the century he had edited the *Fitzwilliam Virginal Book* in collaboration with Barclay Squire. Earlier still, he had joined forces with Lucy Broadwood in the publication of a joint contribution to the folk song movement, *English Country Songs*. Maitland could look back over a lifetime of experience and influence in the musical world; by an older generation he was still remembered as a pianist and harpsichordist. Now, living at Borwick in comparative seclusion, his pen was still engaged in contributions to the *Musical Pilgrim* series of handbooks, a two-volume analysis of Bach's Forty-eight Preludes and Fugues, and a survey of Schumann's piano music.

It was wonderful for me to have such a friend and to be invited to visit him as often as I could. In the music-room on the first floor there were two Broadwood grand pianos of exceptional quality, and a harpsichord. It was a beautiful setting; memory tells me that the sun shone brilliantly through those long mullioned windows whenever I was there. A small adjoining room gave me my first glimpse of linen-fold panelling and it housed one of the many organs on which Handel was supposed to have played.

Fuller Maitland was tall, erect and dignified; his silvery white hair gave him an air of Edwardian elegance. To my mind, he bore a striking resemblance of the portraits of Elgar that I had seen. His kindness and, incredibly, his interest in my musical efforts were inexhaustible. I could only marvel that he was willing to spend so much time on a callow and immature teenager. With infinite patience he listened to my playing and drew me out in long discussions of both technical and interpretative problems. His chief concern was for good taste, a quality in musical performance which is often elusive and not easy to define. His advice and guidance was a logical extension of the work I was doing at Lancaster but it went deeper. Only in later years was I able to appreciate just how profound his influence had been.

Sometimes he would continue his discourse as we walked in beautiful gardens. Now and again some guest would be staying in the house and I remember that once we came upon a small, slight figure dressed in black and wearing a veil. "Let me introduce you to Lady Stanford," said my host.

I was thrilled but quite tongue-tied. Then, on several other occasions, there was the actor, Robin Farquharson, a strange and exotic character, I thought. I had never before met anyone so colourful, nor with such wonderful manners. In later years we were to meet now and again in London and become more closely acquainted. Robin was Fuller Maitland's executor after his death in 1936 and was kind enough to regret my absence from the sale of the Borwick instruments. "Such a pity!" he said; it appeared that I could have acquired the harpichord quite cheaply. To have done so would have given me the greatest pleasure, in the unlikely event of my being able to find a thousand pounds at that time. To Robin that necessity had not occurred.

In his music room Fuller Maitland helped me to discover the repertoire of music for two pianos. To join forces with him at the two Broadwoods was an entirely new delight. A memorable day came when he produced Schumann's Andante and Variations in B flat. It was not easy to read at sight, I was nervous as always, and the result cannot have been very satisfactory. But this was music such as I had never heard before, of a beauty beyond anything I had imagined and I was quite bowled over. For days afterwards I could think of nothing else. Fifty years have done nothing to erase the memory of that magical afternoon, nor my conviction that this was a landmark on my journey towards musical awareness. The sad thing is that over the years since then there seem to have been so few opportunities to hear the work performed.

Later on this most generous benefactor of mine invited me to accompany him to Leeds for the week of Festival concerts. Although my memories of it are far from complete, I recall a Mozart Concerto played by Myra Hess and a performance of the *Mass of Life* by Delius which Sir Thomas Beecham conducted. Nervous and overawed, I heard this from the front row of the circle, my host on my left and H.C. Colles, his successor as music critic of *The Times*, on my right. At its conclusion Colles leaned across me to whisper to Fuller Maitland: "This Beecham really is a bounder, but he does deliver the goods!" This was the occasion (or was it the following day?) when Sir Thomas's sock-suspender sprang into view during a particularly energetic passage. Unperturbed, he brought everything to a halt at a suitable moment, sat down on his rostrum to repair the damage in front of the audience and then proceeded smoothly to the next movement. The following morning the newspaper posters outside the Queen's Hotel announced, with a rare touch of wit: 'Collapse of the Beecham Trust.'

IT had never been a foregone conclusion that I would enter the musical profession. Up to the age of sixteen such a career had formed no part of my ambitions. At one time there had been some vague idea that I might aim to become a lawyer, and in that direction there was much that appealed to me, not least the logical thinking and factual precision essential to such a calling. I had little justification for believing that I possessed ability of that kind, but I enjoyed Walter Mitty-like dreams of myself as a barrister swaying the emotions and controlling the reactions of judge, jury, and a crowded court by sheer magnetism and the histrionic art. Wherever could those ideas have come from? But at sixteen I turned the last corner of indecision and the choice was made. It was to be music – somehow.

At school it was not understood at all. The pursuit of music had made me something of an oddity, but to make a career of it was odder still. There could be no doubt that to my companions both on and off the rugger field I was an enigma, though that did not worry me at all. I had lived largely in a world of my own, I had made very few friends, and to a great extent I had denied myself, albeit unconsciously, the pleasures of companionship. My failure to realise the value of human relationships probably sprang from my antipathy to sport, an activity which plays so large a part in bringing people together. I honestly preferred to be on my own. If I sat in a café in the town I would invariably read a book and hope that no one I knew would appear. If someone did, I would try to remain unnoticed. It happened many times, not because I felt that others had nothing to offer me. On the contrary, it was more my belief that I had nothing to offer them. I was wrong, and the loss was mine, but I could not accept then that anything had been lost. A time would come when I should see it differently.

CHAPTER 3

The right wrong notes

A DECISION to embark on advanced musical studies can never be taken lightly; in my case it could not have been taken at all without the understanding and full co-operation of my parents. This was long before generous government grants became available to offset the financial obligations of further education. In those days such responsibilities belonged firmly to the student or his parents. Mine readily accepted the burden with no hint of sacrifice, and they were quite prepared to live with the unavoidable implications. Even if tuition fees were to be reasonably modest, the cost of travelling from home on two or three days a week would be considerable. Furthermore, to study for at least three years would preclude the possibility of my contributing anything to the family income before I reached the age of at least twenty-one.

Twelve months later it happened that the Lancashire County Council awarded me a scholarship which covered tuition fees for the following three years. That eased the situation to a limited extent, but it in no way diminished the debt I owed to my parents. For the all-important start which they gave me, and for then enabling me to continue, I have never ceased to be grateful. Incidentally, the scholarship was not by any means a gift. The examination for it took the form of a recital performance in competition with a number of other candidates.

In September, 1925, I was admitted as a student at the Royal Manchester College of Music and came immediately under its spell. It was a spell woven by tradition. The College was rich in traditions and from them came the

24

first powerful impulse. The very names of those who had taught there – Wilhelm Backhaus, Max Mayer, Egon Petri among them – aroused in me an overwhelming respect for the past. So far, I had given little thought to such things but now the impact was striking. As I came to know my fellow-students I had the impression that many of them shared these feelings of mine. We talked at length; we compared our hopes and fears; we dreamed of what we might achieve in the future. I doubt if we could have put it into words, but behind those dreams lay the certainty that for any success which came our way we should be indebted not only to the present but to the fruitful and enduring influence of the past. Things have changed since then, not always for the better. If, as I have sometimes suspected, there is a tendency for the present-day student to believe that the world began on the day he was born, then he is all the poorer for it. Fortunately, we suffered no such deprivation in 1925.

The piano department was led by R.J. Forbes, who was to become Principal after Dr Brodsky's death, and its professors included Frank Merrick and Claud Biggs, to whom I was allotted. My first surprise was to discover that I would have only one piano lesson each week. Surely, I thought, for a first study piano student there would be one every day! I had overlooked the vital point that between lessons there has to be time for practice. Without that the next one would be useless.

Claud Biggs had come to Manchester not long before with a reputation as a soloist both in England and America. His earlier studies with Leonard Borwick who was himself a pupil of Clara Schumann established a line of descent which I could boast about, but which, in fact, was very humbling. In Beethoven and Brahms, Claud Biggs' playing was big and powerful, in Mozart of a wonderful sensitivity. Everything he played was notable for clarity; in his hands the most complex passages became entirely comprehensible; everything was there, clearly to be heard. He had many technical devices of his own and an ingenious approach to fingering, often suggesting a redistribution of notes between the two hands. That is a simple thing in itself but it has proved more and more valuable throughout my life. He had a series of exercises of his own invention, each one designed to solve some technical problem which it did successfully more often than not.

Beyond any doubt, the quality of his playing owed a great deal to his particular affection for music of an earlier period, the Sonatas of Scarlatti, the Suites by Couperin and, above all, the keyboard works of Bach. This was his field and his knowledge of it was encyclopaedic. I have never heard elsewhere such control of tone as he displayed in a miniature such as Couperin's 'Les Barricades Mysterieuses'. In Bach his technical precision and clarity of texture were at the service of a musicality which illuminated the music. Such playing was stylistically opposed to that of many pianists who earnestly imagined that they had captured the Bach style and were little concerned that the result was dry, mechanical and dull. Could they really have believed, I wondered, that that was how it ought to be? The heart of the matter is, of course, the phrasing which was so vital to the harpichord's power of expression, and which Bach so often left to us to decide for ourselves.

In his interpretative suggestions Claud was never dogmatic. Drawing my attention to alternative ideas he would say: "There's much to be said for . . ."; it was a phrase he often used. But his own solution was usually convincing enough to rule out other possibilities. In furthering good taste and developing the ability to make the best choice from a selection of interpretative options, this was teaching of the highest quality. The Forty-eight Preludes and Fugues, all of which he played from memory, were a revelation. He would demonstrate how the phrasing alone, without increase of tone, could bring into prominence an inner contrapuntal line which would otherwise have been obscure. In his approach to Bach there was also a welcome freshness and spontaneity. I remember asking him one day about the need for a certain ornament in one of the French Suites. He thought for a moment and then said "D'you know, sometimes I do it, sometimes I don't."

His response to contemporary music was not particularly enthusiastic. He tolerated it (that was his own word) but was content to leave it to others. The works of the older masters dominated his interests: they filled his life and that was enough. Many years after my student days he heard on the radio a performance of one of the Bartok Violin Sonatas in which I had taken part. He wrote me a letter afterwards in which he said 'there was not only clarity but subtleties of touch and withal a welcome dignity; and you got all the right wrong notes in the Bartok!' He would frequently say in his lessons "You must always be a 'right-note man' ".

They were happy lessons. He inspired us with gentle tact to give of our best, and we worked hard not from fear of any wrath to come but because of our respect and affection for him. It would have been unthinkable to take him anything shoddy or ill-prepared.

He was terribly absent-minded and suffered a lifelong handicap of seriously defective eyesight. He told me once that he was fourteen years old before he discovered that sparrows had two legs. Such detail had escaped him completely. He never seemed to be able to recognise his own hat and overcoat, and he was frequently to be seen walking down Oxford Road wearing garments which obviously did not belong to him. He was an inveterate smoker and loved his pipe; but any pipe within his reach invariably found its way into his pocket to emerge later to his utter consternation. We often wondered about the contents of a small attaché case without which he was hardly ever seen. One day it fell open and all was revealed. It contained a clean collar, a handkerchief and the cadenza of a Mozart Concerto.

Before his marriage I used to visit him occasionally in his rooms in Fallowfield where we would share tea and toast in front of a cheerful fire. On one of these visits he was wearing a pair of boots the laces of which passed, not through the usual eyelet holes, but around a series of hook fasteners. When the time came for me to leave and I stood up, Claud attempted to rise from his chair but hurriedly sat down again. He had crossed his feet, the hooks were inextricably entangled and the boots were held fast together. Our strenuous efforts to get them apart were entirely unsuccessful. "D'you know?" he said, "I don't think

I'm going to be able to see you out." When the problem was finally solved he came with me to the front door in his stocking feet.

Claud had little time for hobbies, but apart from music he had an absorbing interest in the British railway system. He could recite page after page of *Bradshaw* by heart, and he liked nothing better than to sit in a railway carriage, watch in hand, engrossed in calculating the speed of the train by counting the number of wheel-beats per minute. He would plan some imaginary journey by train from one remote corner of the country to another, working out the most efficient route and solving the knotty problems of connections between available railway services. Among musicians he was not alone in this. He often spoke of his old friend, Henry Ley, formerly of Christ Church, Oxford, and later Precentor of Eton College. Apparently, Ley was once asked to furnish a reference for one of his students. 'A pretty good chap on the whole,' he wrote, 'though a bit weak on Sunday locals!'

In my first week at the College I was admitted to the ensemble class directed by Carl Fuchs, principal professor of 'cello. Having known Adolph Brodsky at the Conservatoire in Leipzig, he had been in Manchester for many years, teaching at the College since its foundation. He was also a member of the Brodsky Quartet. With him in that group was the second violinist, Rawdon Briggs, a Manchester player and pupil of Joachim, and the violinist, Simon Speelman, a Dutchman.

Later on in my student days I came to know Simon Speelman's widow who had a large house in Cecil Street, some rooms of which were let to students. For a brief period I had lodgings there with two friends from the College and several wild and irresponsible medical students from the University.

Perhaps this story is apocryphal but it certainly appears in Carl Fuchs' *Recollections*. Simon Speelman, it seems, never really mastered the English language. It so muddled and defeated him that when one day he asked a young lady of his acquaintance to tell him the time she understood him to be proposing to her. She accepted and Speelman always said that he had married her to avoid an action for breach of promise.

Carl Fuchs was a man of culture and charm. At home in Germany he had been brought up to observe habits of thrift and for the rest of his life he practised extreme frugality. Hanging from pegs in his studio were various pieces of cloth which, as his teaching day began, he would tie around his garments to protect any place which might possibly be chafed by his instrument. Usually he wore a workman's shirt to which he added a pair of celluloid cuffs, very fashionable at that time. They caused unbelievable complications! A piece of tape attached to a cuff passed up and under his sleeve, across his shoulders and down again to terminate at the other cuff. He also wore a velvet jacket which, in the warm summer weather, he would remove, together with the cuffs, then roll the sleeves of his workman's shirt to the elbows. By now, he was ready to teach, but only if his student happened to be male. It would have been a most painful embarrassment to him to be seen in any casual state of dress by a young lady. "I think it is time for Miss —," he would say. "I must prepare!" On would go the cuffs in the vain hope that just the right amount would show below each sleeve. The velvet jacket on again, the result would be entirely unsatisfactory, several inches of cuff plainly visible on one side, none at all on the other.

Little as I then foresaw the part that chamber music would play in my life, I was soon aware of my good fortune to come under the care of such a master. Vast experience and indisputable authority illuminated all his teaching. Those lessons were graced by a courtesy of rare quality. A new world of duo-sonatas, trios and quartets opened up, a complex world full of intricacies of balance and blend of tone, of rhythm and rubato when playing with other instrumentalists. I had everything to learn, but Carl Fuchs knew the value of encouragement. After a very few weeks I was allowed to join Michael Collins, a very talented new student from Liverpool, in a public College performance of Brahms' E minor 'Cello Sonata. It was a first appearance for both of us. Although that revered critic of the *Manchester Guardian*, Samuel Langford, felt that we had approached so austere a work somewhat mildly – and I am sure he was right – the ice was broken.

In all departments of the College it was a period rich in promise. The ambition of many of the best young violinists in the country was to work there under the guidance of Dr Brodsky, or Arthur Catterall, leader of the Hallé Orchestra. They came to Manchester in large numbers with a very high overall standard. Among them were Leonard Hirsch, Clifford Knowles, later to be leader of the Liverpool Philharmonic Orchestra, Harry Blech who was eventually to bring the London Mozart Players to world-wide recognition, Maurice Ward who later turned to the viola, Jessie Hinchcliffe and Norah Winstanley. The list could go on; these are but a representative few. In 1930, the newly-formed BBC Symphony Orchestra was able to draw very largely on young violinists from Manchester.

In the 'cello department the story was the same, through the inspiration of Carl Fuchs as a teacher and his Chamber Music classes. His students included Leonard Baker, Haydn Rogerson, Michael Collins, Alan Ford and his younger brother, Frank.

Nor did the piano department lag behind. In it were Gordon Green who after an outstanding career as a soloist was to become one of the foremost teachers in the country, Stephen Wearing, Lilian Grindrod, Phyllis Eley, Michael Brierley, and John Stirling, son of the actor, Harcourt Williams. There was also Alan Rawsthorne who, in addition to his piano studies under Frank Merrick, was already developing his gifts as a composer. In March, 1927, three of his songs performed in a College concert may well have been the first of his compositions to be heard in public. First class pianists were numerous and the competition was intense.

Behind the scenes came Administration in the person of the Registrar, Stanley Withers. In the earliest days he had been secretary of the fund-raising scheme which had enabled Sir Charles Hallé to establish the College in 1893. I hardly knew him and so am indebted to my friend and colleague, Gordon Green, for his recollections.

His was a purely administrative post, and administering the College in those days was a much more easy-going business than it was to become. It was generally supposed by students that Mr Withers began his working day by sitting down in his office to read the *Manchester Guardian* from end to end – no small task when the paper had about as many pages as a Mahler symphony. Having read it, he would answer a letter or two and perhaps write out one or two notices, all in the most incorrigible hand-writing. At that time the College did not possess a typewriter. He was never seen at a students' concert but the Annual General Meeting, so much dreaded by our Principal, was Mr Withers' one yearly moment of triumph. Resplendent in white tie and tails, his gold watch dangling across his waistcoat, his bald head gleaming under the electric lights, he addressed the Council, friends, and students rather like the Chairman of a Company of Directors and shareholders which had had a particularly successful year. Having dealt with College affairs, his rhetoric pouring like a stream from his lips, he clearly regretted the moment when, his speech at an end, he was obliged to sit down – to contemplate now a further fifty-two rather dreary weeks of bad hand-writing.

Gordon Green has mentioned the Principal's dread of the Annual General meeting. He anticipated it with considerable alarm for there he had to make his Annual Report. He would read his speech from a sheaf of papers held tightly in his hand. As he came to the end of each page it would be carefully placed behind the batch. The speech concluded, the process was repeated, but now he was once more facing page one, and the speech would start again! In the absence of a helpful tug on his coat tails it could have been an interminable da capo.

CHAPTER 4

A visit to the Embankment

IN 1925 the British Broadcasting Company, as it was
then known, was just three years old. Under the dynamic
leadership of J. C. W. Reith the problems of providing
a significant and worthwhile service were being tackled
seriously. For most people, however, the 'wireless' was
still very much a novelty. Receivers were to be found in
only a minority of homes, and those who had fallen to the
temptation of owning one had to accept uncertain reception
and an untidy accumulation of gadgets inevitably festooned
with wire. From the start, music formed an important part
of the programmes but so far it had made little impact
and the tremendous potential of the medium was far from
being realised.

As a schoolboy I had been fascinated by the technicalities,
and I had read all the constructional magazines currently
on the market. To build a crystal set for oneself, as they
urged, seemed a reasonable possibility and one which I could
attempt. All my pocket money was spent in acquiring the
necessary parts, and since it was woefully inadequate I was
lucky to be able to supplement it by extra piano practice at
seven in the mornings. That was an arrangement agreed by
my parents, and one of the fugues from the '48' still takes
me back to those early vigils. In the end, my efforts to
assemble those parts were only partly successful because
at home we were too far from the Manchester transmitter.
It was only on very rare occasions that the temperamental
cat's whisker could be persuaded to touch the right spot
on the crystal. Only then could faint, ethereal sounds of
speech or music be heard.

Nevertheless it was thrilling. Sounds by 'wireless' were still so intriguing a mystery that an enterprising dealer set up a stall on the Promenade at Morecambe. There, for a fee of sixpence, one could hire a pair of earphones and 'listen in' standing there in the open air. His trade was brisk and I was one of his most enthusiastic customers.

My next step was more ambitious, nothing less than an attempt to build a one-valve set, though now I needed to master a much more complicated electrical circuit diagram. My passion grew; surrounded by panels of bakelite, accumulators, condensers and rheostats I spent uncounted hours absorbed in my hobby, piano practising neglected and my father becoming more and more irritated. Fired by an indignation such as he had rarely shown, he took me very seriously to task. I was wasting time on foolishness; first things should come first, he said, and went on to tell me that I would never make my living with wireless. (I could tease him about that in the years to come!) When eventually my efforts were crowned with a little success and the voice of the bass singer, Joseph Farringdon, came through clearly audible, I hoped that he might perhaps be a shade mollified. But the headphones were anathema to him and he hated wearing them.

I badly needed a loudspeaker but they were expensive and in any case my primitive apparatus would have been unequal to its requirements. The answer, I was told, was to put the earphones in a tin basin and that would amplify the sound. Thin, strangulated sounds could certainly now be heard from a distance of two or three feet, but from a musical point of view the experiment was disastrous and soon to be abandoned. It was a long time before the up-to-date horn loudspeaker graced our living room.

In 1925 some of the senior students at the College were already casting shy glances in the BBC's direction. As the musicians of the future they were possibly a little in advance of the general public in recognising the potential power of the broadcasting medium. A number of older and established performers would have nothing to do with it, but the younger generation saw it as a wonderful opportunity and eagerly welcomed the enlarged scope which broadcasting might offer. A few of my fellow students had already been to the studio and one or two had acquired a special aura of distinction in my eyes because they had actually broadcast. In those days we used the past tense of the verb, broadcasted. My respect for Leonard Hirsch, for example, knew no bounds when I discovered that he was a member of something called the 2ZY Quartet, by virtue of which his portrait had appeared on a cigarette card!

Day by day there was much talk about auditions and after each one we waited eagerly to hear all about it in the minutest detail. So far, I was not personally involved. As a first-year student and still something of a new boy it had not yet occurred to me to seek an audition for myself. But by now, practically for the first time in my life, I was making friends and I was playing both officially in the ensemble class and unofficially with several instrumentalists. Before long, one of them asked me to accompany him at his BBC audition. I think he was a violinist, but to my sorrow I do not remember his name. Together we went to the Manchester studio in the Parsonage, and I recall my great surprise when the lift into which we stepped went down and not up. No one had told me that all this magic originated underground.

The studio was small and heavily draped with thick curtains which absorbed every sound. It seemed that no trace of resonance could be permitted. To play in such surrounding was a strange, even eerie experience. It had never fallen to my lot to play the piano in the middle of an open field (nor has it yet) but I imagined that, were I to do so, the sensation would be exactly like this. The microphone stand, imposing and massively constructed, supporting a large box-like frame covered with silk, commanded attention from the middle of the room. Inside it, the microphone rested on a thick rubber sling. We played our three pieces and all went reasonably well. The two of us were quite alone in the studio and because of that it was extraordinary difficult to believe that anyone could have heard anything.

At the end of the audition, and only then, an idea occurred to me. I asked diffidently if it would be possible for me to play some solos and be auditioned as well. Such was the informality of the proceedings in those early days that my request was immediately granted and I was given the freedom of the studio for another fifteen minutes or so. I little realised that the consequences of that far-away afternoon in 1926 would reach forward through so many future years and that this was the start of an association with the BBC which was to last for more than half a lifetime.

Both my partner and I were genuinely surprised to learn later that our auditions had been successful. In due course, my first BBC contract was in my hands, stipulating a short recital of piano solos at the 2ZY Studio in Manchester. On August 3rd, 1926, I broadcast for the first time, playing Schumann's Arabesque, the Chopin Study in E major together with the Scherzo in B flat minor.

As yet, no broadcasting policy on a regional basis had been formulated although there were a number of BBC stations in various parts of the country. They were not yet linked very closely to London; each one, whether in Cardiff, Birmingham, Manchester, Newcastle, Glasgow, or Belfast, was able to arrange its own programmes autonomously. The idea of a countrywide network was still to come. From the performer's point of view this meant that he could seek engagements in any centre irrespective of home base, and for the most part it was necessary for him to be auditioned in each place. Administratively it was a state of affairs which proved very helpful to me.

In the summer of 1926 it happened that my parents arranged to spend a holiday in Northern Ireland. I was going with them and what better could I do than apply to Belfast for a hearing. The Music Director and Conductor of the Belfast Wireless Orchestra was E. Godfrey Brown, a native of Barrow-in-Furness. Perhaps his courteous interest in my enquiry owed something to the fact that I came from his own corner of the British Isles. He granted my request and in due course, accompanied by my mother, I presented myself at the studios in Linenhall Street. We were admitted by the commissionaire, climbed the stairs and were shown into a very large studio. Of what works I played that day I have no record, but no doubt the B flat minor Scherzo was among them. My repertoire was far from extensive. When it was all over Godfrey Brown said "Well, we should like to offer you a concerto with orchestra." I was overjoyed. "But," he went on, "if you will please wait a little I should like you to come to the office so that we can discuss something else." It was intriguing, a delightful mystery. What could he possibly mean? The next half hour or so passed very slowly.

When all was made clear it appeared that the Belfast station pianist had just resigned and a replacement was needed. The duties of the post were explained; the accompaniment of singers and instrumentalists formed the main part of it but there was also a responsibility for a more general musical usefulness. Would this be of interest to me? I could hardly believe my ears. A very tangible offer was being made to me, and my thoughts were racing. It was marvellous, the chance to do exactly the kind of work I wanted to do; I would stand on my own feet, and at a princely salary of £400 per annum. Mr Brown went on to mention the opportunities of solo playing which there would be – it was all sounding more and more attractive – whilst I waited for the moment when I could find enough breath to say that I would accept. Alas! my mother's reaction was entirely different. I was not yet nineteen, she said. I had been at the College for only one year and it was vital that I should have the benefit of two more, if not three. She felt very strongly that it would be quite wrong to accept such a position when my musical education was still so incomplete; the course I had started must be finished! That strength of character and tenacity of purpose which I have already mentioned was never more evident than at that moment. As she developed her arguments, my dazzling prospects rapidly receded and the promise faded away almost completely.

Mr Brown listened very carefully to all she had to say. He respected such firmly stated views and thought her objections sound. But he suggested a compromise; would she allow me to go to Head Office in London to see Percy Pitt, the BBC's Music Director? There I would play for him and he would decide. My mother considered this a splendid idea, and after all I saw a ray of hope, dimmed though it was by my natural pessimism. It could never be said that I found it easy to look on the bright side of things, and at that moment even the firm promise of a concerto engagement did little to raise my spirits.

The arrangements were made and a few weeks later I was walking along the Strand, finding my way to those already well-known headquarters of the BBC and worrying more than a little about the outcome of the coming interview. The buildings in Savoy Hill, quite near the Embankment, looked very imposing and even forbidding. But no fears were necessary; it was to be a very pleasant visit. Percy Pitt, elderly, white-haired and dignified, received me sympathetically and devoted his attention to what must have seemed to him a small problem. He was anxious to ensure that no mistaken decision should be made. In the end, he upheld my mother's views and agreed that a return to the College to complete the course would be all for the best in the long run. Perhaps then it would be possible for the BBC to make a similar proposal. It was disappointing though oddly enough less depressing now than I had expected. I was slowly beginning to see the sense of it and coming to admit, reluctantly, that they were right and I was wrong.

The interview over, I was taken on a fascinating tour of the London studios. How impressive and up-to-date they were then! How very old-fashioned they would look today! Was there really a member of the staff whose sole job it was to look after the ash-trays? Fortunately, I did not dare to ask if that story had any truth in it. In the corridor I was presented to two young members of the staff whose names were rapidly becoming known to countless listeners. Stanton Jeffries was then Uncle Jeff of the Children's Hour and would later succeed Percy Pitt as Director of Music. Stanford Robinson was with him, and they both greeted me in friendly fashion. When I finally left for home I took with me Percy Pitt's comforting assurance that I would not be forgotten and also his promise that there would be some playing engagements for me at Savoy Hill in the more immediate future.

CHAPTER 5

More mysteries unravelled

MY return to the College was naturally tinged with regret for the lost opportunity which had been so nearly mine. But the days now become so full of interest and so worth-while that disappointment was quickly forgotten. Week by week my piano lessons made greater demands and became still more enjoyable. They covered more and more of the basic repertoire – the Studies of Chopin, the Concertos of Grieg, Schumann and the Brahms D minor, Sonatas by Beethoven and Chopin, all leading eventually to the Brahms Variations on a Theme of Paganini. Throughout, there was a clear emphasis on the music of Bach for which there grew in me an abiding affection. This was and always will be a vital part of the essential curriculum for keyboard skill as well as for the development of musical understanding. Now I could see that the study of the Forty-eight Preludes and Fugues could in itself be the foundation of a full technical equipment.

But not all our work was on this serious level. It was natural for a pianist of his generation that Claud Biggs should have a fondness for transcriptions, and he introduced me to some dazzling examples of a genre once very popular but later somewhat outmoded. Among them were the Dohnanyi version of Delibes' Waltzes from *Naila*, and an astonishing arrangement of the Serenade from *Don Giovanni* which had been made by Backhaus. Many years later, when I had the pleasure of a conversation with that legendary giant of the piano, it was surprising to find that he had actually forgotten its existence! The very severe technical requirements of such pieces were invaluable for promoting the high standard of accuracy on which Biggs always insisted. His constant injunction to be a 'right note' man cropped up in every lesson.

With Carl Fuchs we explored a good part of the piano trio repertoire. Beethoven, Brahms, Schubert, Mendelssohn, and Smetana followed each other in fairly quick succession. The Brahms E minor had quickened my interest in the duo-sonata form, and now I could revel in that vast treasury – Beethoven, Mozart, Grieg, Delius, Franck with the violin, and corresponding sonatas with the 'cello. Whenever our grasp reached an acceptable standard the fortnightly concerts in the College Hall offered a splendid chance for performance. It was a feather in one's cap to be chosen to play there, and to do so seemed to set the seal on the work we had done.

We soon discovered how much more difficult it was to play equally well under the psychological pressures created by the presence of an audience. From hard and sometimes bitter experience we learned how true it was that standards in public performance could not be expected to be as high as in the more relaxed atmosphere of study or classroom. This is something the performer has to live with and allow for. We became aware, rather dimly at first, of the inexplicable unpredictability of musical performance, a mystery which surrounds the work of all singers and players. How can it be that on some occasions, and for no apparent reason, the music will catch fire, everything will go right and the performance will be illuminated by some quite new magical insight? Yet at other times, and again for no apparent reason, something dies. Try as we will, the music refuses to come alive and we can cast no spell. Every performer knows this, and he knows, too, how hard he must work if he is to reach a degree of spontaneity and avoid a mere routine level. Understanding, preparation, experience, bodily health and physical well-being – all these are vital factors. Inspiration is another and perhaps the most important of all. It can only come from imagination, instinct, and the command of a quiet mind.

The Press devoted generous space to these early efforts of ours; from the critics we could invariably count on helpful and often penetrating comment. Among them were Neville

Cardus, Granville Hill, and Samuel Langford; all men of wisdom, experience and erudition. Waiting in the green room for the concert to begin, one of us would peep through the red curtain at the side of the platform to discover at whose tender mercy we would be that evening. When we caught a glimpse of Langford, sitting as he always did in the front row, head bowed forward, white beard nestling closely on his waistcoat, we would carry this news back to our nervous companions, and add yet more stress to those anxious minutes. Those judicious ears missed nothing; the reviews we read next morning could be very critical, but they were never unkind and never destructive. If a pat on the back was deserved it was not withheld, and there would be a word of encouragement as well. Very often, some happy turn of phrase would throw a clear light on something we had certainly been taught but not yet fully grasped. In all their writings it was possible to detect a note of optimism, a hint of faith in a new generation into whose hands the musical life of the nation would pass. They were the guardians of artistic integrity and good taste.

These were not the only opportunities for playing in public which came along during our student days. With the encouragement of Carl Fuchs two friends, Eric Roberts, violinist, and Rowland Carr, cellist, joined me in forming a piano trio. We had a few standard works in our repertoire which we had studied in the class, and with these we gave concerts in seven or eight towns in the area. Some of these we organised ourselves; they naturally attracted very small audiences. The smallest of all was in Todmorden where we owed a deep debt of gratitude to twelve listeners who were faithful enough, and perhaps misguided enough, to turn out on a wintry night to hear what we had to offer.

There were also sonata recitals in various places; one or two with Michael Collins in Liverpool for the British Music Society, some with Harry Blech and another, much more venturesome, with Maurice Ward which we put on at our expense in Manchester's Memorial Hall. Here we dared to include the D minor Sonata of Brahms and one of the Delius Sonatas. This last aroused a certain degree of interest for as yet the music of the Yorkshire-born composer was only infrequently performed. Alas! We failed to arouse in Neville Cardus any warmth of enthusiasm for our efforts. His notice in the *Manchester Guardian* was a scholarly appraisal of Delius as a composer of chamber music. It ended with the reflection: 'It is bad luck for Manchester and Delius alike that the city nowadays hears his music at a point below its greatest – that is, when we hear it at all.'

That a musician of such fame and distinction as Adolph Brodsky should be Principal of the College was a source of intense pride to every student. It was difficult to believe that this short, stocky man who walked slowly across the Hall, and sometimes even smiled at us, could have been the friend of Brahms, Tchaikovsky, Grieg, and many other legendary figures of the past. To be lucky enough to find oneself sitting next to him at a Hallé performance of Brahms' Fourth Symphony (as Gordon Green once did) and to listen to his reminiscences of its first performance, at which he had been present, was awe-inspiring. We all knew the story of the Tchaikovsky Violin Concerto – that Leopold Auer had declared it to be unplayable, and that it had been our Principal who gave it its first performance in 1881 with Richter conducting the Vienna Philharmonic Orchestra. When Brodsky walked across the Hall, history came to life.

As a teacher he was demanding and difficult to please so there was always trouble if anything we played for him was not meticulously prepared. We took care to see that did not happen too often! Now and again I took part in his ensemble lessons in the Hall. We played on the platform as though in a formal concert whilst he sat below in the front row, a glass of Russian tea always at his side. At other times I would attend one of his violin lessons in his own room in order to accompany some concerto or other. That could be a nerve-racking experience for his temperament was mercurial and his moods could range between a kindly geniality and a wrath so fearful that it was as though the heavens would open. There were many things wrong with our playing, but more often than not it was his passionate insistence on a faultless rhythm that caused the storms to break. As though it were yesterday,

41

I remember those terrifying moments when the opening of the last movement of the Brahms Violin Concerto failed to satisfy him. His eyes flashing, he might seize the copy from the stand, tear it from top to bottom and scatter the pieces around the floor. Once, he snatched the bow from his student's trembling hand and broke it across his knees. The earth shook beneath us both! If only some merciful power could have whisked us away at that moment, far from that fury! Yet, it usually came right in the end; when finally the elusive character of that Hungarian rhythm was truly captured a breath-taking transformation took place. A blissful smile would come over Brodsky's face, he would nod approvingly and say, very softly, "So!" Suddenly, all was peaceful and it was as though there had never been any problem at all. Now we could do it exactly as he wanted, as it ought to be, and as it always must be. That was all that mattered, everything else was forgotten. But for the two of us, emerging pale and shaken from his room, it was something never to be forgotten.

During the remainder of my student days I renewed my acquaintance with the studios of the BBC and in time began to feel at home in surroundings which had once seemed so strange. In Manchester there were more solo engagements and in Belfast Godfrey Brown had not forgotten his promise. My first concerto there, the Grieg, was in the summer of 1927, and eighteen months later it was the Schumann which took me over the Irish Sea again. The overnight crossing from Heysham was becoming quite familiar.

Percy Pitt, too, was as good as his word. Three months after the interview with him I was back at Savoy Hill for the first of a number of broadcasts on what was known as the Daventry wavelength. To begin with, these were solo engagements, but before long there was a new development, a partnership with a 'cellist in a duo-sonata. Vyvyan Lewis was a pupil of Madame Suggia and a player of marked sensitivity. I no longer remember how it was initially arranged for us to come together, though we both shared north country connections for she was the daughter of a former vicar of Ramsbottom and had appeared as soloist with the Lancaster Orchestral Society. She lived now with

1. *Brahms*

2. *Adolf Brodsky (standing) with Edward Grieg (centre), Madame Grieg (left) and Madame Brodsky (right)*

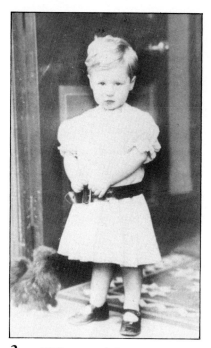

3. *Clifton, aged 2*

4. *Margaret and Thompson Helliwell*

5. *The author and Claud Biggs*

6. *Endre Wolf, Maurice Lindsay and the author in the television studio*

7. *Gordon Green*

8. *The Forces Music Club, with Clifton Helliwell standing left and Sir Adrian Boult conducting Reproduced by courtesy of the BBC*

9. *The author with Willis Grant*

10. *Vlado Perlemuter and John Manduell (right)*

her widowed mother in Chelsea and it was there that we met for rehearsals. Our first work was the 'Cello Sonata by Jean Huré. Musically it was a most enjoyable experience, but a little daunting for me from another point of view. I gratefully accepted Mrs Lewis's invitation to stay for dinner but was quite unprepared for the imposing grandeur of a Cheyne Walk dining-room. The demeanour of my hostess was exceedingly formal and correct; an expressionless butler – forbiddingly austere – stood behind my chair. Worst of all, I found before me a multitudinous array of cutlery, utterly confusing in its variety. As course followed course, the problem of which implement to choose could only be solved by surreptitious glances to right and left. And whatever should be done, I wondered, with those pretty little paper frills which decorated the cutlets? In the end it all passed off smoothly enough, but it struck me forcibly that to enter my chosen profession was going to need much more than purely musical expertise. My lessons in the social graces were beginning. There was much for me to learn, and in the meantime the ground seemed much firmer, to my great relief, when we got back to our rehearsal.

In all, Vyvyan Lewis and I shared three broadcasts, adding to our joint repertoire the Beethoven Sonata in A and the E minor of Brahms. A little later the A major Violin Sonata by Brahms brought me to Savoy Hill again.

Not all the engagements of these student days were on this level. There came one day to the College an urgent request for a pianist to go post-haste to a cinema in Lloyd Street, not far away. The talkies had not yet arrived and all films, of course, still needed a musical accompaniment of one sort or another. For its evening performances this establishment could boast a smallish orchestra, but the music for the matinées was provided by a lone pianist. His failure to appear on this occasion had created an emergency, and I was to take his place.

I was taken first to the manager's office. He was a gloomy, humourless man, obviously submerged by a sea of troubles, one of which, at least, he hoped had just been solved.

"You've done this before, of course," he said.

43

For the first time in my life I was in the presence of an employer. "Well, no," I replied with some diffidence. "Actually I haven't."

"Oh well," he assured me, "there's no difficulty at all. It's quite straightforward – nothing to it!"

He took me to the orchestra pit. There on the piano, on a specially strengthened and built-out stand, was a pile of music some seven or eight inches thick. "All you do," said my mentor, "is to start at the beginning, play right through this lot, and be sure to stop when the lights go up. It should work out about right." He disappeared, if anything rather more dejected than ever, but content to leave me to it.

The lights went down, the screen which towered above me flickered into life, and I began to play. First the overture, followed by an endless assortment of waltzes, drawing-room pieces, marches – everything had a place in that mammoth collection. I never discovered whether any attempt had been made to arrange all this music in some kind of synchronising order. For a time, I was too busy to look at the screen at all, and anyway, I told myself, that was not in my brief. But after twenty minutes or so, I risked it. There above me, monstrously distorted at that angle, were pictures of a desert, an oasis, waving palms. Very nice, and the temperature by now was exactly right. But alas! At that moment I was playing a catchy little Scottish tune called 'The Wee MacGregor Patrol'.

It seemed certain that something was going disastrously wrong, but there was nothing for it but to plough on for another two hours. When, with blessed relief, the lights came up again, I had disposed of most of the pile of music, my fingers were sore and aching, and I was in a state bordering on complete exhaustion. I reeled back to college, filled with admiration for the stamina of countless pianists who could do this sort of thing all day and every day and also for those among them (and there were many) who had cultivated the art of improvisation so brilliantly that they needed no printed copies at all!

One or two further visits to the cinema followed this first initiation, not to play the piano in the afternoons but to join the orchestra for the evening performances. Now, I was required to play a large and somewhat repulsive harmonium which filled in the harmonies left incomplete by the inadequate number of players. There were lengthy sections when I had had nothing to play and this meant counting empty bars, which I had never had to do before. There was no conductor; the little orchestra was directed by the violinist and there was no visible beat. That would have been a great help, but in its absence I found it very difficult to come in in the right place. In fact, I was lost for much of the time, and when occasionally I ventured a chord or two it was all too obvious that my guess was wrong. It was infuriating but I could hardly resent the pain on the leader's face, nor the scowls which he directed towards me. Fortunately, there were very few of these uncomfortable sessions, partly because I was now coming to the end of my time at the College, but after one of them the long-suffering violinist-leader allowed himself one indignant and clearly heartfelt criticism: "A right b---- orchestral player you are!" sent me away feeling very small indeed.

The curriculum of the College laid down that all students should take a second practical study. For mine I was allotted to Dr Thomas Keighley for organ lessons. Half an hour in each week was very little and opportunities to practise on the small organ at the end of the hall were limited, even if time could have been found. It did not seem to matter a great deal to either of us. It was inevitable that little serious work could be done, and of those lessons I remember hardly anything. My tutor had many extra responsibilities as Professor of Harmony and Composition. Perhaps because of these pressures he was addicted to very precise time-keeping, not so much in musical performance, but rather as a constraint dictated by the clock. Accordingly, at the exact moment which marked the end of a less than inspiring half-hour, the lesson was abruptly at an end. It mattered not at all if I happened to be in the middle of a bar. With an unresolved chord hanging miserably in mid-air one awaited his valedictory comment, and invariably it came: "Continue on those lines".

Oddly enough, there was an outcome. During the fourth year of my course the parish church of Brathay in Wesmorland advertised for an organist and choirmaster. On many visits to the Lake District I had seen and admired the old church which stood high above the river, halfway between Ambleside and Skelwith Bridge. Truth to tell, my determination to obtain this post was prompted by a purely non-musical consideration. For a long time I had wanted my parents to own a car. They had no such intention but, I thought, if this appointment could be mine, a car would be a necessity. After all, Brathay was some thirty miles from Carnforth. Another vital factor in my little scheme was the offered salary of an attractive £50 per annum.

There was one real problem. I knew nothing of the liturgy of the Church of England, with its forms of worship far removed from the comparative simplicity of Nonconformist services. Not only that, no grasp of psalm-pointing had so far come my way, though I was well aware of those dangerous pitfalls. Nothing daunted, I set to work, embarking on a close study of all the relevant portions of the Book of Common Prayer, and seeking help and advice from every possible source.

My trial Sunday, approached with not a little trepidation, must have passed muster. Although the Brathay authorities knew that I was not a member of their Church, the post was offered to me, and accepted. The car was bought (for fifty pounds) and my parents fell in with my little plan, which they had clearly seen through from the start. Then came some lessons in driving, and my first Sunday duty drew near. I viewed it with some concern both for the niceties of Matins and Sung Eucharist and the coping with unaccustomed gears on the hills of Lakeland.

The incumbent was Canon Baines, now an old man and seemingly very tired. He had great charm of manner, an authority born of age and experience, and a deeply held belief in the value of music as an adjunct to worship. He expected the highest possible musical standards and to share those responsibilities with him was inspiring. I was to learn something of his difficulties. The congregation consisted largely of wealthy families who, being now retired from prosperous businesses in Yorkshire, lived in splendid houses on the shores of Lake Windermere. We held an occasional choir practice in one or other magnificent home.

Shortly after my arrival, Canon Baines received a letter which represented the views of about half the congregation. It demanded the adoption of new and up-to-date hymn tunes, failing which subscriptions would be withdrawn. Instructions accordingly were passed to me for action. But in the course of the next week or so a second letter arrived, this time from the rest of the parishioners, threatening precisely the same sanction unless there could be a return to the old, familiar and well-loved tunes! How the matter was finally resolved I cannot remember, but there can be no doubt that the Canon's diplomacy was equal to the strain.

Year by year, in the last week of the summer term, the College maintained the tradition originally established by its founder, Sir Charles Hallé, of presenting the Annual Examination Concerts. Their rather unusual title derived, not from any connection with our own examinations, which by then were all completed, but from Hallé's insistence that at the end of the year the College itself must be examined – by the public. A series of concerts, representing all departments, and held on each night of the week, would offer a progress report by which the year's work might be judged. This annual review had long been a feature of Manchester's musical life, and it continued without interruption until the College itself was no more.

In the Summer of 1929 my course was at an end. Claud Biggs decided that my contribution to the concert on June 28th should be the first book of Variations on a Theme of Paganini by Brahms. It was a fitting work with which to mark the close of four extremely happy and rewarding years and with which to say farewell to a College which had inspired my deepest affection. There were two appearances for me in the programme. It ended with a performance of the Sextet for Strings and Piano by Paul Juon, for which I joined five of my colleagues from Carl Fuchs's ensemble class.

With this, however, my evening was not yet finished. The College had arranged a programme of music to be given in the Council Chamber of the University following the

47

conferment of Honorary Degrees by Professor Alexander. At 9.30 p.m. I took my place there at the piano to play two transcriptions of Bach Chorales, the F minor Fantasie by Chopin, and to accompany some groups of songs.

As we drove home through the night at the conclusion of this second concert, I knew full well that this busy evening had been a turning point in my life. My student days were over. Manchester and all it had meant to me now lay behind. I looked back over four marvellous years, realising the treasures they had brought me, the friendships I had made. It had been a prelude to a new world. But now was not a time for looking back. A stronger impulse was to look forward, though with that my spirits fell. As I saw it that night, the future looked hazy, ill-defined, and very uncertain. At that moment I could count on the organ work at Brathay, and a handful of pupils scattered over the Northern countryside. But of what, if anything, might lie ahead in the larger world I knew nothing at all.

CHAPTER 6

"Like a shaft of light . . ."

AMONGST us there are some who are fortunate enough to have an instinctive grasp of the art of living. They are the lucky ones; they are convinced beyond doubt that everything is for the best; they are equally certain that as one door closes another will most surely open. Their faith in the ultimate rightness of things is unshakeable; they are happy, blessed people and they are to be envied. Perhaps now, in more mature years, I can claim some small share in their comfortable philosophy but at the age of twenty-one I certainly could not. As I look back, I have to admit that I had no entitlement whatever to the anxieties, the doubts, and the fears which filled my days, but nevertheless they were very real at the time. I had no means of knowing that the smile of fortune was already turned in my direction, nor that all was being neatly arranged for me by a beneficent fate.

In the brilliant sunshine of a July morning the waters of Belfast Lough gleamed and sparkled in the wake of the Heysham boat as it neared the end of its nightly journey across the Irish Sea. I stood on deck, the gentle slopes of County Down already visible on the horizon to my left, and more distinctly on my right the hills of Antrim in a haze of blue. With each moment, the shipyard gantries of the docks and the taller buildings of the city became more clearly focussed. It was a breathtaking scene.

An hour or so later my steps took me past the City Hall as I made my way once again to that gaunt building which was the BBC's home in the city. By now, after several visits, it was not unfamiliar but this time there was a difference; I was here to stay. The miracle had happened and its timing could not have been more precise. On the first morning of the summer vacation the BBC's unexpected letter had offered the post which three years earlier had been so nearly mine. This time it could be most eagerly accepted; this time nothing stood in the way. Here I was, climbing those narrow stairs in Linenhall Street, starting out on what was to be a very long journey.

In 1929 the BBC was seven years old. Its Belfast outpost, small as it was, enjoyed a considerable measure of autonomy with a broad commitment to offer to the listeners of Northern Ireland a range of home-produced programmes, a good proportion of them of a specialised regional interest. It was well-equipped for its task, with a permanent orchestra of some sixty to seventy players, a good number of local performers of professional standard in both music and drama, and a close association with the University and bodies such as the Belfast Philharmonic Society. The Drama Department was already held in high esteem. It had been developed and vitalised to a dynamic degree by Tyrone Guthrie, who had just left to pursue a career elsewhere. He was replaced by John Watt, a producer with whom I was to enjoy a happy and stimulating partnership in many ventures.

All told, the staff were few in number, but any lack of strength in that respect was more than matched by enthusiasm. Even after seven years of broadcasting there was still the feeling of being in at the beginning. That was not surprising; every day brought its experiments, its discoveries and its excitements. Countless ideas were yet to be tried out for the first time and in every project to be tackled there was a sense of adventure. It would naturally be impossible to recapture that atmosphere today. That sense of co-operation and adaptability of which we were then aware could only belong to a time when the potential of radio was beginning to emerge.

Technically, we all had our own particular job to do. My participation was under an agreement for service as a pianist, and even before my arrival I was already committed to play the B flat Rondo for Piano and Orchestra by Prince Louis Ferdinand – incidentally an attractive work which I have never since seen programmed – shortly after that, Beethoven's C minor Violin Sonata. But at Linenhall Street the departmental divisions of staff were blurred, and constantly we all found ourselves in the midst of activities for which we were not primarily engaged. Consequently, my duties in the first week included becoming an Uncle in the Children's Hour, reading a story and announcing the all-important birthday greetings. That was not all. I helped out in the percussion section of the orchestra, worked the 'thunder' sheet in a play production (nothing could have been more satisfying) and then became involved in the creation of sound effects. Far removed as all this was from the keyboard, I gleefully grasped every commitment which came my way.

The Children's Hour brought me two important benefits. Informality was the keynote of the programme and, to begin with, it was terrifying. There was no telling in which direction our improvised chatter would take us and there was certainly no time for inhibitions of any kind. There was also a good deal of improvisation at the piano. It all quickly ensured an easy familiarity with the microphone, which otherwise could have long retained its terror. It was not immediately visible, but we knew that it was there, hidden away within its framework of mahogany, decently draped with panels of purple silk. We gathered closely round it and it became quite friendly! The second benefit was equally important – and equally necessary. In one week, all trace of my Lancashire accent disappeared. The teasing and leg-pulling by my colleagues was not to be endured a moment longer; something had to be done about it, and it was. Oddly enough, in the years to come, the BBC for specific reasons went out of its way to make use of a regional accent, and there are many who will remember Wilfred Pickles' reading of the wartime News, short-lived as that experiment was. But in 1929 only the already well-established 'BBC voice' was acceptable.

I can no longer remember why I should have had anything to do with sound effects, but it was certainly true that any help which those of us around the studio could offer towards the solution of a current problem was always welcome. On one occasion there was a certain drama production which badly needed to simulate the sound of frying bacon. At that time I had the impression that the opening scene of every Irish play seemed to be set 'in the kitchen of a farmhouse in County Down', and so the requirement was not surprising. Numerous trials proved unsuccessful, quite hopeless in fact, and we knew all too well that to fry real bacon anywhere near the microphone would produce an excellent impression of a riotous Guy Fawkes night. The enticing sound remained stubbornly elusive until at the last attempt the sprinkling of a pinch of health salts into a glass of water held near the microphone provided the answer. Not only was the sound absolutely right, the inviting aroma was there as well for those with sufficient imagination! But all this sort of thing, fascinating as it was, remained on the fringe of my main task which was to contribute to the music programmes.

The Director of Music and conductor of the orchestra was Godfrey Brown, whose strange habit it was to wear a somewhat decrepit pair of slippers throughout the day in both office and studio. He was tall, loose-limbed, and in late middle-age his greying hair gave him a distinctly austere appearance. But his personality was friendliness itself and certainly he was a good friend to me. His professional life in music had been based on a hard school in his more youthful days; he would tell me about his early work in his native town of Barrow-in-Furness where his winter rehearsals with an amateur orchestra were held in an intensely cold hut, warmed only by a single, centrally-placed iron stove. To begin with, the clarinettist could never play anything decently because his chilled instrument was far below pitch. He would then sit close to the stove, warming his instrument, only to find eventually that it was now impossibly sharp. Much time would then have to be spent holding it out of the window to cool down, and in the whole evening the poor man's contribution could never have been more than a few bars.

Probably it was the kind of experience that had developed Godfrey Brown's acute concern for perfect intonation. It often amounted to an obsession. Of course it was important, but I have known him spend many minutes on end discussing the merits of a variety of low B flats with the tuba player, quite oblivious of the ill-concealed impatience of the whole orchestra. The unfortunate victim once gave vent to his own discontent by letting his long-held note fluctuate as wildly as an Irish banshee. "Let it settle down somewhere," I remember G.B. saying, "and then I can criticise it!" It could be cold in the Ulster Hall at ten o'clock on a wintry morning, yet I have known him to begin with Mendelssohn's *Midsummer Night's Dream* Overture and then happily spend the best part of an hour on those first four cruelly exposed bars, tuning the woodwind. Nothing could have been more unrealistic; a lost cause, if there ever was one.

For all that, his craftmanship and powers of organisation commanded respect. Under his direction the orchestra had been brought to a high standard of performance. Its programmes were invariably planned with imagination, and they reflected G.B.'s lively interest in contemporary music. Any new work which had made an impact elsewhere could be reasonably sure of a hearing in Belfast within a short space of time. This was particularly so in the field of large-scale compositions for chorus and orchestra, which were performed either in the studio or in public concerts arranged in conjunction with the City Corporation, the YMCA or the Philharmonic Society of which Godfrey Brown was also conductor. The city had every reason to be proud of its orchestra and it can be justly said that the audience well appreciated the chance to come to grips with works such as Arthur Bliss's *Morning Heroes* so soon after their first London performance.

Quite frequently there were visits by distinguished guest conductors, among whom Sir Henry Wood was always given the warmest welcome. To me, a newly-fledged member of the profession, Sir Henry's rehearsals were a revelation. His preparation was planned down to the smallest detail. Not a moment was wasted. Here was craftsmanship of a unique quality, an object lesson in superb musical organisation. In all his work there was an impressive honesty of purpose. Not the least of his gifts was an exceptional command of the felicitous word which in itself could be both an illumination and an inspiration.

One instance remains clearly in my memory. At the marvellous entry of the clarinet in the thirteenth of Elgar's 'Enigma' Variations he called out: "Like a shaft of light from a window!" The effect of this on the player, who knew exactly what was wanted, was magical. Sir Henry knew precisely how to make his intentions crystal clear. Most important of all, nothing was changed when it came to the performance. Inexperienced as I was, and playing under him for the first time (in Lord Berners' Suite, *The Triumph of Neptune*) I was profoundly and most comfortably aware of a sense of security. There were those who complained that Sir Henry's performances lacked imagination and insight, that in his concentration on detail the panoramic vista was lost, or at least neglected. It was left to the perceptive commentator of the local *Newsletter* to present a compensatory view. 'If that administrative ability,' he wrote, 'and that fidelity which declines to yield to passing impulses, may deprive us of some of the glorious moments that a more adventurous leader might provide, we have the solid compensation of security from the disasters that so often overtake him who rides for a fall.'

In later years, a closer association with Sir Henry allowed me an opportunity to look through some of his scores. It was an intimate glimpse behind the scenes. Blue pencil markings were plentiful. Every change in the number of beats per bar was clearly indicated, every variation in tonal values boldly underlined. Everything was there, even rehearsal reminders – 'Tell the 2nd Clarinet he is out of tune!' 'Tell the story about ...' – a little puzzling perhaps, but my admiration for his skill was in no way diminished.

Godfrey Brown saw to it that Belfast audiences and the radio listeners of Northern Ireland could hear the foremost artists of the day: Szigeti, Albert Sammons, Gaspar Cassado, Antoni Sala and Antonio Brosa were among the string players who came. The pianists were numerous: Egon Petri, Clifford Curzon, Moiseiwitsch, are names which come to mind. The Norwegian pianist, Johanne Stockmarr, was a particular favourite. Her performances of the Beethoven Fourth, Schumann and Grieg concertos were marked by clarity of understanding and the subordination of a superb technique to musicianship and artistic integrity. Those were qualities which reflected her warm and engaging personality. Here again, as at the College, was a link with the past which I treasured. I felt a tremor of excitement when she told me one day "I must be home on Thursday because I shall be having tea with Mrs Grieg."

Then, to my great delight, there was my own teacher, Claud Biggs, who had also chosen to play the Beethoven G major. That was a studio performance on a summer evening. As absent-minded as ever, Claud was not to be found when the moment for the announcement arrived. Amid the general alarm, it occurred to me to lean out of the reception room window, looking along Linenhall Street towards the City Hall. There in the distance, still some hundreds of yards away, I could see him proceeding very casually in the direction of the studio. Godfrey Brown's solution for the emergency was to invite me to play the five solo bars with which the concerto opens, calculating that the ensuing orchestral tutti would allow time for Claud to be in position at the piano. It was an embarrasing moment. It seemed to me quite wrong that so important a work should begin under such false pretences, and I made some demur which fortunately was accepted. In due course, Claud arrived to give a beautiful, and complete, performance; how the delay was explained to a waiting world I never discovered.

There were, however, plenty of opportunities for me to play with the orchestra in my own right and I valued the chance to gain experience as soloist in several of the well-known concertos. Our musical director must have been strongly drawn to the music of Liszt, for, in addition to the E flat Concerto, I had to prepare and play the 'Wanderer' Fantasia, the 'Hungarian' Fantasy and the Busoni transcription of the 'Rhapsodie Espagnole'. Works for piano and orchestra also tempted him to explore some out-of-the-way corners of the repertoire. Consequently I found myself undertaking the solo part in works such as 'Mon Lac' by Witkowski, which, truth to tell, made little appeal to me – so little, in fact, that I organised a sizeable cut in the score, much to the disgust of a certain member of the staff who had persuaded G.B. to include it. Then there was Hely-Hutchinson's 'The Young Idea' – 'cleverly scored,' said the critic 'and those who like jazz would like it' – 'The Rio Grande' by Constant Lambert, almost immediately after its first performance in London, the Toccata for Piano and Orchestra by Respighi and the marvellously effective Fantastic Suite by Ernst Schelling.

The great singers of the day were well known to the Belfast public; artists of the calibre of Peter Dawson, Muriel Brunskill, Horace Stevens, Elsie Suddaby, Dennis Noble; and many of them made repeated visits to perform both in public and the studio. The usual pattern of programme building at that time was for the soloist to appear with orchestra in the first half of the concert, and again in the second with piano accompaniment. For me to be able to associate as accompanist with such fine artists was of inestimable benefit. I began to learn many things. There were differences, I discovered, in their approach to performance, in degrees of tension and nervousness and its bearing on the final result. Rehearsal procedures were never identical; there were some who encouraged the accompanist to contribute an element of positive leadership; there were others who did not. There were the perfectionists who rehearsed thoroughly with never a detail unrevealed, quite unlike those who would risk a great deal for the sake of freshness and spontaneity on the night. Some were easy to work with, some were difficult. That there existed a positive relationship between personality and performance became abundantly clear, and it was not long before I saw that tact and diplomacy had a place among the most important requisites of the accompanist's art.

To me, the greatest experience of those years, and the most artistically demanding, was to accompany Elisabeth Schumann in two concerts. Here was the art of a royal line of *lieder* singing, a perfection of grace and friendly charm. The voice was of great beauty, though not particularly powerful. Its glory lay in the subtlety of the colouring, especially in the lower register, and she had at her command an ethereal pianissimo. Flexibility of tone was allied to perfect diction and a consummate technique which allowed her to span an extended phrase with the greatest of ease. To the songs of Schubert, Brahms, Strauss and Hugo Wolf she brought a mastery of style but also a winsome happiness which on occasion could put even her powers of characterisation at some risk.

Elisabeth Schumann was kind enough to invite me to accompany her on a lengthy concert tour and it was bitterly disappointing to be unable to accept, but my BBC duties made it impossible.

Years later, we worked together on a number of occasions. By then she felt that her powers were diminishing, though any such possibility would surely have been imperceptible to her audiences. But, with the integrity of the genuine artist, she was fully prepared to accept the truth as she believed it to be. We discussed the choice of songs for her recital and I tried to help. But to some of my suggestions her answer was "No, no, not that one – not any more". She knew exactly what remained to her.

Finally, I accompanied her on what proved, sadly, to be her last appearance. It was not long before her death in 1952, a television broadcast for which the set was designed to represent a small drawing-room. Arranged around it at various vantage points was a series of souvenirs of her life in music – a piece of china, a programme, an item of jewellery, and so on. The plan was that as she walked round the room each object would prompt some reminiscence and have a bearing on the song she would sing. Alas, she was required not only to sing but to speak into the microphone, and that did not come easily to her. She was terribly nervous, visibly trembling. At the rehearsal she was quite unable to remember the proper sequence and so a large blackboard on which helpful cues were chalked was carefully placed out of camera range. Now all seemed to be well, at least for the moment. But at the live broadcast itself, she was even more nervous. Halfway through, the moment came when suddenly everything had gone. Her mind was blank and she could no longer think what she should say or do. A few silent seconds seemed interminable, and then she turned helplessly towards me and said, very simply, "Play, Clifton!" The opening notes of Wolf's 'Mausfallen Sprüchlein' brought the programme to life again.

Elisabeth Schumann was not among those singers visiting Belfast who attempted to pay the city a compliment by singing an Irish song. Those who did, and there were not a few, little knew what risks they were taking, nor what rough critical handling might ensue. '- - -' said one writer, 'arranged his own Waterloo when he elected to sing "Father O'Flynn" as an encore. One could imagine no better voice than his for the song, which, not pretending to be "good" music, is always enjoyable as good humour if properly sung . . . But let them not try Irish songs unless under qualified guidance. For, in the first place, what they sing, they sing, as a rule, badly, and in the second, what they sing is in itself bad, as a rule. It is mostly of the *genus* music-hall, *species* stage-Irish. What an insult it is, if they but realised it, to serve up these emanations from places East of the Irish Sea to people of a nation which possesses a music of its own nowhere surpassed.'

The real music of Ireland repeatedly found its way into our studio programmes and I quickly came to know and love this 'music of its own', both in its original form, untouched in any way, and in those more sophisticated versions created by composers such as Stanford, Hamilton Harty and Herbert Hughes. The songs of Harty, in particular, were a special joy, their accompaniments of marvellously judged texture, written by one who was himself an accompanist *par excellence*. His orchestral works, too, contributed frequently to our programmes, the 'Irish' Symphony, for example (in its Scherzo, virtuoso playing by the flautist, Harry Dyson, could be guaranteed) and that beautifully evocative tone poem, *With the Wild Geese*.

The vigour of the Drama Department periodically received extra stimulus from the visits to the studio of the players of the Abbey Theatre in Dublin. Lennox Robinson, Barry Fitzgerald, Maureen Delany, Eileen Crowe, F.J. McCormick, Sara Algood – these are names which build a bridge of memories for me over a span of more than forty years. Their days in the studio were crowded, exciting and alive. Since their productions usually called for incidental music of some kind, I was often there on the fringe, listening to the lilting cadences of Irish voices and watching, fascinated, the miraculous character transformations when the red light glowed and we were on the air. Sara Allgood is remembered for her vivid portrayals of Sean O'Casey's characters, some of which had created a sensation on their first nights in Dublin. In addition to her career as an actress, she was also a singer. On a number of occasions she gave recitals of Irish songs and for me it was a great pleasure both to accompany her and to claim her friendship. Once, I remember, I crossed the Irish Sea specially, breaking into a holiday, just to accompany her in three songs. Her singing of an Irish melody, authentic in its original simplicity, was intensely moving. The accompaniments were of necessity simple and very slender; elaboration in the style of the modern arranger would have been hopelessly out of place.

From time to time a 'country' singer would be engaged to do exactly the same thing. He was usually quite untrained musically, and one such occasion was not without its hint of comedy. When we met in the studio for our rehearsal he came empty-handed.

"Have you copies of your songs?" I asked. Assuring me that he had indeed, he produced from his waistcoat pocket a closely-folded piece of paper, perhaps an inch and a half square. Spread out, it proved to be a single page torn from something like the *Daily Express Song Book*. His three tunes were there, set out merely as melodic lines without accompaniment. Obviously I was going to have to invent some suitable harmonies and make up a background. I was thinking about this as I sat at the piano, when nervously he came up to me.

"You know," he said, "I'm very frightened about all this."

"Why is that?" I asked in as sympathetic a tone as I could muster.

"Well, you see, these tunes are all written in the treble clef, and I can't possibly sing up there."

"Would you like me to transpose them?"

"Could you possibly do that? I'm sure it would help me a great deal."

He had brightened considerably until I asked how much transposition he thought would be necessary. He had no idea!

Eventually, perhaps a shade wickedly, I said: "What about an octave?"

"Could you really do it that much?" he asked eagerly.

So I played them exactly as they were printed and a very happy singer exclaimed: "That's absolutely marvellous; I don't know how you did it!"

All went well. It was a nice little broadcast, and when it was all over he very shyly produced half-a-crown from another waistcoat pocket. I declined it as politely as I could.

The leader of the orchestra was Philip Whiteway who, as a student of Dr Brodsky, had preceded me in Manchester by about a year. His playing was extremely musical and marked by a security and reliability for which his generally relaxed approach must have been largely responsible. His natural talent, his capacity for hard work, and the warmth of his personality made him an invaluable member of the Music Department. He and I lived under the same roof in Fitzroy Avenue where Mr and Mrs Patterson let rooms to 'young gentlemen'. For full board we paid two pounds ten shillings a week. Behind the lace curtains at the front of the house we shared the communal dining-table with an ever-changing population of mostly non-musical lodgers. To them, we were something of a mystery. They knew that we had something to do with music, but where was our real work, they would ask. To play an instrument was obviously a distressingly inadequate means of earning a living.

Each day we would all be there at the right time, awaiting the arrival of our cooked 'tea-meal', Mrs Patterson sweeping in to check the laid table, to throw up her hands exclaiming, "Lord save us, there's no plates," and to bustle out again muttering invocations to "Ess, ess, Peter and Paul." Everything being put to rights, she would then announce: "Well now, there's beans on toast, eggs on toast, cheese on toast;" and after a brief pause, say invitingly, "The baked beans are very nice today!" The list never changed, except in its order of precedence. The daily ritual notwithstanding, we knew well that we were expected to choose the first-mentioned dish; it was a lesson soon learned.

My first impression of Belfast people was disappointing. I found them dour, humourless and unimaginative, though as time went on this proved to be a hasty view. Of Ireland itself and its tortured past I knew nothing at all. Some vague idea that it had once been a troubled country was all that had emerged from the cold print of history books at school. It was therefore something of a shock to find that the troubles belonged not only to the past, but to the present as well. I was sitting one day on the lower deck of a tramcar, passing the City Hall, when suddenly the conductor ordered us all to lie on the floor. There had been no warning of anything amiss, but since every passenger obeyed with remarkable promptness, so did I. Seconds later a machine gun opened up from an uncomfortably close vantage point. It was all over in a moment, the firing stopped, no one was hurt and as far as I could see little or no damage was done. A pointless episode, even if momentarily alarming. I took my little story home to Fitzroy Avenue, eager for enlightenment. "What ever is all this about?" I asked. I was told that on some previous occasion, another Englishman, equally mystified, had asked exactly the same question, adding further, "Has it anything to do with religion?" The reply he received was, "It's nothing whatever to do with religion at all. It's all those b----- Protestants!" I had to make do with that.

Philip Whiteway and I became good friends. Naturally we shared many interests. More often than not, a little portable gramophone played Gershwin's 'Rhapsody in Blue' as a background to breakfast, giving the day a cheerful start. In every spare moment Philip practised diligently and I therefore acquired even closer familiarity with the Glazounov Violin Concerto. We worked together a great deal in the studio, of course, not only in serious and demanding chamber music but in something much lighter. Philip was in charge of the Radio Quartet, a combination of two violins, 'cello and piano, which contributed several quite lengthy broadcast programmes in each week. Its repertoire of suites, marches, waltzes and selections from musical comedies was extensive. Nowadays it would be called wallpaper music, but in spite of its unpretentious purpose a good deal of careful preparation was essential. At the piano, I soon discovered how much concentration was needed if the way through the repeats and da capos of a Johann Strauss waltz was not to be lost altogether. There were times, I fear, when it was!

Looking back, it seems a little odd that the Radio Quartet should have enjoyed so much popularity, but in those days when broadcasting was young, it was a novelty for background music to be available at the turn of a switch. The whole exercise provided a useful introduction to one aspect of music-making which to me was quite new. We played from 'cued' parts which, for the uninitiated, enabled a piece of music requiring a large group of players to be performed by very few. A melody for a missing instrument such as, in our case, the clarinet, would have to be filled in by the piano, unless it was already planned for a violin to take it over. Hence the need for prior rehearsal and a clear understanding of what one might call 'lines of demarcation'. Without that there could be disaster. Such 'arranged' versions of music could, of course, tempt the unwary into indiscretion for, quite obviously, there are important orchestral works which ought never to be performed in anything less than their original form. The most striking example ever to come my way was an edition of Rimsky-Korsakov's *'Scheherazade' Suite* which bore the inscription: 'Not recommended for performance by fewer than five players.'! Needless to say, it formed no part of our Radio Quartet programmes.

At that time, the usual pattern of orchestral concerts to which I have already referred, kept me unoccupied until the moment for the group of solo items with piano accompaniment arrived in the latter part of the programme. That I should be doing nothing for quite lengthy periods seemed to cause Godfrey Brown some concern. From his point of view this would not do at all, and so before very long I found myself required to help out in the orchestra's percussion department. The tambourine and the triangle offered few technical problems and for a time my contribution was limited to those two instruments. The important thing was to count the number of 'rest' bars correctly. Eventually I could do it without too much anxiety, though some of the Wagner excerpts demanded much concentration. In time, when more trustworthy, I graduated to a pair of cymbals, and actually played them in a performance of *The Dream of Gerontius* conducted by Elgar himself. Still later, at a public performance, the tubular bells in Tchaikovsky's '1812' were left to my tender mercies. They are much more difficult to manage than they look, and if their full sonority is to be achieved, they must be struck on the rim, not on the side. The repeated pealing of their downward scales begins towards the end of the overture and sets up so much noise and reverberation at close quarters that every other sound, even that of the full orchestra, is overwhelmed. Nothing else can be heard. I began in the right place, I struck them all fairly and squarely, keeping my eye firmly on those top rims. To be responsible for that mass of sound was thrilling, and so I continued with unflagging energy and determination until at last a tug on my coat-tails drew my reluctant attention to the fact that the overture had come to an end quite a few moments earlier. A highly entertained audience was waiting to applaud!

Not very sensibly, I began these adventures in the 'kitchen' department of the orchestra with some slight degree of resentment. Was I not engaged as a pianist, and was it not a somewhat unwarranted use of my free time? Only much later did I realise that it had been a marvellous opportunity for me to become familiar with the standard works of the orchestral repertoire, and even better, to study the principles of orchestration and instrumental colouring at first hand.

CHAPTER 7

Ventures and temptations

MY days in the studio were varied. I would go from accompaniment to chorus rehearsals, from the Radio Quartet to percussion in the orchestra. There would often be a new concerto to learn or a recital group to prepare – and there was always the Children's Hour. When plays or sketches called for incidental music of some kind I welcomed participation in a dramatic production. It was in this area that I became fascinated by the possibilities of sound radio. Day by day the experiments of my producer colleagues revealed more of the potential of sound effects – the use of echo chambers, for example. or the facility of mixing music and speech originating in separate studios. What was soon to be known rather grandly as 'multi-studio technique' was still in its infancy, but it could already be seen that it would add a new dimension to broadcasting. Much of what we were trying to do would now be seen as quite primitive, but it was far from being so regarded at the time.

When the moment of truth arrived and the red light glowed everyone concerned shared excitement, tension and anxiety. The goddess of luck had an important part to play and on occasion she played it very positively. I recall a programme for St Patrick's Day which was daringly planned to include the relay of a scene from a play being performed on the stage of the Abbey Theatre in Dublin. It was an ambitious project that created a number of problems. To begin with, the engineers reported that the microphone, comparatively insensitive as it was then, could not be positioned unobtrusively whilst still remaining efficient enough to pick up the stage dialogue. It was a real difficulty until someone cunningly thought of hollowing out a loaf of bread which lay on a kitchen-table in the centre of the stage. From that hidden vantage point the microphone proved fully equal to its task!

A more serious hazard was caused by the lack of spare lines between Belfast and Dublin; adequate communication was obviously essential but unfortunately non-existent. The intention was that the play should be preceded by orchestral music from the the Belfast studio – not surprisingly, it was to be 'The Londonderry Air'. This was duly played at what was calculated to be the right moment in advance of the change-over. Then, by the happiest of accidents it turned out that a trio in the Abbey Theatre was also playing that same music. By sheer chance, our listeners were imperceptibly transferred in a shared identical bar from one to the other – and the goddess received heartfelt thanks for her gracious assistance.

I found the temptation to become involved in the existing mysteries of radio production irresistible and constantly looked for ways in which more opportunity might come my way. Browsing one day in a dusty second-hand bookshop, I came across the tattered libretto of an early eighteenth-century play, *The Farmer's Wife* by Charles Dibdin. Nearby, a heap of yellowing sheets in considerable disorder proved to be songs and choruses with piano accompaniment, composed for that self-same play by Henry Bishop. A torn title page revealed that, as a comic opera, it had been performed 'with the highest applause' at the Theatre Royal, Covent Garden, in the year before Waterloo. No orchestral parts were to be seen, and there was no score, but the arm of coincidence could not have been expected to stretch even further than it had already. Could this be turned into a radio programme, I wondered. Impossible to answer that question then, but I bought the libretto and as many of the bedraggled music sheets as could be found and hopefully carried them away.

I waited impatiently for some spare time. When it came at last, a closer inspection of the libretto revealed that the plot centred on the machinations of a bold, bad baronet, Sir Charles Courtly, who runs away with Mistress

Cornflower, the farmer's wife. The farmer, a simple soul, suspects nothing until he finds that his wife is missing. She has abandoned country joys for the sophistications of the town and he must bring her back. There was some enchanting music for vocal ensembles and chorus, and among a number of vividly characterised solo songs there was one of particular beauty, 'Fly swift, ye Zephyrs'. The plot offered plenty of scope for sound effects, the clattering of hooves, the jolting of carriages, the watchman's bell and so on, and it would all come to a happy ending with a rollicking chorus for the whole company. So far so good; it was worth a try.

In a matter of weeks the adaptation of the script and the orchestration of the music was completed. At 10 p.m. on May 19th, 1930, the orchestral, drama and effects studios silently awaited a steady red light. With it, a blue cue light in Studio 1 signalled the start of the overture and *The Farmer's Wife* was on the air, Philip Whiteway conducting. I had learned a great deal about what was necessary for everything to be ready for that moment. All went smoothly. Studio opera was not yet by any means a familiar radio event and perhaps it was for that reason that the broadcast attracted a generous measure of kindly comment in the Press.

It had been a happy venture and encouraging enough to whet the appetite. Before very long, I was tackling something new, a radio version of Offenbach's sparkling operetta, *Geneviève de Brabant,* a work famous not least for its well-known and very popular duet, 'The Two Gendarmes'. This time there was no need for re-orchestration but there was a good deal to be done in adapting the play for the microphone, and in solving some awkward problems of selection and condensation. When it was broadcast some months later Godfrey Brown conducted and the cast was headed by Herbert Thorpe and Foster Richardson, two singers of the time whose names, in the world of radio, were well-nigh inseparable.

I counted myself fortunate. Life had much to offer; golden opportunities tempted ambition in more than one direction, even to the extent of inciting me to dabble, very briefly, in the composition of light music. It came about through some persuasive pressure from John Watt, a producer of light entertainment. he was to leave us before very long, transferring to London to create his *Songs from the Shows* series, but at this time it was Belfast which enjoyed the benefit of his inexhaustible imagination and puckish sense of humour. His revues, variety programmes and miscellanies followed each other in quick succession. He had also evolved a series of afternoon broadcasts which went out every day under the title of *Stop Press* an ingenious amalgam of up-to-the-minute topicality and music (which was why I came to be involved). As yet, there was no recording facility; everything had to be done live. I cannot be certain that John Watt ever carried out his plan to take a microphone outside the building for an eye-witness account of the road-mending activities at the front door, but it would have been entirely typical of him.

I remember one example of his quick-witted resourcefulness. He was in charge of a revue for which he had written both script and lyrics. Towards the end of the actual broadcast he could see from the control panel that the programme would run too short. That would have been unforgiveable, even then. The final song was already in progress, but there and then John wrote the words for an extra verse and walked out into the studio to hand them to the singer; the conductor signalled a further repeat to the orchestra and the extra verse brought everything to an end exactly on time.

It was 1930 and the talkies had just reached the cinemas of Belfast. Their arrival had inspired John Watt to a mischievous flight of fancy which far outstripped reality. His *Talkie Town* was announced as a 'hundred per cent talking and singing super-special', and the original music for it was written by Philip Whiteway and myself. Why we should have tackled such an assignment now passes my comprehension but it was tremendous fun, though I hardly think that our score could claim any striking originality. A theme song was naturally essential and our 'Mile End Melody', after two broadcasts of the complete show, found its way into several other light entertainments.

Another turn of events led to my accepting the responsibility of writing the music for a play, this time on my own. *Masquerade in Moonlight* was the work of a staff colleague, Henry MacMullan, and described as a romance, set in the fashionable Assembly Rooms of eighteenth century Bath. A *Radio Times* commentator, having read the script, suggested in his advance publicity that romance was almost too tame a word and expressed his view that if this was the way they carried on romances in the days of highwaymen and the Bow Street Runners, we should be thankful to be living in these quieter days of speed records and gangsters!

In those early days of radio, the power of music to suggest and sustain atmosphere was becoming more and more recognised, and in this sense the script of *Masquerade in Moonlight* presented an admirable challenge. Not only that, it offered an opportunity for a musical style which could combine echoes of the eighteenth-century with a more contemporary lyricism, not to mention the experience to be gained in writing a score for a large number of singers, chorus, ensembles and small orchestra.

Although the outcome was encouraging I was in no doubt that this kind of success was of a superficial nature. I certainly did not see myself as a composer who would have anything of genuine creative value to offer on a more serious level. Nevertheless, there was to be one more foray, one more attempt to place a tentative foot on the lowest slopes of this particular Parnassus, and this time it was of a much more serious nature. It took the form of a Theme and Variations for full orchestra, which was performed at a public concert in the Wellington Hall in 1934. The critics were right to attribute its thematic content to the influence of Elgar, but they were kind enough to give it detailed analytical comment and the *Northern Whig* was good enough to describe it in a headline as 'an engaging work'.

Godfrey Brown, helpful as always, sent the score to Colonel Fritz Brasse, a German conductor living and working in Dublin where he was in charge of the Irish Free State Army Band. 'Your first work for orchestra,' he wrote to me, 'is very interesting and I have studied it carefully.

My advice to you is: work, hard work, write and write and never stop writing; remember that only hard work brings mastership and the talent given to you by our Creator makes it a duty to yourself to work and develop that talent to mastership.' In a postscript he added: 'Wagner copied the score of the IX Symphony of Beethoven!' Splendid advice from one who had himself spent four years in Max Bruch's master class for composition. But it was not to be. A door, partly opening, had revealed a long, hard and stony path leading to an undisclosed destination. In this direction I lacked the essential confidence and conviction, and I was not to follow it.

In making certain that my time was well filled, Godfrey Brown's ingenuity was limitless. In my view it was not a serious problem! The accompaniment demands were increasing, I had chamber music commitments, and public concerts required my participation either at the piano or in the orchestra's kitchen department, quite apart from the many hours needed for practising. It was probably my involvement in various productions, both musical and dramatic, which prompted his latest idea. I now found myself needed for the training of the chorus and that made an immediate appeal to me. To strive for accuracy of intonation, dynamic gradation and the utmost clarity of diction with a willing and gifted group of singers was an endless fascination. We spent much of our time on the preparation of oratorios and large-scale choral works for the public orchestral concerts, but there was also the more intimate challenge of madrigals and part-songs. There was a studio concert in which I conducted a selection of these and in which sonatas for violin and piano were played by Winifred Small and Maurice Cole. At the end of our first group I stepped down from the rostrum and received an agitated signal from Maurice Cole, sitting at the piano. His gesture was clear – would I turn the pages for him? I was at his side without delay to be much surprised by his whispered and very clearly concerned enquiry, made during the announcement. "You do read music, don't you?" he asked, anxiously. I imagine that he was satisfied with my efforts, though I never discovered. Years later, I teased him about it, but he had no recollection of the occasion.

One of my first professional engagements outside the BBC took me to Dublin in 1934 to accompany, I thought, one recital for the Royal Dublin Society. It was an occasion which exposed my lack of experience in business matters. The fee which I stipulated must have been absurdly modest, even for those days, and it was accepted with alacrity. I was told that I was to partner a violinist, but somehow or other it proved impossible to find out what works were to be played. (That was a situation with which I was to become all too familiar in later years). On arrival in Dublin, it transpired that there were to be two recitals, both lengthy and exacting. In the afternoon there would be a Handel sonata, a Mozart concerto, a group of smaller pieces which included the Nocturne by Szymanowski, and finally the Ravel Tzigane. The evening concert would consist of Corelli's 'La Folia', the *Symphonie Espagnole* by Lalo, Saint-Saens' *Rondo Capriccioso*, and again some shorter items.

My soloist was Henri Temianka, a violinist of great technical skill, though, to my mind, some qualities of grace and sensitivity were more elusive. We set to work in a hotel bedroom which happily boasted an upright piano, and our rehearsals proceeded. He was not particularly sympathetic by nature; he was far from easy to accompany and he was not easily satisfied, although perhaps there was some justification for his impatience. But his playing had a splendid authority and there was much that I could learn, not only of his musical approach but also of that diplomatic tolerance which is always essential to an accompanist, especially when a genuine rapport is not easy to find. In the end there were no hitches, and the two concerts went smoothly.

When all was over Temianka was affability itself, but as we left the hall he became very much the business man. he had one final question for me: "By the way," he asked, "was it pounds or guineas?"

After those two strenuous days it was with some release of tension that I presented myself at the studios of Dublin radio, situated then in the famous Post Office Building in

O'Connell Street. I had been engaged to give a solo piano recital and enquired now about the scheduled time for a balance test. "That isn't necessary at all," I was told. "We know where to place the microphone, so just come about five minutes before the broadcast." What a change, I thought, from the highly organised procedures of the BBC. There were to be other differences. In the evening I sat at the piano ready to begin but puzzled by the apparent absence of a red light. Where was it I asked, whereupon a somewhat embarrassed lady announcer (a very charming Irish girl) explained "Well, actually, it's been broken for three weeks, but I'll tell you when to begin." Moments later, she did.

The recital over, I walked out of the studio and ran into Dr Vincent O'Brien who was then the station's Music Director. (Incidentally, it was he who years earlier had 'discovered' John McCormack.) He greeted me warmly and in the course of our little chat he asked: "How much are we paying you for your recital?" I told him.

His reply came with a friendly and rather deprecatory gesture: "That's not very much, is it? We must see if we can't do better than that.". There was a slightly awkward pause. Then he followed on: "But you don't mind if we don't pay you tonight? At the moment, you see, we have no money in the building at all."

Some three months later I received a cheque for just twice the amount of the originally agreed fee. It was all very charming. Surely, I thought, it could not be like this anywhere else in the world. That visit to Dublin, the first of many, inspired in me an affection for the city which has remained unchanged over the years.

Much as I already owed to Godfrey Brown, I was more in his debt when he began to create opportunities for me to conduct the orchestra. So far, I had had no experience in this direction. Perhaps he felt that by now I had served a satisfactory apprenticeship in several fields, but to put the orchestra in my charge was nothing less than an act of faith on his part, if not a considerable gamble. My first programme, which he planned himself, showed his dislike of half-measures; if I were to swim at all, it would be in

71

the deep end. Devoted entirely to the music of Haydn, it included the *D major Overture,* the aria 'With Verdure Clad', the 'London' Symphony, and movements from the Sinfonie Concertante for violin, 'cello, oboe and bassoon. This was music after my own heart and for me, he could not have made a better choice. I studied every detail of those scores determined to ensure, if at all possible, that some of the essential character of Haydn's music, his elegance and wit, his grace and tenderness, could be captured. In the end, I had every reason to be grateful for the skill, artistery and sympathetic goodwill of a truly excellent orchestra, and I owed much to the art of the four instrumental soloists, Philip Whiteway, Gethyn Wykeham-George, the leader of the 'cellos, David John, a shy and retiring son of Augustus John who played the oboe superbly, and our very highly respected first bassoon, W.S. Bates.

A few weeks later, Mozart's 'Prague' Symphony was entrusted to me in another programme, and on this occasion I was allowed to include three pieces by Scarlatti, a Burlesca, Sarabande and Gigue, which I had transcribed as an orchestral suite.

What little spare time escaped the eagle eye of Godfrey Brown I devoted affectionately to the maintenance of a car. I had brought the maroon-coloured Singer from home, the four-seater which had made possible the organ work at Brathay. It was followed by a succession of second-hand machines, Alvis, Riley and Austin models among them, and for a very brief period I was the proud owner of an ancient Lagonda. They were models in name if not in character. All had seen better days before coming to me and they must have rejoiced the hearts of numerous previous owners. Eventually, when no alternative was left, I drove out of a Belfast garage at the wheel of a brand new MG Midget, breathlessly excited and quite unable to believe that this delectable object actually belonged to me.

I was therefore well equipped to discover the beauties of the Northern Ireland countryside, to see for myself the Giant's Causeway at Portrush, to spend a free day within the shadows of the Mountains of Mourne, and to become familiar with those enchanting villages of County Antrim,

Cushendall and Cushendun (where saucers of milk were still placed nightly on doorsteps for the fairies).

Beyond the studios of Linenhall Street, I had many friends to visit. Among them was the artist, Humbert Craig. At that time he was completing a series of Northern Irish landscapes which afterwards were reproduced as railway posters to be admired by travellers throughout the British Isles. He would invite me to spend an evening in his studio where I watched him at work and marvelled at the skill by which those seemingly inconsequential dabs of brush could miraculously become, in seconds, a flock of sheep. Humbert Craig was happier in the Glens of Antrim than anywhere else in the world. He would tell me in all seriousness of sitting there in the forest with his paints and easel for hour after quiet hour, whilst gradually in the silence the 'little people' would shyly approach within a few feet, ready to fly at the slightest sound. He had seen them; they were real, friendly but intensely shy – and they were eighteen inches tall. He was completely and sincerely convinced and I could summon no scepticism with which to resist that Irish charm.

How splendid it would have been if Humbert Craig could have known the composer, Thomas Wood! They would have had much in common. As far as I know, they never met and I wish that I could have arranged for their paths to cross. Both could claim personal experience of the kind for which no rational explanation can be found, and both were content to accept such things without question. In his book, *True Thomas,* Wood sets out his views on the supernatural together with the evidence which supported his belief. It appeared about two years after the time of which I write, but an earlier work of his, *Cobbers, a personal account of a sojourn in Australia, Tasmania and some of the reefs of the Coral Sea,* was already being widely read.

I count myself fortunate to have known Thomas Wood. Performances of his music, in particular his effective *Master Mariners,* brought him to the studios in Belfast on a number of occasions. Despite the appalling handicap of seriously defective eyesight he achieved distinction in several walks of life – as Lecturer and Precentor of his College in the

University of Oxford, as composer, and as writer on a wide range of subjects, not least the Merchant Service, of which he had dramatic personal experience.

We had wide-ranging discussions on many aspects of music. He furthered my photographic efforts, with practical advice and I was greatly interested in his invention of a system for the colour-coding of band parts, which went a long way towards a solution of the problem created by music arrangements for a reduced number of players. Most important of all, he was one of the few writers who have attempted to analyse the thought processes of the composer. I treasure my memories of a man of such imagination and resource.

My visit to some friends in Enniskillen who invited me for a weekend's fishing on Lough Erne was an occasion which proved to be memorable, not so much for the thrill of actually catching from a rowing boat a sizeable pike, but for the eventful journey from one side of Ireland to the other. A Saturday evening concert delayed my start from Belfast; it was very late as I drove along the narrowing roads of Tyrone and Fermanagh. Mile followed deserted mile until suddenly, the night at its blackest, a figure sprang from the hedgerow into my headlights and was immediately joined by a second man from the other side of the road. They were not 'little people'; they were both far from eighteen inches high, nor were they shy. Both were brandishing revolvers which pointed alarmingly in my direction and their signal to stop left little room for argument. I was ordered out of the car, and questioned. What was my name, where had I come from, where was I going, why so late at night? My typically English reaction of resentment and indignation quickly gave way to a considerable measure of anxiety. The car was thoroughly searched; everything movable was taken out, closely examined and eventually replaced before I was allowed to go on. By degrees the mood of my interrogators changed to something a little less menacing and finally they grudgingly explained that there had been much gun-running in the area. We were, in fact, very much nearer the Irish Free State border than I had imagined; every traveller was suspect. I drove on, more than a little shaken, thinking over the mystery of Ireland – a strange country, an enigma over the centuries, beautiful but unpredictable. Would an Englishman ever succeed in understanding it? How many more of its faces had I still to see?

But for that, as it turned out, time was running short.

CHAPTER 8

London Calling

THE establishment in 1934 of a new BBC department marked a significant policy development, the setting up of an overseas broadcasting service specially directed towards the areas of the world which were then known as the British Empire. No such decision could have been taken without the advances which had been made in the technique of short-wave radio. The newly-projected programmes were to include not only news and talks but features, drama, outside broadcasts and music. The Music Director of this Empire Department was Eric Fogg and there was to be a small, permanent orchestra of sixteen players. In the autumn of that year I transferred to London as its pianist.

In an orchestra which has the full complement of players necessary for the symphonic repertoire the piano has normally no place, but here it was essential because of the reduced number. It eventually proved to have been a mistake to plan the orchestra on so modest a scale, though it was no doubt an economic necessity at the time. Eventually it was enlarged, but for the time being the more ambitious programmes required extra players, at extra cost, and for the rest it had to fall back on arrangements. The limitations encouraged ingenuity. We found, for example, that in the absence of a second oboe we could still play Rossini's *La Scala di Seta* overture by giving his part to a muted trumpet. A number of similar expedients proved to be satisfactory over the microphone.

The orchestra had to contend with an unusual schedule of duties; it was fortunate that on average its members were comparatively youthful. In the history of musical

76

performance it is unlikely that an orchestra had ever before been required for rehearsals and concerts at literally any hour of the twenty-four. For this new service, that was the order of the day. If its programmes were to be heard overseas at a suitable listening time it was obviously necessary for the various time zones throughout the world to be taken into account. Consequently, our programmes for Australia and New Zealand went on the air at about 6 a.m. with a rehearsal some two or three hours earlier. Broadcasts to India were in the afternoons, to the Far East in the mornings, whilst for Canada and North America we would be playing two or three hours after midnight. For the time being, everything had to be live. Recording was not yet perfected, although in the course of the next year or so there were experiments with the Blattnerphone system which used not tape but thin steel wire.

Four or five concerts each week disrupted normal daily life. No two successive days followed any recognisable pattern. Occasionally we saw the sun rise, now and again we saw it set. In the middle of the night we walked to the studios through deserted streets, London asleep around us; we went home to bed against the tide of the city waking to a new day. In the studio all sense of day or night was missing. Outside it, our main concern was to achieve something approaching the requisite amount of sleep between one commitment and another. A very odd existence indeed!

For me there was a further complication. The music programmes included vocal and instrumental recitals in addition to the orchestral concerts, and many of these I was invited to accompany. Since these took place when the orchestra was absent the intricacies of my time-table became more and more involved. Such difficulties of mine were matched by those of the unfortunate singers who had to try to persuade their voices that the clock could be ignored, however unusual its indication might be.

For so small an orchestra the limitations of repertoire were challenging. There was no initiative expected of me in this respect, but I determined nevertheless to embark on a little private enterprise. Somewhat ambitiously, I set out to devise a version of Wagner's *Siegfried Idyll* for performance by sixteen players. I was encouraged by the thought that there could hardly have been a greater number on that Christmas morning of 1870 when its first performance was given on the stairs at Triebschen.

In due course I submitted my score to Eric Fogg who welcomed it as a useful addition for those occasions when we had no supplementary players, and he was kind enough to give it an airing. Later on, I made a reduced version of the orchestral accompaniment of Elgar's *Sea Pictures,* though this was for a rather larger orchestra. When Astra Desmond came to the studio to sing them she had just returned from a visit to Elgar. She told us that when going through the score with him, he had sat at the piano playing the final song, 'The Swimmer' with tremendous gusto, then turning to her to say, with a satisfied smile: "It *is* a good tune, isn't it?"

By then, a step-up in the world had brought me to the centre of the department's activities. I had been appointed assistant to Eric Fogg, and Assistant Conductor of the orchestra. My duties included the building of programmes. To weigh the balance of one item with another, whether vocal, instrumental or orchestral, and to plan a sequence of keys and moods with contrast of styles, was an absorbing task. I began to learn something about the ideal shape for a programme and to understand how much a piece of music can owe to the context in which it is heard. I also ran into difficulties of a rather different kind, superficial perhaps, but still troublesome.

Now and again we engaged one of the many excellent Salvation Army Bands to give a concert, their items interspersed by groups of songs. I sent a completed draft of such a programme to the Band's Director and was more than surprised by his vigorously expressed reaction. We had scheduled a popular singer of the day, Samuel Worthington (Bass), to contribute two groups of songs. Herein lay the trouble! Whilst the director assured me that there was no question of any personal objection to the artist we had chosen, he could only take great exception to the juxta-position of two words in the billing. Worthington and

Bass constituted an affront to deeply held principles of temperance! For the Band to be so associated was quite unacceptable and therefore it would withdraw from the engagement, with apologies.

Coming to know Eric Fogg, I found that his personality was two-fold. On the one hand he had tremendous gaiety of spirit and an impish sense of humour. As a radio Uncle in the Children's Hour at Manchester he had been extremely popular. He could be witty, amusing, and the best of good company. But his changes of mood were frequent, abrupt and quite unpredictable. He was, in a way, the victim of his own temperament and I suspected that he was much concerned to conceal a high degree of nervousness. As a conductor he seemed to be convinced that the control of an orchestra was entirely dependent on an attitude of autocratic severity, unrelieved by any measure of human understanding. But if a conductor is to be successful in welding together a group of players into an instrument of his own, he needs not only a dynamic personality but a warmth of fellow-feeling which will initiate a co-operative response. It was unfortunate that between Eric and the orchestra there could never be the all-important sense of mutual involvement. It would have made a world of difference. It was hardly surprising that members of the orchestra should tell me privately that when Eric walked into the studio, his face an expressionless mask, the will to play died within them.

If only he could have given free rein to that humanity of which he had so generous a share. I found it difficult to believe that this was the man who had written the highly successful Bassoon Concerto, a work of irrepressible wit. As a composer, Eric had a rare gift. There can be no doubt of that, and it is perhaps to be regretted that his five years as Empire Music Director may possibly have stifled even more significant contributions to British music.

Amongst his works the Overture, *September Night*, was much admired. He used to recall its first performance, which he conducted himself, at a Promenade Concert, and which produced a characteristic sidelight on the businesslike approach of Sir Henry Wood. As always, Sir

Henry sat in the wings to keep an eye on everything when he was not conducting; he hardly ever disappeared into the artists' room. *September Night* at an end, Eric walked off to the sound of tumultuous applause. H.J.'s comment, as he passed, was not the conventional "Bravo", but instead: "Heard every note – takes eighteen minutes!" It reminded me that once, in the second half of a public orchestral concert I had accompanied the tenor, Frank Titterton, in a group of songs, the last of which was perhaps just a little too sentimental in character. As we left the platform Sir Henry's rather withering comment was: "Now go back and sing 'Because'!"

I was now facing the orchestra for rehearsals and concerts two or three times a week, determined to acquire a measure of authority. I was inexperienced, and it did not come easily. But I had a great respect for the players; in my view we shared an equal artistic responsibility. As it turned out, we made music together in a spirit of friendly co-operation and our sessions were happy and productive. The orchestra could play beautifully and did so more often than not. Because of the limited complement of players the music of Mozart figured largely and we spent a great deal of time on works such as the Divertimenti, always aiming for what Bruno Walter so aptly described as 'the most loving and faithful elaboration of detail.'

The study of scores occupied many hours and my reading ranged widely in the search for concepts of philosophy and an understanding of musical style. Two books in particular played an important part – Bruno Walter's autobiography, *Theme and Variations*, which led me to explore even more deeply the miracle of Mozart's genius, and *Buffets and Rewards* by Felix Weingartner. One of his paragraphs, I remember, set out an important maxim for conductors, chamber music players and accompanists; in fact for all who make music in consort.

He recalled that in early life he had been prone to uttering sharp criticisms too light-heartedly, so making unnecessary enemies. With maturity, he found that kindliness and friendly feelings were invariably returned to him in some form or another and he realised that bitterness and a carping spirit not only have a hardening effect, but stand in the way of a natural development. Such indulgence, he maintained, contributed nothing whatever to the art of living.

In 1938 I heard Weingartner in Queen's Hall with the London Symphony Orchestra in Brahms' Third and Schubert's Seventh Symphonies. It was revealing to compare this experience, with my disappointed reaction to Mengelberg's performance of the Brahms a few months earlier, when rubato and rhythmical distortions had, I though, actually made it sound dull. On another memorable occasion I heard Weingartner with the Vienna Philharmonic in a programme of Strauss Marches and Waltzes. That was an evening of sheer enchantment.

In the studio the challenges presented themselves in quick succession. A sudden indisposition of Eric Fogg gave me a first chance to take over a concert of symphonic proportions at a few hours' notice. This was my first solo concerto assignment, the G minor for piano and orchestra by Saint-Saens, brilliantly played by Leslie England. The lengthy, slow-moving first movement provided a marvellous, though perilous, exercise in control. It was more comforting to find that the principles of accompaniment – balance and anticipation among them – whether at the piano or with orchestra, were identical. Over the next year or so I enjoyed taking charge of quite a number of concertos, notably a Mozart with Karl Ulrich Schnabel, the Beethoven Violin Concerto with Max Rostal and another for that instrument, much less well-known, by Castelnuovo-Tedesco played by Eda Kersey.

To describe the activity of the Empire Department as lively would be something of an understatement. Serving so many time zones throughout the world, its output was extensive; despite the awkward hours with which everyone had to contend, the staff were fired by enthusiasm. We were all very conscious of our distant audiences, and the BBC made successful efforts to maintain the closest possible contact with listeners on the other side of the world. A weekly magazine, *London Calling,* the overseas equivalent of the *Radio Times,* publicised our programmes and carried introductory articles; some of them on musical subjects I wrote myself.

The Engineering Department strove to ensure the best possible reception of these short-wave transmissions. The technicalities were far beyond my grasp, though I understood that our broadcasts were beamed towards the Heaviside layer of the atmosphere, there to bounce off at a pre-determined angle which would direct them to a particular area of the globe. Conditions of reception varied from time to time and therefore a device which automatically limited the range of signal strength had been perfected. Its purpose was to make sure that the quietest musical passage would not fall below an acceptable level. The results were not always artistically desirable; I remember once listening to a recording of the orchestra (on that steel wire) and finding that a long diminuendo which I had organised very carefully had actually become, on transmission, a crescendo.

Occasionally the orchestra was required to collaborate with one of the other services in feature or drama productions. An example was Lawrence Gilliam's *Life of King George V*. Robin Farquharson played a leading role and I had charge of the chorus and orchestra. The whole undertaking was elaborate and complicated, making use of all the recent developments on sound radio technique. Those advances had been rapid and were already making the earlier experiments which I remembered from Belfast look primitive. But it still seemed strange to direct the music in the concert hall, wearing headphones, and fitting it all to voices which were coming from a studio six floors above. This was my first involvement in a 'transcription' programme; it was not intended for use in the British Isles but recorded on large wax discs for distribution to radio stations in various parts of the world.

For the Empire Service we had producers of our own. There was William McClurg, a stimulating and congenial colleague with whom I went to Germany in 1937. He combined a creative gift with administrative efficiency; two desirable characteristics which are not often found together. And there was John Pudney, whose gentle nature contained a trace of diffidence. All his work bore the imprint of a rare and imaginative sensitivity. Those qualities, which in later years were to be widely recognised in his poems, are evident in a *Ballad for Music* which I now find among my papers. He had sent it to me with a pencilled note: 'I wonder what you make of this.' It is too long ago for me to recall any plan we may have had for a musical setting:

BALLAD FOR MUSIC

At Collioure a castle guards the sea:
and, drawn in a masted line upon the quay,
are the painted craft that fish for anchovy.
It is but an hour from there to Perpignon.

Beneath the walls, old women clack all day
mending the nets. And still you hear them say:
What a fool was Pierre, who threw his soul away,
over the butcher's widow of Perpignon.

Not for boat's stem or stern cared he;
nor for sardine or anchovy;
and lay each day alone upon the quay,
caring only for the butcher's widow of Perpignon.

O widow, widow Jeanette, I've loved you this whole year
come back with me to Collioure, said Pierre.
'Tis but an hour's ride from here
You can close your butchery at Perpignon.

Do you think, she said, I care for anchovy:
for nights alone and cold, and my man at sea?
Would I join the gossiping wives that whisper on the quay?
I have better to do with meat at Perpignon.

So she chopped neck and knuckle and rump steak.
While at Collioure they saw the black waves break
and tolled the bell on the quay for Pierre's sake,
who was lost in the night at sea, but dreaming of Perpignon.

At Collioure she passes upon the quay,
behind the masted craft that fish for anchovy.
She likes to say that twice a widow is she,
once for Pierre and once for the butcher of Perpignon.

Before long I found the perfect antidote to the tensions of Broadcasting House. As a member of the Players' Theatre Club in Covent Garden I enjoyed the congenial and light-hearted company of a group of young and ambitious actors and actresses. They were mostly all at the outset of a career which might bring them to the top of a difficult profession and they dreamed their dreams, as I did. The founder of the club, Philip Ridgeway, assisted by Leonard Sachs, had just then evolved his Victorian Music Hall, an entertainment which was to become a feature of London's life at night. The performances began around midnight; the audience sat at small tables throughout the improvised theatre and were plied with suitable refreshment. The archives were ransacked for the well-loved songs of long gone days, the playlets and the sketches, the comedy and the monologues of the Victorian age.

It all revealed a store of talent and among the many who took part and, went on to achieve fame I particularly remember Patricia Hayes, Harold Scott, Alex Clunes, Robert Eddison (who had just devised his remarkable act – an impression as 'the only fish-mimic in the world') and Bernard Miles whose dialect sketches of opera synopses produced gales of laughter night after night. On one of my visits he sought my ideas about what opera he might tackle next. He was thinking seriously of *Tristan and Isolde*, I remember. A youthful Peter Ustinov was often with us, though I do not recall that he took any active part. Once, for a whole week of very late nights, I accompanied at the piano, though how I managed that within all my oddly timed commitments elsewhere it is difficult now to fathom. But the exquisite singing, the outstanding artistry of Gabrielle Brune remains vividly in my memory.

> The boy I love is up in the gallery,
> The boy I love is looking down at me,
> There he is, can't you see?
> Waving of his handkerchee,
> As merry as a robin that sings on a tree.

That was her song, a simple melody of great charm; and I have never heard it since.

To be able to claim the friendship of the violinist sisters, Jelly d'Aranyi and Adila Fachiri, was for me a great stroke of good fortune. Their kindness knew no bounds and I came to owe a very great deal to their generous interest in my professional progress. I spent many evenings with them in their house in Netherton Grove, Chelsea, where music was made for fun as well as for more serious purposes. Their music-room was large and often crowded by a gathering of young string players invited there to play together for the pleasure of trying out some music, new or old.

Jelly and Adila would both play, drawing largely on the works for two violins, a repertoire they had made completely their own. In the concertos of Bach and Vivaldi, or the sonatas of Handel and Tartini, their mutual understanding was so perfect that it was as though they were one and not two players. To accompany them, either at the piano or directing the little orchestra, was for me an incomparable experience. In the spring of 1937 we gave a charity concert together at Londonderry House in the presence of HRH Princess Marina, Duchess of Kent. It was a programme of music and poetry which included Helen Waddell reading some of her unpublished poems, and we ended with the Bach Double Concerto.

There were other rather different gatherings at Netherton Grove. The dinner parties were legendary; to be invited so often was a delight, though more than a little mystifying to me, for I feared that I had little to offer to what was invariably a distinguished assembly from many walks of life. Pablo Casals, an old friend of the Fachiri family, would be there whenever he happened to be in London. He was never separated from his villainous tobacco and the tiny black pipe he loved so well. There was the author and composer, Bengt de Törne, the only musician Sibelius had ever accepted as a pupil; his book, *Sibelius – a Close-up,* was just about to be published. Another guest was the actress, Margaretta Scott, and sometimes there was the 'cellist, Gaspar Cassado, whom I had already met a few years previously when accompanying his recital in Northern Ireland. On one occasion, Cassado joined forces with Jelly and Sir Donald Tovey for an after-dinner performance of the Brahms Trio in C major. My diary rather bluntly records that Tovey played the piano 'not too well'. It was not my first meeting with him for he had once come to Belfast to play the Schumann Concerto in a public concert. At the afternoon rehearsal he had announced that it was not his intention to play the work from memory. He would use the score, and a miniature score at that! He would not tolerate an ordinary solo copy. With not more than a few bars to each tiny page, he would be in urgent need of a page turner. That task fell to me. The first two movements went smoothly enough, but when it came to the 'Allegro vivace' of the finale, I found myself springing up from my chair at intervals of a few seconds. They were taxing moments! When it became doubtful which of us was making the more active contribution to the performance, I had no alternative but to remain standing, much too prominently, until the concerto was at an end.

That evening at dinner Tovey held the floor. It was obvious that he loved to talk, and equally clear that he had no great preference for listening. But he was brilliantly entertaining. The inflections of a beautiful voice, the command of vocabulary, the mastery of phrase and the originality of his commentary were compelling. It was as though one of his distinguished *Essays in Musical Analysis* had come to audible life. This time, he was recalling the first performance of some opera at Covent Garden, Sir Thomas Beecham conducting. (How I wish I could remember which one it was!) For Tovey, it had been an event of overwhelming importance. Well in advance, he had acquired the score and for countless hours he had studied it to the point of close familiarity. Eagerly he awaited the day of the *première* and at last sat in his box at the theatre in a fever of anticipation as he prepared himself for the opening chord. The moment arrived.

"Thomas, the Beecham," said Tovey, "slowly approached the rostrum, bowed, turned to the orchestra, flew into three pieces and conducted the National Anthem! – a libellous performance." As always, Tovey had the exact words. Now that we thought of it, we had all seen Sir Thomas 'fly into three pieces' at such moments.

A frequent guest was Baron Erik Palmstierna, the Swedish Minister in London and a close friend of the Fachiri family. His life had embraced a wide range of interests and activity. In his youth he had seen service in the Swedish Navy. Later, he had written studies of the political history of his country and he was now a respected member of the Diplomatic Service. At this time, his book, *Horizons of Immortality,* was not yet written. In it, he traces the curious history of the rediscovery of the Violin Concerto by Schumann, in which, with Adila and Jelly, he was intimately involved. That such a work existed was not unknown. Both the first and third editions of Grove's *Dictionary of Music and Musicians* had made a brief reference to a three-movement concerto in D minor for violin and orchestra which Schumann had composed between September 21st and October 3rd, 1853. The autographed score, it was stated, had been in the possession of Jelly's great-uncle, Josef Joachim. Nevertheless, there were musicians who had completely forgotten its existence; there were others who believed that even if it were to come to light it would fail to do justice to Schumann, written as it was a mere six months before the final mental collapse which brought his creative life to an end.

The events of the rediscovery, if that is what it may be called, began in 1933 when Jelly was drawn by friends into playing planchette games with an upturned tumbler and a circle of letters – a diversion popular in some quarters at the time. By some of its participants it was taken very seriously, for others, it was a light-hearted amusement to which scorn or scepticism was the only possible reaction.

For Jelly, there was an extraordinary consequence. The moving glass spelt out a 'message', clearly addressed to her.

87

It seemed to have come from Robert Schumann and it was a plea. Would she find and play an unpublished concerto for violin? It was to be found in Germany, possibly in a museum. The story of the events which followed, leading eventually to Jelly's performance of the work in Queen's Hall on February 16th, 1938, Sir Adrian Boult conducting the BBC Symphony Orchestra, is long and involved. It has been thoroughly researched and clearly recounted in *The Sisters d'Aranyi* by Joseph MacLeod, (published by Allen and Unwin in 1969), who acknowledges the assistance in many details of Palmstierna's *Horizons of Immortality*. It was Baron Palmstierna who traced the manuscript to the Prussian State Library and who saw it there for the first time after its long disappearance.

It will be recalled by those to whom the story is familiar that the autograph manuscript needed revision if a performance was to be given, and that task was initially undertaken by Paul Hindemith. But the changes he made were not approved by Jelly, nor indeed by the composer who was approached again *via* the planchette table. Whatever was needed, Jelly was told, could be done by herself. Although she was far from confident about her ability to do so, she made alterations in some two hundred bars of the solo violin part, guided by her own innate musicianship and supported by the certain knowledge that all was being left to her own judgement.

That was the background throughout my visits to Netherton Grove in the latter half of 1937. It was impossible to be unaware of the mounting excitement as, with each new development, the performance of the concerto drew nearer. To become personally involved, in however slight a capacity, was for me a very great privilege. My diary for February 11th, 1938 (just five days before the Queen's Hall *première*) records: 'I visit Jelly and Adila tonight and conduct a small string orchestra specially gathered together for the purpose of rehearsing Schumann's Violin Concerto, of which Jelly is to give the first English performance on Wednesday next. I like the concerto and am honoured to be associated with it at this early stage. But I have a feeling that the critics are even now prepared to dislike it.' It was not an altogether accurate forecast. Although the last movement was not felt to be satisfactory, the first two were warmly admired. It has to be admitted that certain passages betray Schumann's fading powers and it cannot be said that the work has taken its place in the violinist's repertoire.

The writing out of numerous slips of manuscript paper, recording the alterations to which Jelly had given so much thought, was a necessary step. To be entrusted with this was an assignment I gladly accepted. My diary for a few days later registers a note of satisfaction. 'Have at last accomplished the task of preparing the new score of the Schumann Violin Concerto. Have pasted all Jelly's alterations into the original score, and so hope that an accurate version is now in existence for the first time.'

CHAPTER 9

The BBC Presents

TO any young musician, eager to make the most of every opportunity of enlarging his experience, London in the 1930s was a paradise, a treasure-house inexhaustible in its variety. London was, as it is today, the centre of the international musical scene. The greatest artists of the day were drawn as by a magnet to a capital where successful performance could set a unique and coveted seal of endorsement on the career achievements of a lifetime. That was more valuable than anything else the world could offer. For its musical judgement London could claim universal recognition; the glories of the 1930s contributed in no small measure to the respect which it could command.

The greatest of those glories was undoubtedly the London Music Festival of 1936, that brought Toscanini to conduct the BBC Symphony Orchestra. His performances of Beethoven's 'Pastoral' Symphony and 'La Mer' by Debussy are still clearly remembered, after more than forty years, by those who heard them. History was being made. And there were many other memorable events. At the Queen's Hall there was Beecham and a Sibelius Festival, Adrain Boult, Weingartner, Mengelberg, Furtwangler – there was Eugene Goossens with Stravinsky's *Le Sacre du Printemps*, Prokofiev conducting his *Romeo and Juliet* music, the young Rafael Kubelik with the visiting Czech Philharmonic Orchestra – the list could go on.

In opera the story was the same. The brilliance of the Beecham season at Covent Garden has passed into the folklore of more than one generation. It was fortunate for me that the BBC had a lease of a box which I was able to occupy fairly frequently. Of the many productions I saw, the most memorable, beyond doubt, was *Die Meistersinger*, which I had never seen before. Beecham conducted and the Walter was Torsten Ralf. Starting at 5.30 p.m., with dinner in the long interval, the last majestic chord of C major came at 11.45 p.m. Then, in a transport of delight, yet with a real sense of regret that never again would I hear it for the first time, I walked slowly in the night to Broadcasting House, there to while away some hours in the restaurant before beginning my own rehearsal and concert at 4 a.m.

Impressions of Furtwangler's *Siegfried* with Frida Leider and Lauritz Melchior, of Martinelli in *Carmen*, of the voice of Gigli and Vittorio Gui's marvellous orchestral sound in *Tosca* are with me still, never to be forgotten. On May 4th, 1938, I was there in the box for the performance of *Der Rosenkavalier*, Lotte Lehmann as the Marschallin, Tiana Lemnitz as Octavian, Erna Berger in the part of Sophie; Erich Kleiber was the conductor. Towards the end of the first act, just before the Marschallin's long soliloquy, Lehmann, swayed and faltered. She stopped singing, we heard her say, "I can't go on"; she left the stage, and down came the curtain. (It was said afterwards that current events in Germany were causing her untold worry and concern for members of her family.) It was a sensational upset, but the performance continued after some twenty minutes, Hilde Konetzni taking her place without rehearsal. A week later I was happy and grateful to hear Lehmann in the complete role her glorious voice fully restored.

Opera was not solely to be heard at Covent Garden for these were the great days of Sadler's Wells, where the problems of a small stage were solved in productions of *Die Meistersinger*, *Don Giovanni* and *Fidelio*. There was, too, in that year my first visit to Glyndebourne for Carl Ebert's production of Verdi's *Macbeth*, conducted by Fritz Busch. It was staged with dramatic splendour and magnificently sung by Vera Schwarz as Lady Macbeth and David Franklin as Banquo. It was, moreover, a making of history for it was generally believed that the work had never previously been heard in England. It was not long before its ballet music found its way into our orchestral programmes for the Empire.

Bright as was the musical scene, the storm clouds were gathering overhead. For the evening of September 12th, 1938 I was scheduled to conduct a performance of Vaughan Williams' cantata, *In Windsor Forest*, a work which had already come my way on several occasions and for which I had a great affection. The rehearsal with chorus and orchestra took place quite normally in the afternoon; nothing was amiss. Just as it ended, a message was brought to the studio; the concert was cancelled. It transpired that Hitler was to make an important speech on the problem of the Sudetan Germans. All schedules would be disrupted, news bulletins would be extended and there would be no time for music. It was a first hint of things to come, an initial intrusion of the darkening political scene into my small world. In the weeks and months to come, I doubt whether I or my colleagues fully realised that a way of life was coming to an end, that nothing would ever be quite the same again. But all around us the BBC was making vital and essential preparations for war.

Two days after *In Windsor Forest* had failed to materialise, we were once again in the Concert Hall of Broadcasting House. After only a few bars of Weber's Overture, *Peter Schmoll*, we were assailed by noises, an uproar of hammering and knocking which seemed to come from inside the walls of the studio. Our announcer, Frank Phillips, immediately left his table and departed, to return minutes later carrying a card on which he had written in large letters: 'Can't stop it - war work!' We continued, as best we could amidst all the disturbance, with the two Minuets from Brahms' Serenade in D, but uppermost in my mind was the big question – how could we expect our soprano, May Blyth, to sing Beethoven's 'Ah! Perfido' in such distressing circumstances, quite apart from the devastating result for the listeners? Happily, the noises ceased just as the aria was announced and her performance followed, entirely undisturbed. But the edict had gone forth. Nothing, not even a live broadcast, was to be allowed to stand in the way of transforming

Broadcasting House into a state of readiness for every eventuality.

Without delay, the lower floors were separated from the rest of the building, becoming a complete broadcasting unit in miniature with control rooms, studios, tape machines, telephone exchange. Nothing was left to chance. There were even gas-masks fitted with interior microphones. Wherever bound, we clambered through steel doors, rubber-lined.

There were times when the storm seemed directly overhead, ready to break at a mnyoment. We were not to know that there would still be a few short months before the tumult, and we put no faith in Mr Chamberlain's optimistic assurances or his piece of white paper. Restless and uneasy as those months were, musical life went on much as before, though for me there was something distinctly incongruous in becoming involved in a series of programmes devoted to light opera. The gaiety of *Die Fledermaus* and the romantic charm of *The Rebel Maid* seemed worlds apart from the ominous uncertainties of life beyond the studio.

By the summer of 1939 my concerts with the Empire Orchestra numbered more than five hundred. They were coming to an end. For Friday, September 1st, the fateful day of Germany's invasion of Poland, there was to be an operatic programme. It was cancelled and I had to telephone every individual player and instruct him not to come to the studio. I could also bid him farewell and wish him luck. In effect, the orchestra ceased to exist at that moment.

My own position was vague and uncertain. The staff had been allotted to various categories and in my case it was essential that I should find work of a kind which would contribute to the war effort. The BBC would then make up whatever salary I received to its former level. Eric Fogg had transferred immediately to Manchester; for the time being I remained.

It would be tedious to recount the events of the next few days in detail. Starting out in the early mornings, I journeyed across London, presenting myself to officials in one office after another offering my services in any capacity whatever to a variety of organisational headquarters, to National Service Offices, the Central Recruiting Office, the Air Ministry, the Fire Services, the Ambulance Service. The list was endless and my notes on the activity of those few days cover three pages. It was natural that the sudden declaration of war should have produced some temporary administrative chaos, but the absence of any positive response to my applications was both frustrating and extremely depressing. As far as the armed services were concerned, no enlistment of any kind was possible, at any rate for the time being. For the rest, no applications could be considered unless preliminary training had been undertaken, and for the moment no courses were available. The Drill Hall at Edgeware produced a gleam of hope; I was asked to return on the following day. It was another fruitless effort. After a wait of two hours, there was one question only: Was I a qualified electrician?!

I was realistic enough to have discounted altogether any possibility of musical work, but to see no alternative prospect of any kind was distressing. I wrote to Eric Fogg: 'It is a dreadful feeling having nothing to do and I feel desperately unemployed! If this letter seems tinged with depression it only reflects my bewildered state of mind.' I was but one of millions for whom the world had turned upside down.

But in a matter of days, the situation was changed by an instruction from the BBC. I was to go to Bristol, to which city several departments, including the Symphony Orchestra, had already been evacuated. Hundreds of staff members were in urgent need of accommodation in Bristol's private houses and I was to be a Billeting Officer. Splendid! – I was more than ready to turn my hand to anything. Additionally, I was to join a team of programme monitors. It was already officially laid down that no speaker on the air could be allowed to depart in any way from his prepared script, not by a word or even a syllable. The logic of the ruling was obvious. any alterations of the spoken word might possibly be subversive, a subtle form of 'Fifth Column' activity conveying some message to enemy territory. For a tour of duty of several hours, the monitor listened to his loudspeaker, following every word of the typed script before him, his hand on a switch by which the speaker could be silenced at a moment's notice. As far as I know,

94

it never happened, but it was an essential precaution, and one which called for a good deal of concentration.

My BBC duties to date had already covered quite a wide range, but this was something new. Billeting, a different matter altogether, was even stranger, physically exhausting and not without its embarrassments. Day by day and hour by hour, I explored the residential areas of the city, knocking on doors, stating my authority to question alarmed housewives about the number of bedrooms in the house and how many people slept in them. All in all, my unwelcome enquiries were met by courtesy and a willing desire to help. Although only a few weeks had passed since the declaration of war, there was a general realisation that normal life must suffer disruption, that what would have been intolerable in peacetime must now be accepted, however reluctantly. Naturally, there were some less than amiable, and there were some for whom my appearance on the doorstep created a dilemma. Not seldom, a dismayed lady of the house would take me timidly into her confidence – "I would like to help, and I know I ought to help, but, you see, the fact is I haven't been getting on with my husband too well just recently...' Then would follow an involved account of internal geography and, more often than not, a recital of domestic complaints and grievances. I learned much of life behind closed doors!

In one rather superior area of the city a courtly, white-haired old gentleman answered the door. I stated my business and he heard me out politely.

"I am eighty-four years of age," he said, "and my wife is eighty-two. We have a housekeeper who is seventy-six; we are just waiting for her to pop off, and then we shall leave here to live at the seaside!" The sparkle in his eye boded well for a future which he clearly anticipated with impatience.

They were anxious days, but in due course everyone was safely accommodated, even if the subsequent smoothing out of all kinds of difficulties kept the billeting office constantly busy. Naturally enough, no one knew what to expect in those fateful early days of September, 1939. Amidst all the uncertainty, it was generally thought that the whole format of radio programmes would be completely changed. There had never been broadcasting in time of war; there was no experience to draw on. But, as the weeks went by and we entered, unknowingly, the period to be known as the phoney war, the output settled down to a semblance of normality. There was time to consider how this powerful medium, apart from its all-important dissemination of news, might best be used as a contribution to the morale of the nation. Music would obviously have a significant role.

Billeting and programme monitoring were not, after all, to be the sum total of my efforts. A turn of events brought a move which I welcomed, bringing me on to firmer ground. Dr R. S. Thatcher, who was Deputy Director of Music, and with whom I would now be working closely, gave me an outline of what was required. With the imposition of the blackout and the consequent necessity for listeners to spend much more leisure time in their own home, it was believed that music programmes could and should be more attractively and more helpfully presented. The announcer, in providing an introduction to a performance, would play a larger part in capturing the listener's interest. But his material would have to be prepared for him, and it was seen that some form of presentation department would have to be set up. This was the plan, in a nutshell, and this was the work of which I was to take charge. Before very long, I was joined by two colleagues – the writer, C. Henry Warren, and the music critic, Alec Robertson, who was later to become known for his numerous talks and commentaries on musical topics. Ours was a wide-ranging task. Above all, we quickly came to appreciate the subtle difference between the written and the spoken word. One could hardly ever be quite certain that a written phrase, however neatly turned, would be entirely acceptable to the announcer who was to use it.

Much later in the war – it is difficult to maintain a strict chronology – a story of Bruce Belfrage reading the one o'clock news in London caused us all great delight. It was strictly laid down that all *communiqués* issued by the War Office had to be read precisely as written. Not a word could be changed. The day came when Whitehall put out a particularly colourful statement which referred to the 'valour of our troops scaling the escarpment' and in that vein it continued. As it stood, Belfrage considered it impossible to read, and made a vigorous protest to the News Department. It had to stand; nothing could be done. Belfrage thereupon took the matter into his own hands and telephoned the War Office. But, being transferred repeatedly from one office to another, he made little headway. At long last, he found himself in touch with a Brigadier, who, having finally grasped that this was the BBC, said, "Oh! You have to read it out, do you? We pin ours up on the wall."

I cannot be certain that our efforts to present musical performances were crowned with marked success, and some of them met with the disapproval of the critics of *The Listener*. We had prepared the presentation material for a symphony concert which Sir Henry Wood conducted before the nine o'clock news one evening. The timing caused me some anxiety because it was essential that it should finish precisely at the right moment, neither too early nor too late. Even seconds were important, for any gap before the chimes of Big Ben would have been promptly filled by some nonsense from Lord Haw-Haw.

At the rehearsal I asked Sir Henry to confirm once more the exact timing of the Fifty Symphony of Sibelius which ended the programme.

"Put it this way," he said, very helpfully, "what time do you want it to end?"

"Ninety seconds before the hour," I told him whereupon his comforting reply was, "Leave it to me!" It was all perfectly safe in his hands; the final chord was reached at precisely the required moment.

In his introduction to the work which we had prepared, the announcer described the final movement as "a triumphant ode to the courage and perseverance of man". Our researches must surely have found some justification for that comment, but to the critic, W. McNaught, it was 'Blah!' 'Annotations,' he wrote, 'should depend on the needs of individual works, not on a daily prescription of twenty or thirty nice words to be taken before listening.' It was a lengthy and good-natured column which he devoted to that concert and one could only be grateful for his witty and final comment: 'The last time this symphony was broadcast it had to be faded out with two-thirds of the last movement still to come. Sir Henry seemed determined that this should not happen again, and he beat the clock by a minute and a half, thus securing a triumph for the courage and perseverance of the BBC Symphony Orchestra.'

At the beginning we undoubtedly made mistakes. But developments which stemmed from these endeavours, and which led in a somewhat different direction, had greater significance.

There was still the belief that broadcasting could in some way be more helpful to the musically-minded listener who was now handicapped by wartime restrictions of all kinds. Was it not reasonable to suppose that many would now be making their own music with increased involvement? Could we not offer something of value to the amateur musician? I was reminded of an entry which Samuel Pepys had made in his diary more than two hundred and fifty years ago. 'The little knowledge in music which I have, never was of more use to me than it is now under the molestations of the mind which I have to contend with.'

In January, 1940, a new weekly series of programmes was launched. *Music Makers' Half-Hour* offered practical advice and encouragement to pianists, choirs, amateur orchestras – the scope was enormous, and the response was immediate. Day by day the letters came in, telling us of the wartime musical societies which were being formed, of the little groups of singers and players who were meeting every week in out-of-the-way villages, and of the many pre-war societies who were determined to continue to keep their flags flying. One town in Hampshire which, like many another, had received its full quota of evacuees, had actually formed what was described as a 'Drop-in-and-sing-the-*Messiah*' choir.

We soon realised the obvious. One of our important tasks would be to give our large audience an opportunity to hear some of this music which was being performed in the countryside in spite of all kinds of difficulties. Fortunately, that was quite possible, for by now the BBC had a van fully equipped to record on discs. We took it out into the West Country and the music we brought back formed the basis of four programmes featuring 'the real thing' from Hampshire, Wiltshire, Cornwall and Devon.

Later in the year a second series was entitled *Music at Home*. It brought to the studio a number of speakers, each an expert on some aspect of performance, among them Trevor Harvey on 'The Mixed Choir', Thomas Dunhill on 'Chamber Music', Reginald Jacques on 'The Amateur Orchestra' and Imogen Holst on 'Carolling'. There was plenty of evidence to show that programmes of this kind were helpful and answering a genuine need. This time we took the recording van further afield, to makeshift studios in Kendal, Barrow-in-Furness, Bolton and Manchester. We brought home an even wider range of amateur music-making by school orchestras, brass bands, mixed and male voice choirs, a string quartet, and even an orchestra of banjos, mandolines and guitars. For one of the programmes we engaged Wilfred Pickles as narrator.

To select the musical examples, to write the linking material, and to achieve a balanced half-hour which would do justice to a spare-time activity inspired by enthusiasm and undertaken for sheer pleasure was a task both challenging and fascinating. Much of this preparation and the broadcast itself was carried out in conditions of uncertainty, for Bristol had became a target for the nightly visitations by the Luftwaffe. We had a number of small and impermanent studios in various parts of the city and a heavy raid often made it necessary for the whole programme to be moved at very short notice to an undamaged location.

In common with the majority of my colleagues, I was a member of the BBC contingent of the Home Guard, attending early morning parades in the grounds of Bristol University under the command of Stuart Hibberd and finding myself standing to attention in the ranks with Sir Adrian Boult at my side. Throughout every raid – and they were often of nightly occurrence – we were on duty, with orders to lend a hand in whatever emergency arose. The 'incidents', as they were known, came in quick succession. The house in which I had first been billeted suffered a direct hit. Sadly, the whole family from whom I had had such a friendly welcome were killed. For some forgotten reason I had left there just a few days earlier, moving to share with a BBC colleague in another house a few streets away. Here we found ourselves under the wing of a lady who had spent her professional life as a music-hall artiste. Even if we had not known that already, it would have become clear when, one dark night at the height of a severe attack, she stepped out into the street, breaking all the rules, for a glimpse of enemy aircraft caught in the criss-crossing search-lights.

"How lovely those planes look," she said, "with the limes on them."

Over forty years or so, the tensions and dangers of those days have faded. What remains uppermost in my mind is the warmth of companionship which they generated. It was now that one of my new friendships quickly assumed a very special significance.

Earlier in London, I had known Jessica Mountfort of the Public Concerts Department only very slightly. As we pursued our separate ways along the corridors of Broadcasting House we had merely exchanged a nod of recognition. Now, here she was in Bristol with responsibilities in music administration, and we were seeing more of each other. Over many a meal in the canteen (the cast of ITMA often sitting at tables nearby) we chatted at length, and found that we had much in common. That she had so passionate a love of music was not surprising for in her family music had played an important part – her mother a highly respected teacher of piano, her father a dental surgeon and amateur 'cellist who, with his string-playing friends, devoted every available moment to the study and performance of string quartets. With those sounds in her ears from an early age, the world of chamber music for Jessica was familiar and much loved territory.

There always seemed to be so much to talk about. We shared a sense of humour, and, as the days went by, I came to know and appreciate her unfailing kindness and consideration for others. Above all, it was her positive outlook on life which I found so challenging in that time of stress and uncertainty. I was to realise how much this friendship meant to me one day when we walked up the road in search of a lunch-time drink. Daylight raids were comparatively rare, but on this occasion an enemy aircraft, without warning and apparently coming from nowhere, swept the length of the road, its machine-gun chattering viciously. As we dived together for the meagre shelter of a doorway we could hear the bullets striking the ground a few feet away. In a few seconds, all was quiet and we emerged, more than a little shaken. For me, it had been a moment of illumination.

The story of Bristol's war, the appalling casualties and the complete overnight disappearance of Park Street, one of its main thoroughfares, has been told many times and need not be repeated. A small part of that story, however, provided for me one of the most bizarre episodes of my life.

Many of the BBC Symphony Orchestra's performances came from a church hall near Pembroke Road, and there its instruments were stored. In one of the fire-bomb raids, the building suffered badly and those of us who were on guard were hastily ordered there as a matter of extreme urgency. Though the point of no return had not been reached, the hall was well alight in a number of places. My companions concentrated on an ante-room which housed the harp, the double-basses in their coffin-like wooden boxes and all the rest of a well-nigh priceless collection of instruments. My orders took me to the main studio which was practically empty except for a black and gleaming Steinway Concert grand piano which stood proud and lonely in the centre. The ceiling above it was ablaze. A stirrup pump was thrust into my hands with an order to direct it on to the piano and give it a thorough soaking! If there had been time to think, that instruction could have been seen as quite incomprehensible for the instrument was about to be completely ruined, if not in one way, then in another. But in the streets outside lives were being lost and a piano was of comparatively little importance. I did as I was told, though it needed an extraordinary effort of will. There can surely be few musicians who have been obliged to carry out a duty so painful and distressing.

In planning a new series of broadcasts to run alongside those for the amateur music-maker, our thoughts turned to the many thousands of men and women who had been uprooted from their normal surroundings and replanted in the Forces. The music-lover in uniform, we argued, could surely not be expected to accept a deprivation of that which he felt to be an essential part of life. Why should it be assumed that the Forces were interested only in the lighter forms of entertainment? Something was already being done about it. ENSA was hard at work providing concerts, ballet, and other forms of relaxation and diversion. Each Army Command had its own experienced musical adviser whose function it was to encourage and co-ordinate music-making among the troops themselves. In some of these Commands it had been possible to form an orchestra, and in one there was even a string quartet. But much more needed to be done to narrow the gap between the man for whom music, recapturing past experience, could provide a spiritual anchor and the man to whom music meant nothing at all.

With this thought in mind, we embarked on a fortnightly half-hour series of programmes. *Forces' Music Club* placed the BBC Orchestra at the disposal of selected members of the Armed Services who were invited to the studio. They chose the music they wanted to hear, and which they felt others would enjoy. With Alec Robertson and myself they discussed the reasons for their choices and told us about the musical events in their units. Very few suffered from microphone nerves! Our hope was that such a broadcast, whilst meeting its main objective, might still retain a sufficiently popular appeal to those who claimed to have no interest in music whatever.

It was an ambitious project, and its organisation was complicated. The preliminary researches took us to the four corners of the British Isles, to units of all three Armed Forces, to the ATS, the Home Guard and a number of Convalescent Depots. Moving around the country in 1942 was not without its problems and I carried with me a number of official authorisations without which a visit to certain locations would not have been allowed.

The response was distinctly heartening. Our innumerable contacts were infinitely varied. There were those who were extremely knowledgeable, those who had not yet discovered music, and those with special interests such as film and ballet music. There was one leading stoker whose knowledge of opera was positively encyclopaedic! In small groups we brought them to the studio and there, quite uninhibited by the microphone, they aired their views and the orchestra played. Oddly enough, it was all of great interest to the Press which lost no opportunity for both comment and advance publicity. 'This week,' said one, 'it is the Navy's turn to take part in this programme, which bids fair to becoming one of the most popular broadcasts on the Forces wavelength.'

Some missionary zeal clearly lay behind these efforts of ours. Few professional musicians would have found anything wrong with that. In attempting to share great music with the maximum possible number of listeners, both initiated and uninitiated, we were, moreover, pursuing a policy which the BBC had formulated in the earliest days and maintained over the years. Here in Bristol we were thankful to have a colleague from whose gifts that policy had received an invaluable impetus.

To a new generation the name of Sir Walford Davies may not have the lustre of forty years ago, but he was a legend in his lifetime. He it was who from the beginning had seen the potential of radio, and who through his genius as a microphone speaker had done so much to translate a vision into reality.

As early as 1924, Walford Davies was a member of the BBC's Advisory Committee on music. Through the initiative of Miss Mary Somerville the foundations of a BBC educational system was being laid, and in April of that year he gave his first broadcast to schools. He followed it during the next ten years with more than four hundred lessons by radio. His warmth and ability to communicate, his beautifully-modulated speaking voice, his homely approach and above all his supreme skill in finding an illuminating precision of phrase – all these qualities combined to win for him the affection of countless listeners. They were not school children alone, for in 1926 he began his *Music and the ordinary Listener* talks which were to continue for four years.

Sir Walford took great delight in reading the letters which came to us from his listeners, giving their reactions to his broadcast. Among those he cherished there was one from a tired surgeon who confessed that he listened to the talks simply because that inimitable voice massaged his spine. It was also somewhat salutary to read of the little child who called out to him down his mother's loudspeaker, "Oh, shut up!" Then there was news of another little girl of six years old who, although she did not understand a word he said, refused an invitation to a party because it was "Walford's night." He was equally grateful to an unknown listener who, on hearing his name mentioned, remarked "Oh, Sir Walford Davies; yes, what a benevolent old spook he is!"

After having held the post of Organist and Choirmaster of St. George's Chapel, Windsor, for a number of years, he accepted the appointment of Master of the King's Music in 1934. In that same year he became closely associated with the Corporation's religious broadcasting department, bringing his influence to bear on the musical planning of morning services and the Sunday night Epilogues. Bristol Cathedral had been placed at the disposal of the BBC and, since I often stood in for Trevor Harvey who had charge of the BBC Singers, it was here that I had my first association with Walford. In July, 1940, he embarked on what was sadly to be his last series of weekly talks. Their title was *Everyman's Music* and Walford himself explained:

Under this title it is proposed that we should meet week by week at this hour to discuss together that kind of music which is simple enough and human enough both in its rhythmic and melodic aspects to gain the regard of Everyman, whatever his special taste in instrumental or vocal qualities . . . One of our poets wrote "My mind to me a Kingdom is". Suppose that somewhere near the centre and citadel of that Kingdom of man's mind there may be a small field of music where the mind itself is made audible, where every listener may hear imaginative (that is creative) thought in process. Let us take then the title of these talks to refer to that as yet small but truly limitless mental field common to the listening mind everywhere.

The new project fell within the orbit of the Presentation Department and so the organisation and production of the talks brought us into closer contact. We spent many hours of discussion in the small flat which he had taken in Queen's Court, and I felt his friendship to be an honour indeed. His written notes to me were frequently addressed: 'My dear C.H. (C.H.)' for it amused him to point out that my initials had another connotation.

Walford himself was a stimulating companion. At lunch one day he allowed his lively imagination to run freely, developing at some length his newly-acquired theory that Haydn and Walt Disney would have made an ideal partnership. On another occasion he gleefully told me of a small boy in Wales who, answering a request on one of the Schools broadcasts, had submitted a little tune he had composed. By an odd coincidence, his name was also Walford Davies!

"Fortunately," said the adult Walford, "it was a good tune, so I returned it with thanks and added: 'But we must both do better!' "

As a broadcaster, Walford was entirely unpredictable. His approach was of such spontaneity, his mind so sharp and so susceptible to the inspiration of the moment that the discipline of a prepared script could only frustrate his individual style. We tried once, and only very briefly. For him, the limitation was impossible, and he turned again to his few headings and a bar or so of music notation, roughly sketched on the back of an envelope. That was all he needed. At the start of the series, it made for great difficulties because of the war-time monitoring requirements, but it was soon officially accepted, to my great relief, that Walford would have to be an exception to the rule.

For each of his talks there was naturally some advance plan, but it was never more than an approximate scheme and his tendency to stray from it often led to more than a little confusion for those assisting him. It was no unusual thing for one of his programmes to go on the air without any certainty of what might happen, and that could be unnerving for a group of singers or instrumentalists who were there to provide the illustrations. There was one occasion when Walford was to discuss the Mozart Clarinet Quintet. With him in the studio was the clarinettist, Frederick Thurston, ready with the score to play several of its themes. The talk proceeded smoothly in Walford's inimitable style, but having touched on its first movement he digressed to remind his listeners that there was another superb Quintet for Clarinet and Strings – by Brahms.

"Perhaps Mr Thurston would be kind enough to let us hear the first subject of that most lovely work," he said.

This was quite unexpected. Thurston paled a little, but, musician as he was, played it splendidly from memory. Walford continued and for a few minutes it appeared that the remainder of the talk would centre on the Brahms! Even another illustration was called for before Mozart was finally brought back into the fold.

The broadcast at an end, a very perturbed clarinettist strode across the studio. "Walford," he exclaimed, "you must NEVER do that again!"

The gentle reply came with a disarming smile: "My dear boy, why were you so worried? No difficulty at all. You did it beautifully."

Though never a fully-fledged department of the Corporation, 'Presentation' was making headway. Administratively, it was regarded as an off-shoot of the Music Department, its function to initiate programmes, not of music, but about music. They were now becoming more elaborate.

During the first half of 1941, six performers were invited to the studio to be featured in a new series of programmes entitled *The BBC Presents* . . . Lionel Tertis, Albert Sammons, Yvonne Arnaud, Solomon, Pouishnoff and Florence Austral were all supreme in their own fields. In presenting these artists within a very flexible format, we hoped that we might succeed in revealing some relationship between their artistic mastery and their experience of life. It was an interesting project which needed considerable resources including a symphony orchestra and a number of actors for the occasional dramatisation which would highlight some of the significant events of a lifetime. Perhaps we went a little too far in this direction at times. There were critics who thought so, and felt that where music was concerned, any suggestion of showmanship was out of place. But, in an effort to reach the widest possible audience, we thought it right to make use of the enormously effective dramatic potential of the radio medium. Today, such methods would be seen still more critically, and that in itself is evidence of the greater discrimination which has developed in the last few decades.

To gather the material for these programmes was an enjoyable task in which I was able to count on the helpful co-operation of all the featured artists. Some intriguing facts emerged. How many of our listeners were aware, for example, that Albert Sammons, one of the world's foremost violinists, was practically self-taught, and that in his early youth he had earned a living by playing in one restaurant or another before graduating to the orchestra pit of theatre and music hall? He remembered that on one occasion, when directing the orchestra in London's Waldorf Hotel, he noticed Sir Thomas Beecham among the diners. Here was a heaven-sent chance to make an impression and so, naturally, the next item was a movement from a concerto! It earned more than the usual amount of applause and as Sir Thomas departed, his meal at an end, he sent his card to Sammons. It was not, alas, a note of thanks or congratulation. Scribbled on the back was the correct metronome marking of the concerto movement he had just played . . . For all that, it was not long before Sammons became the leader of Beecham's Opera Orchestra. He played for us some extracts from the Violin Concerto which Delius had dedicated to him, and from the Elgar Concerto which he had played more than a hundred times in this country alone. We were also delighted to have John Ireland in the studio to discuss his Second Violin Sonata with Sammons and to join him in a performance of its slow movement.

To Lionel Tertis, 'virtuoso of a neglected instrument', as we described him, our programme paid tribute to his immense achievement in revealing the potential of the viola as a solo instrument. To that initiative he had devoted a long life and the consequences were to be far-reaching. Among musicians, there were some who were not slow to express reservations about the principle involved in the adaptation by Tertis of certain works such as the Elgar 'Cello Concerto. But over the perspective of the years it can be seen now that projects of that kind made, at that stage, a vital contribution to the advancement of the viola's cause. They pointed the way to a new repertoire and our British composers were ready to accept the challenge, creating a number of original, important, and welcome compositions for viola with orchestra or piano.

In later years, it was a particular pleasure for me to collaborate in performances of these newer works with some of our finest players; almost invariably they had studied with Tertis himself. A broadcast of York Bowen's Rhapsody, in which I had partnered Maurice Loban, brought a kindly note of appreciation from the composer: 'Bravo!' he wrote. 'I listened last night to what I consider a very fine performance of my Rhapsody. Both of you contributed to a real sense of satisfaction by the composer who has by no means been satisfied with the piano parts played by others at times, and I send you my warmest thanks and appreciation for the evident trouble you both had taken to produce a safe and beautiful performance. It was grand! I shall telephone Maurice Loban to thank him – what a beautiful viola player!'

It was no easy task which Tertis had set himself. There were those of our profession who did not see the viola's future as he saw it, and their doubts remained for a lengthy period. Our tribute to Tertis merited some attention. Whilst in no way opposing the movement inspired by Mr Tertis, William McNaught, the critic, reflected on the Cinderella-like characteristics of the viola, its voice low and gentle, its domestic nature reserved and always happiest in the company of violins or 'cello in quartet or orchestra. That was how it always had been, and that was how it always would be. Today, in the light of the striking advances which the viola repertoire has made in the last thirty or forty years, these comments lack something of a prophetic ring.

The programme for Yvonne Arnaud, artist, actress, concert pianist, diseuse and singer, was especially memorable and not only for its content. The time for the broadcast coincided with one of the worst of all Bristol's air raids, which continued, as I remember, for six or seven hours.

With Lance Sieveking, who was joining me as compère, Douglas Cleverdon, producer, and the actors, Norman Shelley, Hedley Goodall and George Holloway, the whole cast spent the night in a cellar until at last dawn broke and a welcome All Clear sounded. Although there were fearful things happening above us, it was certainly the most enjoyable raid of my experience, the long hours enlivened by Yvonne Arnaud's gaiety, her irrepressible spirit and that high-pitched squeak of voice which belonged to her alone. A live broadcast that night was out of the question, but somehow we managed to record the programme which finally went on the air some months later. The *Radio Times* then explained, with masterly understatement: 'Owing to war-time conditions becoming a bit prominent on the night in question, the programme was not broadcast.'

Some of *The BBC Presents* . . . series I wrote and produced myself. For others I enjoyed the collaboration of the writer Leslie Bailey and the producer Maurice Brown.

Day by day, the ways in which radio might be used to bring serious music to a new audience were becoming clearer. The projects which we now had in mind were elaborate enough to suggest that the possibility of some conflict between the Corporation's Music and Feature Departments might arise. The problem was of an administrative nature, the solution of which, I suggested at one point, might be my secondment to Features. A move of that kind would not have been so unusual at the time, when staff responsibilities on a personal basis were accorded a degree of flexibility, although departmental boundaries remained firmly drawn. My suggestion was not taken up, which, in the light of events soon to unfold, was just as well. In the end, the difficulties were smoothed away by an arrangement which allowed one or other Features producer to be made available to us as necessary.

We were beginning to engage specialist writers. The script for the programme of September 1941, celebrating the centenary of Dvorak's birthday, was written by Dr Viktor Fischl of the Czechoslovak Ministry of Foreign Affairs in collaboration with Joseph Schrich. Here, we were able to include the recording of an interesting interview which

Maurice Brown and I had had with Jan Masaryk. He reminded us that when Dvorak first visited this country he had said 'The English are a kind, affectionate and music-loving nation, and it is well-known that if they once get fond of a man they remain faithful to him. Please God that it may be so with me.'

The widespread celebration of 1941, to which the Royal Philharmonic Society, the London Symphony Orchestra, the National Gallery Concerts and the BBC contributed, confirmed the depth of an affection which has remained unchanged throughout the years.

My association with Lance Sieveking, which had begun with the Yvonne Arnaud programme, was something which I greatly valued. His knowledge of the arts, his erudition, originality and many-sided gifts commanded my admiration and respect. He was already a legend at Broadcasting House for, as writer and producer, his pioneering work had initiated much of enduring value. As a disseminator of the arts, the debt owed to him by sound radio was widely recognised. Like many others whose province was the creative side of broadcasting, he was concerned at the imbalance brought about by an overweighted administration. In an organisation which had grown so rapidly that was at least a source of danger, and I remember his amusing if somewhat cynical comment that: "If broadcasting were to cease altogether, if there were never to be any more programmes, eighty per cent of BBC staff would continue in their jobs and know no difference!" I cannot think that he was entirely serious; this was more the reaction of one whose over-riding concern was for the quality of the end product.

Sieveking and I worked together on a number of projects, though to him some of them must have seemed little more than a spare-time activity. One of them was to provide a new interval signal to replace the three thin impoverished B-B-C chords played on the piano which had given way eventually to a flat, metronomic beat deservedly known everywhere as 'the ghost in goloshes.' Neither version had ever done more than irritate a nation anxiously awaiting the latest news bulletin. Now, the official policy was 'to preserve the familiar three-note combination, but present

110

it in a more sonorous and virile form. Sieveking and I
went off to Bath to search through the antique shops for
a clock with a suitably mellow 'tick-tock'. Our interest was
naturally limited to the quality of the instrument's sound and
not at all in its appearance. This caused the dealers some
mystification, but the one we found, a beautiful mahogany
mantel clock made in 1830, would have scored points on
both counts. The recording we made gave us the background
to the new B-B-C chords which were superimposed at
intervals of eight seconds and impressively played by two
trumpets and two tenor trombones. The 'ghost in goloshes'
was exorcised at last!

Another of our joint efforts was a somewhat unusual
programme which we called 'School Concert Rehearsal'.
Perhaps prompted by the series on *Making your own
Music*, we realised that music was an essential part of
normal everyday life in many British schools. We decided
to investigate and with the help of Reginald Redman, the
BBC's West of England Music Director, set off with a
recording van for Marlborough College, Dauntsey's School
and Betteshanger School. Informality was the keynote as
we set up our microphones as unobtrusively as possible in
a variety of music-rooms. There were many surprises. These
were not boys who saw music as merely something to keep
them away from the playing-fields. They were involved to
some purpose, and the wealth of material we captured was
bewildering in its variety – madrigals, psalms, woodwind
quartets, the music of Purcell, Mozart, Brahms, Vaughan
Williams – even some movements from one or two violin
concertos. We put the programme together and coped as
best we could with the problem of what to leave out.

The birthday anniversaries of two great British composers
in 1942 provided the occasion for more commemorative
programmes. The first was devoted to Delius and for
this we enlisted the help of Eric Fenby who had been
the composer's amanuensis throughout his last years of
blindness and paralysis at Grez-sur-Loing. Here was a
chance to attempt, at least to demonstrate, if not to
explain, those extraordinary gifts which had enabled Fenby
to share a composer's vision and to capture, in written

111

and permanent form, the product of creative genius. It was a unique story; so vivid was Fenby's account of the composition of the tone-poem, 'A Song of Summer', that we ventured to reconstruct the scene in dramatic form.

Sitting in his chair in the garden at Grez, Delius told Fenby to imagine that they were sitting in the heather on the cliffs looking out to sea. "The sustained chords in the strings," said the composer, "suggest the clear sky and the stillness and calmness of the scene – the undulating figure of the 'cellos and basses suggests the gentle rise and fall of the waves."

This was just the background. The significance of the work itself, dictated to Fenby note by note, was then left to the listener's imagination. With Sir Adrian Boult conducting the BBC Orchestra, with the voices of Fenby himself and of Laidman Browne as narrator, our programme celebrated not only the birth of Delius but the actual creation of a magical contribution to British music.

The centenary of Sir Arthur Sullivan, born on May 13th, 1842, was marked by a series of special broadcasts. From the Royal Albert Hall there was Sir Henry Wood's performance of *The Golden Legend*, and in the studio one of the favourite Savoy operas, *The Gondoliers*. Leslie Baily wrote a splendid script for 'An Impression of a great Victorian', the biography programme which Stephen Potter and I presented jointly. Clarence Raybould was in charge of the orchestra and chorus, and the actors included Grizelda Harvey, Harcourt Williams, Carleton Hobbs, Charles Lefaux and Arthur Young. These names are representative of the company of players who created a golden age of radio drama.

In combining speech, music and sound effects for programmes such as this, our search for the most acceptable dramatic result could lead to complications in production, though we have tried to avoid them wherever possible. It was by no means always possible, and it is therefore all the more remarkable that, without the great advantage of pre-recording, these broadcasts went on the air smoothly and usually without accident. Curiously enough, the Sullivan biography was very nearly an exception. At one point, whilst

112

the orchestra was playing part of the *Tempest* music, we noticed at the control panel that a piece of narration from a separate studio had started without a cue light. The speaker was already a page ahead, though fortunately none of his words had been heard. It was an anxious moment, but the situation was saved by a quick run down the stairs, with an instruction to start again. Happily, such excitements were rare; this particular hitch could have been catastrophic, but in the event, the listening audience knew nothing of it.

CHAPTER 10

Portrait of a Composer

DURING the early months of 1942, the Music Department was transferred from Bristol to Bedford, where its work could continue in a more relaxed atmosphere, free from the stresses, strains and uncertainties which had resulted from the Luftwaffe's almost nightly attentions in the West Country.

The most ambitious project to date was already on the stocks. A tribute to the memory of Elgar was planned for June 2nd of that year, the eighty-fifth anniversary of his birth. From the outset, we were all acutely aware of the importance of the undertaking, for which large resources were to be made available. The time was right, we felt, for such a programme. Those were dark days, and for a nation in turmoil it was no bad thing to be reminded of its heritage. Eight years had passed since Elgar's death. Whilst there might yet be a few anti-Elgarians around, the vast majority of those for whom music was a treasured possession acknowledged his genius and rejoiced in the works which had brought English music to a pinnacle of achievement.

In 1933, the Reverend Basil Maine, author, composer, lecturer and music critic, had published his concentrated study of Elgar's life and works. It was a valuable addition to the bibliography, an appraisal of penetrating insight, inspired by deep affection. Nothing could have given me greater pleasure than his acceptance of an invitation to collaborate with me in the compilation of a programme to which I had already given the title, 'Portrait of a Composer'. No one could have wished for a more expert, nor a more congenial colleague. But good fortune did not

114

end there! A helpful note of introduction from Sir Adrian Boult resulted in a kind proposal by Elgar's daughter, Mrs Carice Elgar-Blake, that I should spend some days as her guest at Broadheath, her home near Worcester. This was an opportunity which I eagerly grasped.

Mrs Blake's bungalow, Woodend, with its magnificant view of the Malvern Hills, stood no more than a few hundred yards from the tiny cottage which was Elgar's birthplace, now acquired by the City Corporation of Worcester as a permanent memorial. The plan to establish it as a museum was not yet realised in full, but under the guidance and inspiration of Mrs Blake the project was under way.

A ground floor room, just inside the front door of the cottage, remained Elgar's study complete with his desk, his pens, microscope, and a display cabinet alongside. The walls were almost completely covered with framed photographs. In the little room upstairs, however, there was as yet considerable disorder. Here were the archives, a treasure-house for the researcher, so extensive that many weeks would have been inadequate for much more than a cursory examination. My hostess was kindness itself. As far as she could, she showed me where my quest might most usefully begin and drew my attention especially to the piles of dusty old music manuscipts which lay on a lower shelf. They all dated, she told me, from her father's apprentice years and were very little known to anyone. Though they were not at that moment directly relevant to my purpose, the temptation to spend time on a closer look was hardly to be resisted. It can be imagined how deeply I regretted the necessity to turn to other things.

As I did so, my eye was caught by intimate and touching reminders of Elgar in his less serious moments – copies of the *Daily Telegraph* for example, in which he had regularly attempted and almost always completed the crossword puzzle, in ink. One, only half-finished, was dated for the day before his death. On all sides there was evidence of his irrepressible sense of fun. A page of a newspaper for November 12th carried a series of photographs taken at the previous day's Cenotaph Service in Whitehall. What oddly incongruous idea had prompted him to embellish that page with lightning sketches of rabbits, with pen and ink?

To be allowed to come so close, even to the minutiae of comparative unimportance, was an emotive experience. It was as though, on entering the cottage, a spell had been woven, my feelings a mixture of wonder and incredulity that I should have the opportunity to step into a past which, as every moment went by, was becoming more real than the present. Could I possibly bring myself to accept Mrs Blake's suggestion that I should work at that desk, with all its associations, in the study below?

With a twinge of conscience and a sense of unwarrantable intrusion, I turned to the diaries which Lady Elgar had kept for many years. There, entries for 1918 caught my notice. "Brinkwells – Monday: E. at work on String Quartet; Tuesday: Last movement of String Quartet finished; Wednesday: E. busy all day with air gun.' (This, surely, explained the Cenotaph rabbits!) I recalled W. H. Reed's graphic description of the old oak-beamed cottage at Fittleworth in Sussex with its splendid view of the River Arun and the South Downs beyond, the environment which had inspired the writing of chamber music, the Violin Sonata, the Piano Quintet and the String Quartet. Somehow, the opening of that volume at that page seemed to have a curious significance, for the String Quartet was the work for which Lady Elgar had a particular affection. Two years after she made those entries in her diary, her funeral service in Hampstead Parish Church ended poignantly with a performance of its slow movement.

Throughout a long period, she had carefully preserved every possible press-cutting. They filled fifteen enormous volumes. Here was the public face of Elgar, the story of his triumphs and disappointments told by those who had known him only at a distance. Apart from the journalists, here were the critics to whom year by year since the beginning of the century, the characteristic Elgarian idiom had gradually become more and more recognisable and familiar. To begin with, their task was not easy; it was not surprising, for example, to find that the first performance in Manchester for the Introduction and Allegro had made no great impression at all. On the other hand, there were those for whom the 'Enigma' Variations in 1899 had removed all doubts about the future of English music. Those Press notices revealed a fascinating variety of reactions to the early works.

My own thoughts went back to the autumn of 1933 when Elgar had come to Belfast to conduct *The Dream of Gerontius* for the Philharmonic Society (a performance in which, very incidentally, I had been entrusted with the bass drum and cymbals – an awesome responsibility). I recalled Elgar's masterly control of chorus and orchestra and the skill with which he had transformed inspiration into living reality. I remembered his dignity, his aristocratic bearing, his beautiful clothes and his amused smile when, at the rehearsal, Godfrey Brown presented him with an empty cardboard box. Throughout a long and eloquent speech of welcome, G. B. had held it behind his back, unaware that the Irish linen handkerchiefs it had contained lay in a neat heap on the floor.

During my work in the cottage that morning, there was a caller – a tall young man in the uniform of a Lieutenant in the Home Guard. Our conversation produced yet another link with the past, for this was Philip Leicester, the son of Elgar's life-long friend, Hubert Leicester, to whom the second 'Wand of Youth Suite' was dedicated. That was a friendship which dated from boyhood days, a period when Elgar's struggles with adversity were just beginning. Turning away from his brief apprenticeship to the law, he had taught himself to play the bassoon, and then joined a wind quintet of which Hubert Leicester was director and first flute. Many of Elgar's earliest compositions were written for that combination. Probably some of them still lay there on that lower shelf. Over the span of years the lives of the two friends ran in parallel, the first flute eventually to become Sir Hubert Leicester, Alderman of the City of Worcester, and the bassoon to become Master of the King's Musick. For my chat with Philip Leicester I could have wished for more than half an hour.

That evening I joined my hostess in tackling *The Times* crossword puzzle, the family tradition continuing.

Not unexpectedly, the solution called for some consultation with a dictionary. I found one, at Mrs Blake's request, in the bookcase across the room, but by mistake I removed its adjoining volume – an old edition of the *Chronicles of Froissart*. Its fly-leaf bore Elgar's signature and on the margins of page after page were the closely pencilled annotations he had made there some fifty years before. I caught my breath; here in my hand was the genesis of a concert-overture which was to be the earliest manifestation of the true Elgar idiom to achieve official recognition.

When my stay at Broadheath came to an end I took away with me a vast amount of material for 'Portrait of a Composer' and still to come were the researches at the British Museum and consultations with Basil Maine. There were some problems and policy changes on the way, but eventually the script was complete. There had been differing opinions on the advisability of impersonating the voice of Elgar. Arthur Bliss, who was now BBC Controller of Music, thought not. On the other hand, Sir Adrian Boult, who was to conduct, saw nothing against it. My own view, shared by Stephen Potter as producer, was that we ought not to run the risk of irritating or even alienating those listeners who had actually known Elgar. In the end, however, it was decided that we should take that risk, and we did. In the event, we were much relieved to be assured by those who knew, that the voice of Arthur Young, a very fine actor, had come as near to reality as could be expected.

We reconstructed the 1905 ceremony in Worcester's Guildhall where Elgar received the freedom of the city, and amongst many other facets of his life we reproduced the conversations he had had in his father's music shop with the ex-actor and Shakespeare enthusiast, Ned Spires, so tracing the source of the inspiration which led to the creation of *Falstaff*.

Basil Maine's influence was far-reaching, enlivening the selection of music with an infectious enthusiasm for those works which were comparatively less familiar. His effective idea of prefacing some passages from *The Apostles* and *The Kingdom* with the relevant portions of the text, read movingly by Maine himself, tempted us to hope that the actual moment of Elgar's imagination had been recaptured.

On the day of the broadcast, June 2nd, 1942, there were more than two hundred singers, players, actors and technicians assembled in a temporary studio at Bedford School. Preliminary rehearsals went on for six or seven hours and in the welcome intervals we stood around on the playing fields in glorious sunshine and a mood of keen anticipation.

Reactions to the programme were largely favourable. It had its critics, of course; among them were those who thought that the smell of incense hung too heavily, that the atmosphere was too reminiscent of a Three Choirs Festival. It was not to be expected that opinions would be undivided, for radio biography was a new art form. It was a venture into comparatively unexplored territory and there were still many discoveries to be made. To find that in certain significant quarters the programme had made a deep impression and had aroused enthusiasm was reward enough. An eighty-fifth birthday anniversary cannot be celebrated more than once. 'Portrait of a Composer' remained a single contribution to radio and was never repeated.

For some time I had been wondering if it would be possible to bring to our listening audience a glimpse of what lay behind the scenes in the preparation of a music broadcast. As far as I knew, no portion of an orchestral rehearsal had ever been transmitted. It seemed to me that an experiment of that kind might well provide material for an interesting and entertaining quarter of an hour and, at the same time, break new ground. The co-operation of a conductor would obviously be essential; by good fortune, that proved to be no problem. The Promenade season was shortly due to open with a concert by the London Philharmonic Orchestra, to be conducted by Sir Henry Wood. His agreement to allow parts of his first rehearsal to be recorded, and to give us all possible help, was typical of his interest in new developments. It happened that a feature of that opening concert was to be the first performance of an *Epic March* by John Ireland to whom I wrote asking his permission to include it in our 'pre-view'. His reply left it to my discretion

119

although he allowed himself a preliminary grumble that 'as a mere composer' he had not been invited to be present. That, too, was in character as I well knew by now.

Tape recording, with all the advantages of minimal equipment, still lay in the future. On the day, an enormous van, equipped to record on discs, was parked in a side street near the Albert Hall and connected by a multitude of cables to various microphones amongst the orchestra with one, on this occasion, for the conductor. We were naturally anxious to avoid any suggestion of interference with the rehearsal work in hand but, as it turned out, Sir Henry co-operated, even to the extent of asking in what order we would like the various items to be taken. He was in particularly ebullient form, appeared to enjoy himself hugely, and at times was clearly far from unaware of the presence of a microphone. Happily, he forgot about it more often than not and became his natural characteristic self.

Throughout the morning's rehearsal, I was joined by my announcer-colleague, Joseph MacLeod, who prepared the linking commentary. By the end of the day his rough notes had been transformed into a sharply observed script, the eighteen discs we had made were edited, and within twenty-four hours our impression of a Prom rehearsal was broadcast twice, to South Africa in the early evening and again in the Home Service at the peak hour of 8.05 p.m. The programme won some approval; it was heartening to have the response of one listener, for example, who had found it a 'wonderful opportunity to get at the real meaning of music. Sir Henry's comments were right on the mark every time.' They invariably were!

Ten days later we put out a newly-edited version for the North American service. Edward Lockspeiser, who had worked for CBS in New York and had recently joined the BBC, provided assistance in adapting the programme for Transatlantic listeners. Its title was no longer 'Prom Preview' but the more formal 'Promenade Concert Rehearsal'. This time we used one of the splendidly equipped studios which by now had been prepared for the Overseas service, situated several floors below the Peter Robinson store in Oxford Street. To my surprise, the junior programme engineer was a girl, one of the many just recently appointed to replace men who had left for the Forces. In a number of highly technical capacities, these young women worked hard and under considerable pressures, being required to cope with a seventy-two hour tour of duty, sleeping in any odd hour when possible, and following that with seventy-two hours entirely free. The young lady who worked with us on 'Promenade Concert Rehearsal' had clearly mastered the art of remaining completely efficient whilst half asleep on her feet.

FOR three years the nation had been at war. For me it had been a period of ceaseless activity with little time for taking stock or looking forward. But in any case, the future in war-time is hidden from us all; to live from day to day becomes habitual. The work I was doing was fascinating, endless in its variety. It answered a creative impulse, offered scope both for imagination and the organisation of efforts other than my own. There could be a great deal of satisfaction, I had discovered, in the successful exercise of one's own powers of persuasion. Nevertheless, I was assailed by bouts of despondency from time to time, and even occasionally a sense of failure. It arose partly from my realisation that whilst the majority of our projects received an official blessing, the allotment of programme time often created some conflict of opinion in high places. It was natural enough, I had to admit, since programmes of this often experimental nature aroused such a wide range of reactions, and they were not yet sufficiently established in the minds of the all-important planners, who, I was sure, would have shed no tears over their absence. I was also finding that it was a mistake to be too ambitious. For the individual who works alone, ambition is the essential spur, but to be ambitious within a large organisation can very easily be misunderstood.

There was a further and very important factor. I was not doing the work for which I had been trained. Apart from conducting a concert with a section of the BBC Symphony Orchestra, a programme of part songs with the BBC Chorus, and the occasional direction of choral music for religious services, I had taken no practical part in music-making for three years. Worse still, in the complete absence of time and opportunity, the piano had been sadly neglected.

So far, the Corporation had been successful in its appeal for the deferment of my military service, but at the age of thirty-five and physically fit as I was, it would have been unreasonable to expect such an exemption to continue indefinitely.

Towards the end of the month, the BBC was notified that their latest application on my behalf had been turned down. Officially, the decision came as something of a surprise; no contingency plans for my replacement had been made. Now it was clear that I would find myself in uniform in some three months time and all doubts were removed. I would be turning my back on a daily round that was never less than stimulating despite its tensions, and for that there could only be a measure of regret. But I also had a great sense of anticipation, even elation. What might lie beyond the new door soon to be opened I could not imagine; but the unknown is always a challenge, it never fails to intrigue, nor is it necessarily menacing. Without doubt, considerable adjustment to a new life would be essential, but to some extent at least, that necessity had already come my way. Moreover, I would be joining the ranks of countless fellow-men who had found themselves in the same situation.

For the time being I could return to the work in hand – a memorial programme for Gustav Holst. That proposal had caused a little difficulty in the early stages. The planners could see no justification for any such celebration since we were still some thirty years ahead of his birth centenary. An opposite view was taken by Arthur Bliss who considered the time to be appropriate, bearing in mind that Holst's music could hardly be said to have been as fully recognised as its importance deserved. At that time, much of it was still comparatively unfamiliar to a wide audience. At the end of the debate 'Gustav Holst – Musician and Friend', which I was to devise in collaboration (it was hoped) with the composer's daughter, Imogen, was scheduled.

At the earliest possible moment I went to Dunmow in Essex to meet Holst's widow and her daughter. Mrs Holst, very handsome, tall, and surprisingly youthful in appearance, combined tremendous charm with domestic expertise of a high order. Their home was the sixth part of a large house, furnished in impeccable taste and bright, modern style. In sharp contrast, the piano was an ancient Broadwood grand which I was told Holst had bought for £12. On that, he had composed *The Planets*.

I had the impression that Mrs Holst attached as much importance to her cooking as her husband did to his music. Even for me she had specially prepared a delightful un-wartime-like afternoon tea of little buns and cakes. In those days of austerity that was something to be recorded in my diary. At the time, Imogen was far from well and consequently reluctant to take on any extra commitment. A good deal of persuasion was needed before she would agree to take part in the programme, but once it was settled we made excellent progress.

As the writing of the script proceeded, the complexities of Holst's character came increasingly into focus; it was soon quite clear that a contribution from Vaughan Williams would be of great interest. They had been contemporaries and friends, and through their shared interest in folk-song they had together brought a new, nationalist influence to bear on British music. There could be no question that the inclusion of V.W.'s assessment of Holst's work, his personality and achievement, would be of significance. Unfortunately, it had never been possible to persuade him to come to the studio to speak; there had already been several attempts and all had failed. Worse still, he had recently expressed some disapproval of the BBC's current methods of attracting a wider public to the enjoyment of serious music. For all that, it was thought that yet another attempt should be made and it was decided that I should pay V.W. a visit and try to bring about a change of heart.

It was not to be expected that he would remember me though we had met once before, very briefly, in 1938. In the summer of that year, in company with Clarence Raybould, Trevor Harvey, Herbert Murrill and one or two other colleagues, I had attended a BBC conductors' conference arranged by Sir Adrian Boult at his home in Peaslake. Quaker's Orchard, an old, beautifully restored and enlarged convent, was the setting for a week of generous hospitality, discussion and study. We spent much time, I remember, on the score of Stravinsky's *Rite of Spring*. Towards the end of the week Vaughan Williams came for tea. It was difficult to believe that this large, ungainly figure could be a composer – a farmer, perhaps, but certainly not the creator of the works I knew and loved so well. That day, over the teacups, we saw him in his most friendly and sociable mood. At one point, our general small-talk touched on the lamentable inefficiency of conductors who failed to study their scores thoroughly – a topic which prompted V.W. to entertain us with a lengthy and amusing, though highly critical account of his experiences at the Three Choirs Festival. They were clearly not among the happiest of his memories.

But all this was four years ago. By now, his relations with the BBC had suffered some strain. It was obvious that my present assignment would not be easy, and I went off to White Gates, his home in Dorking, not at all confident of the outcome.

He received me with the kindliest courtesy, but must have wondered why I was there. Sitting in his study, brilliant sunshine streaming through the windows, we chatted about many things. Eventually, when he began to look a little puzzled, I managed as diplomatically as I could to bring the talk round to the purpose of my visit. When at last all was clear, he was, alas, quite adamant in his refusal to speak into a microphone. This time, whatever powers of persuasion I could call upon were woefully inadequate. He could not be enticed. All he had to say, he assured me, was already being said in his music. I could not possibly argue with that. He was really quite stern, though his kindliness was unchanged.

My mission had failed, but I was glad to have attempted it. It had given me a treasured memory; I had seen V.W. at work. Several months passed before I suddenly realised just what my visit had interrupted. Those large sheets of manuscript paper which had covered his desk must surely have been the Fifth Symphony which received its first performance not long afterwards, a work which, in its sublime affirmation of faith in the future, was to make a surprising impact on world torn apart by bitterness of conflict.

I met Vaughan Williams only once more. Ten years later, on the occasion of his eightieth birthday, he was present in the audience in the Concert Hall of Broadcasting House to listen to the recital broadcast in his honour, and to which I was delighted to make a contribution.

During the weeks which led up to the Holst programme we were already at work on a number of ideas for future projects. One of them, strongly supported by Stephen Potter, was intended to trace the history of the 'Gentlemen and Children of the Chapels Royal'. Stanley Roper, who was also Principal of the Trinity College of Music, was their Master and Organist. His vitality and enthusiasm enlivened our discussions from which a wealth of material for such a programme emerged. Unfortunately, there were problems. On the outbreak of war the boys had first been sent down to Cornwall and soon afterwards widely scattered; technically at that time, the choir did not exist. It was disappointing because much of their history was not widely known. Though there were no recent recordings in existence, we still hoped that something might be done on a purely reminiscent basis.

The possibility of a feature on the history of the Royal Philharmonic Society had interested me for some time. In 1813, the year of its foundation, the musical situation in our capital city was, in one respect at least, deplorable. In his detailed study of the Philharmonic, long out of print, Myles Birkett Foster writes: 'there was no band fit to play really orchestral works, by which is meant those Symphonies, Overtures, etc., which make their entire effect by means of the instruments and independent of voices. The opera and theatre bands were only employed in playing the weak Overtures and accompaniments of the Italian and English operas in fashion in those days.' There were, of course, the 'Concerts of Antient Music' which were still to run until 1848, but these were aristocratic and amateur promotions, restricted by a standing rule which allowed no music composed during the previous twenty years to be performed. Their contribution to the cause of instrumental music, and to the general standard of performance, could only be discounted. With the coming of the Philharmonic Society, possibly motivated by the great success of Mr Salomon's concerts in the last decade of the eighteenth century, all this was to be changed. Its fully realised intention 'to promote the performance, in the most perfect manner possible, of the best and most approved instrumental music' was to have a far-reaching influence.

The story of that achievement would trace the development of orchestral performance in England and offered wide-ranging possibilities for a radio programme. Even a little further research brought important events into closer focus. In 1818, through one of its Directors, Ferdinand Ries, the Society commissioned Beethoven to write two new symphonies and invited him to London to direct their first performances. That project came to nothing, partly because of Beethoven's ill-health, and partly because he demanded a fee in excess of the 300 guineas offered. Four years later, things went more happily. Beethoven now agreed to accept a new commission for a fee of £50 which resulted in nothing less than the immortal Ninth Symphony. But the 'New Grand Characteristic Sinfonia with Vocal Finale', to give it its full title, was not delivered to the Philharmonic until many months after the stipulated date – not, in fact, until it had already been performed in Vienna and dedicated to Friedrich Wilhelm III, King of Prussia. There is something of a mystery here, for the manuscript in the possession of the Society bears the inscription in Beethoven's own hand: 'Geschrieben für die Philharmonische Gesellschaft in London'. In Grove's tactful words, these are facts which are 'difficult to reconcile with Beethoven's usual love of fairness and justice'.

Though a historic occasion in the annals of the Society, the first performance in England on March 21st, 1825, could hardly be described as a success. A work of such unusual design, so full of unsuspected difficulties both musical and technical, presented the conductor, Sir George Smart, the players, singers and audience with well-nigh insoluble problems. (The great double-bass player, Dragonetti, asserted that he would have doubled his fee if he had seen the score before agreeing to play!) The critic of the newly-issued monthly periodical, *The Harmonicon*, did not hesitate to express his view that the Symphony 'is at least twice as long as it should be', and further complained that 'the want of intelligible design is too apparent'. Small wonder that a work so elusive should lie on the shelf for twelve years before being attempted again.

In the last months of his life, the link between Beethoven and the Philharmonic Society was still further strengthened. Early in 1827 Beethoven was seriously ill and suffering extreme poverty. To Moscheles, the distinguished pianist, composer and conductor who had recently settled in London, he wrote: 'What is to be the end of it all? And what is to become of me, if my illness persists for some time?' His letter was a pathetic appeal for help. The Philharmonic had earlier been ready to arrange a concert for his benefit; it was now more urgent than ever.

The response was immediate. At a hurriedly summoned General Meeting it was unanimously decided that the sum of £100 should be sent forthwith 'to be applied to his comforts and necessities during his illness'. Beethoven's letter of thanks, addressed to Moscheles as intermediary, was warm and heartfelt. 'May Heaven but restore my health very soon,' he wrote, 'and I shall prove to these magnanimous Englishmen how greatly I appreciate their sympathy for me in my sad fate.' He would prove his gratitude to the Philharmonic 'by engaging to compose for it a new symphony, sketches for which are already in my desk, or a new Overture, or something else which the Society might like to have.' He died eight days later.

It was a striking episode in the history of music-making in England, and a story well worth telling. The radio script was soon completed but it was never broadcast, nor was the 'Chapels Royal' programme.

They were not the only projects which failed to materialise. Of the others, the one I most regretted to lose was a feature on the early life of Delius in Florida, a period notable for the composition of his opera *Koanga*, the Piano Concerto, and most important of all, to my mind, the tone-poem, Appalachia. That was the work which haunted my dreams for a very long time.

But time had run out. My sojourn in Bedford had come to an end and so, too, had my BBC service, at any rate for the time being.

CHAPTER 11

A pike man in training

Let the pike man march with a good grace, his face full of gravity and state, and such as is fit for his person; and let his body be straight and as much upright as possible; and that which is most important is that they have their eyes always upon their companions which are in the rank with them and before them, going just with one another, and keeping perfect distance without committing the least error in pace or step.

And every pace and motion with one accord they ought to make at one instant of time. And in this sort all the ranks ought to go sometimes softly, sometimes fast, accordingly to the stroke of the drum . . . So shall they go just and even with a gallant and sumptuous pace; for by doing so they will be esteemed, honoured and commended of all the lookers on, who will take wonderful delight to behold them.

William Garrard, 1591
The Art of Warre

IT was a happy coincidence that this charming piece of sixteenth-century advice should have come my way shortly before my own transition to military service. I was delighted to find it, though any romantic ideas which it might have prompted were going to be quickly dispelled. Even so, the writer's accuracy and precision were strikingly confirmed in those first weeks of my training on the square. We tried to march with a good grace, we learned to hold our heads high, and very soon we knew how to 'look proud' even if so far our faces failed to register the required degree of gravity and state.

Platoons of raw recruits, newly formed week by week at the Initial Training Centre in Brentwood, Essex, were graded roughly by age, though in mine I found myself six or seven years junior to many of my companions. That they were all bricklayers was probably the outcome of current calling-up procedures and the ever-changing status of what were known as Reserved Occupations. I was certainly the odd man out; whatever they could have thought of me I never knew – nor did it matter. But they were splendid chaps, some of them surprisingly a little nervous, all of them as staggered as I was by an abrupt transformation. Vocabulary, with a monotonously plentiful sprinkling of four-letter words – and one in particular – was the feature which I found more boring and tiresome than any other. No noun, however insignificant, could ever be used without the addition of its supremely inappropriate but indispensable adjective.

For the greater part of every day our lives were besieged by the ceaseless authority of the NCOs. Freedom, it seemed, was lost for good; our every move was by command; transfer from one training session to another a hundred yards away could only be done under orders. We were no longer considered capable of managing anything for ourselves, however simple. It was dreary, depressing, and positively damaging to self-respect. I had to admit that I had some bad moments; in one of the worst it struck me with just a suggestion of comfort that at least my thoughts were unassailable. But it was the beginning of discipline; I could see that, and the Army knew far more about it than I did. Perhaps it would not always be like this, I thought.

It was interesting to study the effect of authority on the personalities of our NCOs. It rested lightly on the shoulders of the Company Sergeant-Major who had all the qualities. He was logical, he was reliable in his reactions and he knew his job down to the last detail. In contrast, our Platoon Lance-Corporal made every effort to be tough but that only resulted in uncertain temper and a high degree of unpredictability. In between the two extremes there was a Corporal whose one anxiety, astonishingly, was to please, not his superiors, but those who awaited his commands. On one of our innumerable marches from one part of the camp to another he imparted, in a quite apologetic voice, a priceless nugget of military advice – "I say, when we turn to the left, the blokes on the left really ought to slow down a bit to let the others catch up!" What, I wondered, would William Garrard have made of that in 1591?

We were to be at Brentwood for six weeks and into that time an enormous programme of primary training was crammed. Every minute of every long day was fully used, and at breakneck speed. We rushed breathlessly from one parade to another, taking in our stride lectures, examinations in general knowledge, tests of all kinds, medical and dental inspections, physical training, first steps in gunnery – and towards the end, three days on the firing range at Purfleet. All had to be done in half the time it would normally take, or less. Standing for hours at a time proved very tiring to begin with and there were times when muscles I never knew existed screamed a protest. I had still to learn how amazingly adaptable the human frame could be, but I quickly discovered the sheer joy of crawling into my bunk at 10 p.m., even with its rough blankets and tiny pillow made of straw.

With so much time spent out of doors and in very well organised physical training, I had to admit after about a week that I was beginning to feel terribly healthy. Remembering the miseries of school-days, the very thought of cross-country running filled me with horror, but after ten days, my scrappy diary records: 'I can even run in singlet and shorts in the pouring rain and think nothing of it – not much, anyway!' Suddenly, for no apparent reason, it struck me that this extraordinary life need not be all bad. For the time being it was a reality to be accepted, the more wholeheartedly the better. From that moment I was a great deal happier.

The Army loses no time in finding out everything there is to know about its new recruits – their personalities, individual aptitudes, capacities and ambitions. Tests of all kinds were designed to this end. There was an afternoon when we were all marched into a large room, the benches round the walls laid out with a series of mechanical instruments – the lock of a door, an electric power plug, a bicycle pump, and so on. But they were all dismantled.

131

Our task was to reassemble their many separate parts and restore working order. My companions were enthusiastic; here was a chance to show what they could do. Alas, I was entirely at a loss and did very badly; I doubt that I left anything approaching a successful effort at the end of that session. Consequently, it was with astonishment that I learned in later interviews, first with a Personnel Selection Officer and then the Company Commander, that I was to go to the Royal Armoured Corps, one of the most highly technical branches of all. It seemed that the ways of the Army were strange indeed. But both officers had given me an OCTU recommendation and assured me that this was a very positive step towards a possible commission. It appeared to me to be most unlikely.

The six weeks came to an end exactly as planned and on November 12th, 1942, with reveille at 4.45 a.m., we marched out of Warley Camp for the last time. My destination was Barnard Castle in County Durham where I was to report to the RAC 54th Training Regiment. Thick fog, shrouding the whole country throughout the day, lengthened the journey by many hours but I was well fortified by rations from the haversack and pints of coffee supplied by the WVS *en route*.

No greater contrast could be imagined than that between Deerbolt Camp, the home of the 54th, and the only other military establishment I had known so far. Warley Barracks had been a peace-time garrison, the headquarters of the Essex Regiment. In 1942 it had already seen many years of service and, in fact, I was given to understand, had been condemned even before 1939. Nevertheless, as I now knew so well, in its current, frenzied activity as an Initial Training Centre, that had been all forgotten. Here at Deerbolt the camp was comparatively new – and marvellously situated below the town on ground which rises sharply beyond the bridge spanning the River Tees. The many bungalow-like buildings which housed us were built of pinky-grey stone, widely spaced with beautifully tended gardens between, full of vegetables. The paths were being neatly edged by white stones brought hand-to-hand from the river bed; I carried quite a few myself on my first fatigues.

Apart from location, there were far greater differences between Deerbolt and Warley. The whole camp had an air of smartness, efficiency and style. I was warned that the amount of spit and polish needed here was quite frightening though, odd as it might have seemed, that did not alarm me at all. I actually welcomed the prospect. Everything was quieter, more highly organised, and slower, especially the drill – in the Guards tradition, they said. To acquire a new black beret with its silver badge of the RAC, the shoulder flashes and the green lanyard was quite exhilarating; I was a Private no longer, but a Trooper, and the stage was set for a fresh course of training.

Here again organisation was the keynote and its basic emphasis was on physical fitness. We were left in no doubt of its purpose. We were being conditioned for war and were expected to develop endurance, resource and fortitude day by day. It was all clearly explained; the pattern of our training was based on the experience of men of all ranks returning from the battle fronts. They said what was needed and to that our schedule was precisely adjusted. I noticed one curious feature. Our time-table seemed to be kept secret; it was hardly ever possible to discover what lesson, exercise or occupation was planned to come next. Keeping us in the dark was probably intended to teach us not to raise questions of 'where?' or 'why?' but merely to be ready for anything, whatever it might be.

To begin with, it was more often a question of brawn, and here I found myself at a disadvantage. Once again I was the odd man out but this time I was almost twice the age of my companions, some of whom had come straight from school. The difference between us was all too obvious when we came to tackle the Deerbolt Battle Course which was of infamous reputation and practically the sole topic of conversation in the NAAFI. Now I found out what it was like to struggle with almost complete physical exhaustion, the sinews tested near to breaking point. The effort was far beyond anything I had ever been called upon to make. For the whole hazardous round I exceeded the record time by about twenty-five per cent – not good at all, but there was a crumb of comfort in knowing that some of my companions had taken even longer.

Nevertheless, this question of physical demand worried me a great deal. How much easier it might have been if I had spent more Saturday afternoons on the rugger field at Lancaster, with piano lessons relegated to second place! It was this which added to the tensions of those first few weeks at Barnard Castle. I could only hope against hope that I might somehow be able to match up to all that lay ahead.

In our indoor training, such misgivings largely disappeared. Our initial instruction in a number of different categories provided a basic knowledge for all, and also led to specialist grading according to individual aptitude. We could become wireless operators, gunners, drivers, electricians or mechanics, and for some there could be a combination of two qualifications. In my own case, the issue was not long in doubt. I was already enjoying some small headway in the use of Morse code, and it was therefore not an unpleasing prospect to have radio communication chosen for me. The course would take eight weeks and later on there would be 'schemes' out on the moors, first in wireless trucks and then in tanks.

Meanwhile, to my surprise, the Brentwood recommendation that I might be considered for Officer training had not been forgotten. Things began to happen; unfortunately, my particular *bête-noire* immediately raised its ugly head. The first rung on what was to be a very long ladder turned out to be the Assault Course – again! Perhaps this time I felt a shade more confident on the cat-walk across the river, though the water fifteen feet below looked bleak and cold. It was three days before Christmas and the snow was falling. I clambered up the tree platform, grasped the suspended rope, swung myself out into mid-air and managed to let go at the crucial moment. Mother earth came up to hit me, just as she had before. At five minutes for the whole round my time was not brilliant though still quite reasonable according to the PT instructor with his stop-watch. He must have been a man of kindly compassion for he was not averse to telling us that one OCTU candidate had taken ten and some had even failed to get round at all.

Then came the Regimental Board. Before being called, we sat nervously in the waiting-room for an hour which was spent in earnest study of the *Daily Mail* just in case there were any questions on the current military situation. Inside, there were five officers sitting at small tables around the room. My first interview, brief but pleasant, was with the President. He seemed to be mainly concerned to discuss some Regimental concert which had failed to materialise. (My musical background had not gone unnoticed.) I moved on, this time to a Major, very rakish with bushy moustache, cap on the back of his head, a British Warm and many "Hells" and "Dammmits."

"Oh! You're the BBC fellah," he began, and then continued at length about the iniquities of the BBC for whom apparently he had written some stories – and been considerably underpaid! We found we had a mutual friend in Lance Sieveking and before long I was explaining the principles of multi-studio technique and talking about the changes in broadcasting brought about by the war. Not a word about the Army!

At the next table was a Squadron-Commander, another Major. Inevitably we began with the BBC, but this time only briefly for now the interview was more serious and searching. Why did I want to be an officer? I said I thought that I could perhaps serve the Army best by accepting responsibility, having been accustomed to it in civilian life.

"So you want responsibility, do you?" he asked. "Of course, that's a very different thing in wartime, you know – holding men's lives in the hollow of your hand, and all that sort of thing."

This was an interview with a sense of purpose, unlike my final encounter with a charming Captain who seemed to be rather less at ease than I was. He was obviously more than grateful to the BBC for giving him something to talk about, but even so, our intermittent exchanges were broken by long and silent intervals. Eventually, when all else failed, he admitted that there were many questions he ought to be asking me; unfortunately, he could not remember any of them at the moment although they would all probably come back to him after I had left!

135

Three days later I stood stiffly to attention before the Commanding Officer. Slumped in his chair, he looked tired and worn, as though all the burdens of the world rested on his shoulders.

His first words, as he studied my papers, were "How old are you?"

"Thirty-five, sir," I replied.

There was a long silence.

"God! You're old, aren't you?" he said at last. There was an even longer pause before he added "Do you feel your age?"

My answer came very promptly: "No, sir – not at all."

The age-long silence which now ensued allowed me ample time in which to reflect on the unpardonable sin which the calendar and I had conspired to commit. But at long last his reply came: "Well, I'll put you up as a special case – and if not, we'll have to find you something else." Whereupon the Sergeant-Major marched me out.

Hundreds of miles from the German lines as we were, the only enemy we faced in that bleak and wintry January was the weather. The snow fell incessantly, the temperature reached unprecedented depths, and everywhere the ice was black and treacherous. To slip and fall, as I did when simply reading a notice-board, was altogether a stupid and inglorious affair. But to pick myself up and find that the left hand thumb was now where the little finger should have been was startling to say the least.

They were very busy at the Military Hospital in Catterick. I waited there for some five hours without attracting much attention except for a kind and rather elderly VAD nurse who, looking at my hand as she passed by, said with a delightful smile: "Well, it's not exactly as God made it, is it?" And she went on her way. Eventually the diagnosis was a Colles fracture; that night the bones were most expertly set by a surgeon from Trinity College, Dublin. Of that, I have no recollection, but I was conscious next morning when he came to inspect his handiwork. He asked me about my occupation in civilian life. "I play the piano," I said. He was horror-stricken; as he told me how glad he was that he had not known that on the previous evening, his face was quite pale. But I owe him a deep debt of gratitude. What he did he did superbly and with complete success.

The incident was at least partly responsible for a delay of rather more than three months before I could reach the last hurdle of the OCTU stakes. In the meantime, as a wireless operator, I made close acquaintance with Cruiser tanks, discovered the unpredictable hazards of driving Bren carriers in convoy, and made some headway through a jungle of strange technicalities. It was a new world and I was learning to live in it. More importantly, I was at long last beginning to understand the value of comradeship and to realise what a community of spirit could mean when the stresses came.

For those of us who had to face it, the three-day visit to a War Office Selection Board was a matter of unending speculation and growing apprehension as it drew nearer. In the event, some of our fears were justified though it has to be admitted that the experience was far from unpleasant. Everything possible was done to relieve the tension; the atmosphere was friendly and always courteous. We were made members of the Officers' Mess and we lived there, sixty of us in groups of six. For close acquaintance with each other the time was too short and so we each wore a numbered armband. At meals, where we knew that our social graces were under scrutiny, one heard: "Pass the salt, 43, please," and other requests all gracefully and numerically phrased.

It was immediately clear that our numerous tests and trials had been devised with great expertise; even at the receiving end one could only admire the skill and efficiency with which they had been arranged. There was a psychological probe, for example, in which we were shown seven slides on a screen. In three minutes for each we were to write a story, using the picture as an illustration of its central incident. What followed was more difficult; this time, a blank white screen invited the creation of an imaginary picture for similar treatment.

In a written paper there were distinctly awkward questions:

What does your best friend think of you?

137

What does your severest critic find wrong with you?

What is your object in life?

Would you welcome service overseas? – If so, why?

There were some posers here! We suggested topics for group discussions. My far from original proposal was: 'The effect of the cinema on modern life.' Happily, that went down well with the testing officer who admitted to being very tired of talks on post-war reconstruction!

Out of doors there was a Group Obstacle Course which presented a variety of dilemmas. In my case it involved a full-sized telegraph pole, sundry lengths of rope and a large, unmanageable expanse of netting. For any onlooker, there was ample material here for comedy. Laurel and Hardy would have been in their element. Such a thought was far from our minds; we were all in deadly earnest. The 'Obstacle' difficulties faded into insignificance when we finally came to the Group Tactical Situation. Now there were real problems which inspired highly complicated, entirely unpractical, but always optimistic and enthusiastic solutions.

Eventually our ordeal came to an end and at that moment, beyond doubt, none of us felt more than half an inch tall. The uncomfortable conviction which we all shared was that now, after all these wide-ranging and penetrating inquisitions, nothing was any longer concealed. Our interrogators knew more about us than we knew ourselves. For myself, there was very little on which I could build any hope of success.

Yet the miracle happened, and miracle it was. The RAC was willing to accept me, not for an active unit overseas, but for a training regiment. Everything moved with what now seems quite incredible speed. No more than three days passed before that news came through; five days after that I was at Blackdown in Surrey, ready to start out on a nine week pre-OCTU course.

From the first moment of arrival, we were left in no doubt that a constant crescendo of effort would be essential, and expected, if we were to reach the required high standards of proficiency and also survive and undreamt-of rigidity of discipline. Gunnery, driving and maintenance, wireless communication and a host of other subjects followed each other in quick succession. I crawled into bed at night in a confused whirl of carburettors, dynamos, autovacs and cut-outs, all of which could look so dangerously alike!

Four days which were intended to ensure our intimate familiarity with the motor-cycle brought me a completely new experience. Never in my life had I even sat astride one of those malevolent machines and I failed altogether to share the delight and enthusiasm of my colleagues. The one allotted to me had a sullen and unfriendly look – it reminded me of some pianos I had known; a genuine *rapport* between us remained obstinately missing. Even as we rode together at a fair pace round the flat circuit we merely tolerated each other. Then on Bagshott Common we had to learn how to take the jumps without becoming airborne. Our vendetta came out into the open. To discover just how many times we had parted company I could only count my bruises at the end of the day. It was only a small comfort to be told that the Police took four weeks to learn as much as we were supposed to do in four days. Whether I succeeded or not was fortunately never put to the test.

The many stresses of those nine weeks were temporarily eased in an unexpected way. It had never been my intention to become involved in any kind of musical activity during my Army service; I well realised that all my concentration would be needed in other directions. But here at Blackdown we had the Band of the 13th/18th Royal Hussars and their energetic and enterprising Bandmaster, S. T. Vinnicombe. He had the idea that I should play the Schumann Piano Concerto with the Band in a concert which was shortly to be given in the Garrison Theatre. It was a tempting proposal which I found difficult to resist and so I agreed, though to begin with, I was by no means certain that the orchestral score would transfer successfully to a military band. I need not have worried; it proved to be surprisingly effective, and I much enjoyed the experience. The programme billed me as Cadet John Helliwell (which looked very strange to me) and my fellow soloists were the visiting singers, Margaret Eaves and Dennis Noble, both of whom I had partnered on many previous occasions though in very different circumstances.

A week or so later I took part in another concert, this time as conductor of Wagner's Overture to *Die Meistersinger*. It was a heartening and even thrilling moment when we tackled those opening bars for the first time. The bandsmen of the Royal Hussars were all fine players, fully equal to any technical demands, even if in that work they were venturing some way beyond their normal repertoire. I have a happy memory of our final rehearsal in the open air on one of the summer's hottest afternoons. If some essential diversity of nuance was missing from our performance that evening, it was compensated at least in part by an unparalleled precision of attack.

These brief diversions did little to interrupt the serious business in hand. The vital preparation for what was to come filled our days and left room now for nothing else. We all knew that if everything went well the Royal Military College, Sandhurst, would be the last lap – and the most hazardous hurdle of all. Even to the most relaxed and easy-going Cadet amongst us, and there were very few of those, it was an awesome prospect.

When all the final demands of Blackdown were met, we were on our way. As our truck reached the outskirts of the Sandhurst grounds we were met by the RMC Band and marched through the Park to the strains of 'My Boy Billy'. It was a good start, a stirring moment of pride and anticipation. Any lurking tremors of anxiety and self-doubt, I decided, were luxuries I could no longer afford.

Creature comforts were now far more in advance of anything I had so far enjoyed in the Army. In pairs, we shared a neat and pleasantly furnished room. That arrangement brought me a friendly and happy association with David Hodsman, a charming and gifted young man from the north-east of England. With his great interest in music, and particularly the works of Vaughan Williams, we had much in common. Tragically, the brilliant career which seemed so clearly to lie ahead for him was not to materialise. He met his death in northern France some twelve months later, just a day or so after D-Day.

One of our neighbours in an adjoining room was Cadet Althorp, known affectionately to us all as Johnny. As I write this, nearly forty years on, the eyes of the world are focussed on him as Lord Spencer, whose daughter is now destined to become a Queen of England. How little we knew what the future might hold for any of us!

The early morning physical exercises in bare feet on the grass gave us something of an initial shock, though they turned out to be surprisingly pleasant and we soon took them easily in our stride. For the rest, we embarked once again on a fresh bout of military training, this time under the kindly but eagle eye of Captain Gordon-Lennox. In one way or another, each one of us became indebted to him for his personal interest. He saw us as individuals, not as a group, and that made a sharp contrast with Army experience so far. From the start, we were expected to accept responsibility – it was thrust upon us – and for the more youthful members who had seen little of life beyond their schooldays, there was much to learn. It was some surprise to me to be put in charge of the guard on the New Building two weeks after arrival.

The formidable Sergeant-Major instructors were the ones to watch. They saw the rule-book and the letter of the law as sacrosanct; for them, it allowed no flexibility of interpretation nor even any exercise of perception. A deviation, however slight, could spell serious trouble. As a contributor to the current RMC magazine put it:

> There's a Squadron Sergeant-Major
>   Looking viciously at me,
> For my gaiters were not blancoed
>   And that's his cup-o'-tea.
> Oh! the weekend trains are calling
>   And it's on them I should be,
> 'Stead of sweating on defaulters
>   On the square at Camberley.

One of the heavier punishments for a misdemeanour was to complete a run of the long Sandhurst boundary, in full kit and within a fixed allotted time. If that were exceeded the whole exercise had to be repeated until it could be done successfully. It would have presented little problem to my colleagues, who were mostly ten to twelve years my juniors in age. But I was quite certain that if ever that particular penalty came my way I should find myself condemned, like the Flying Dutchman, to lap that circuit again and again – into unending time – with never a hope of release.

The NCO instructors were absolutely right, of course, to take a rigid view of the rules. Only in that way could they carry out the work they had to do – and invaluable work it was. But it could lead to anomalies, and sometimes the lesson we learned was not exactly the one intended.

We returned from an exercise, for instance, at three in the morning. The rain had poured in torrents; we were soaked to the skin, our equipment in a deplorable state. Yet three hours later we were due to be on parade with spotlessly clean rifles for inspection. The rule was that no rifle could be cleaned indoors and another clearly laid down that we were not allowed outside the building during the night. At six in the morning, I stood correctly to attention on that parade, my rifle, miraculously, clean, dry and beyond reproach. I should have been in trouble if it had been otherwise; but I was in trouble anyway, contemplating an answer to the Sergeant-Major's question, how had it been done? I took rather a long time to think of a reply – we both knew how it had been done, and I could already see myself running that circuit! Accidentally, our eyes met, and I was still silent. Furiously, through clenched teeth, he warned: "In another minute, I shall have you for dumb insolence!" and with that he turned away. It was the end of a tiny incident, but it had some significance. I had learned something of the ways of the Army, and I had learned not to find it contradictory if at times it was necessary to break one rule in order not to break another.

It was also laid down that NCO instructors were to address potential officers as 'Sir'. This they did, though long experience had shown them that this single monosyllable could convey unlimited contempt and scorn. No doubt we deserved it, more often than not.

Most of the training was of a practical nature – out of doors, 'on the ground'. We grew rapidly fitter and tougher, able to cope with forced marches of six miles or so within

142

the hour. It was never effortless, by any means, and there were times when my reactions revealed the difference between younger colleagues and myself. I was not offended by the occasionally diverting comment of a waggish NCO who would call out: "Here comes the old gentleman!" It was merely meant to be encouraging. And sometimes my extra years gave me an advantage in staying power. That was very cheering.

The testing climax of physical exertion came during the week-long Battle Course at Capel Curig in North Wales. That was our base, though for the most part we were spread far and wide throughout that marvellous countryside. We waded chest high through the lake shallows, rifles and cigarettes held overhead at arm's length; with live ammunition we put the tactical principles we had learned in the classroom to the test; we crawled face down through the squelchy morass beneath the fixed lines of fire from the Bren guns; and in full kit, with stones in our packs, we climed to the peak of Snowdon, there to drink the finest and most welcome cup of tea ever to be tasted. We nursed our bruises, every bone in our bodies ached as never before, we grumbled and complained. Yet, in the same moment, we were all agreed that this had been the most enjoyable and the most satisfying week imaginable.

The mastery of the elaborate manoeuvres on the square, forming part of Sandhurst's renowned Passing-Out Parades, brought us stage by stage to a new peak of smartness and precision. Periodically, as our senior fellow cadets reached the end of their course, the elusive Sam Browne at last within their grasp, we took our part. Now we moved 'just and even, with a gallant and sumptuous pace'; and from the Elysian Fields, William Garrard no doubt looked on with a half-smile of approval. Time and again, we marvelled at the skill with which the Adjutant, Major James, rode his white horse up the flight of steps and into the New Building. Even for the most cynical, a swelling of pride was inescapable – and not one of us failed to remember that one day it would be our turn.

Another brief visit to a military hospital, this time the Cambridge at Aldershot, threatened to delay that happy day

143

for me. My failure to come to terms with a ten-foot wall on the Assault Course resulted in a broken collar-bone. "Very nice," said the M.O. "A really beautiful, nice clean break of the bone." He sounded pleased, and more than satisfied. There was to be no nonsense about setting it. The thing to do was to leave it just as it was, and it would heal all the sooner. My course hardly needed to be retarded at all and the Army had no intention of being deterred from its purpose. All I needed was a masseuse. She was a very grim, determined young woman who would brook no opposition of any kind. Her conversation was as limited as her sense of humour. "Higher, higher," she would say; "right up – you're not trying – right up, that's right, higher, higher, that's good, now down – slowly!" It was exquisite torture; my pointed references to the Spanish Inquisition made no impression on her whatever. We were neither of us amused.

In the ward, though, where I spent not much more than a couple of days there was comedy to be enjoyed. The anxious bustle which preceded the arrival of the surgeon, and the incredible concentration on tidying-up created an atmosphere of unbearable tension. If a paper or an envelope slipped an inch out of place, if a towel appeared with two folds to the front instead of three, a muster of nurses and orderlies – I counted fourteen – would pounce in to make deprecatory noises and put all to rights. Ten minutes later, the climax past, everyone breathed normally again. As a potential officer, though still very 'potential', I was given a room to myself. (There was a rumour that I was the leader of the London Philharmonic Orchestra – and on the wall a poster which said 'Careless Talk costs Lives.') The two previous occupants of my room had been Germans, I was told – one an eighteen-year old airman, the other a Gestapo agent. How they came to be there I never discovered, but it was an intriguing bit of gossip.

Five days later I was out on an exercise on Salisbury Plain, sleeping on the ground, not at all comfortably but sheltered by a friendly Sherman tank. The only concession made to my temporary incapacity was the privilege of acting as a combined Quartermaster and Messing Officer responsible for feeding some fifty ravenous Cadets.

That the human frame could be so resilient never ceased to amaze me. Obviously, our training had much to do with it, but that did not fully explain the curious fact that, in the services, we could apparently be safely subjected to risks which in civilian life would have courted disaster. I had a striking example.

There was one icy November morning when I was plagued by a streaming cold. We marched to the lake in the Sandhurst grounds and were staggered to be ordered by the Sergeant-Major to jump in, fully clothed. We were to be taught how to stay afloat, whether we could swim or not. His orders were that first we should remove our boots, below water – then the trousers which, with a particular flick of the wrist, were to be thrown overhead so that they would fill with air and could then be used as makeshift water-wings! It all seemed very improbable; we were aghast, and shivering. As the SSM's little discourse came to an end, I happened to sneeze five times in quick succession. His gimlet eye caught mine. "You, too!" he cried. "Go on, you'll be all right." In I went. It was even more of a shock than I had expected, but it worked, and I floated! By the evening of that day, unaccountably, my cold had completely disappeared; I streamed no more.

One by one, our specialist courses came to an end with their respective tests and examinations. As the Course drew nearer to its conclusion, the tension grew day by day. Anxiety was not mine alone; we confided in each other and shared our fears – none of us could escape some sense of impending doom. Already, three of our number had quietly disappeared, apparently overtaken by that fate which hung over us like a black cloud – 'Return to Unit!' Could that terrible rumour be true, we asked each other, that the last straw for one unfortunate victim was that he had left a razor-blade on the top of his locker? No, no, we decided; there must surely have been something far more serious. We would be rational and breathe again. Perhaps, after all, these long and arduous months would have a happy ending.

Then came some official involvement in the question of what was to become of us after being commissioned, and that brought a positive note of optimism. In my case, I learned from Captain Gordon-Lennox that there had been some possibility that I would return to the 54th Training Regiment. That would have been ideal, but for one small snag. To serve there as an officer alongside senior NCOs who had known me as a trooper would, in the opinion of the Commanding Officer, present some difficulty. It was some small surprise to me to discover that amidst all the unimaginable pressures of 1943 the Army could find time for such niceties of tact. Behind the scenes, however, Colonel Hurrell had been busy on my behalf. As a results, I was now told, another training regiment in Barnard Castle, the 61st, would be 'delighted' to have me!

At long last, the day came when the band played, the flags fluttered in the breeze, and we marched on the square with a rare and high-hearted happiness. This was an altogether different Passing-Out Parade, for this was ours and we would never know another. No thought of the future and what it might hold had any place in our minds. Those secrets, bright or dark, could be set aside; the day was sufficient. A new impulse of spirit carried us eagerly through those ritual formalities, the Adjutant rode up the steps on his white horse, and the difference this time was that we followed him into the building. Our transformation was complete; we were "one-pippers'. No matter that some would see us now as the lowest of the low, nor that once again we were starting out at the bottom of the ladder. Characteristically, but kindlier this time, the SSM allowed himself a parting shot: "Now you can go and put on your fancy dress!"

CHAPTER 12

Barney

TO the west of Barnard Castle lies Bowes Moor, a wild and rugged expanse of magnificent vistas, broken only by a handful of scattered farmsteads and a mosaic of grey stone walls. It is an area which by 1943 had become all too well known to thousands of men who had toiled and sweated throughout the severities of the School of Infantry's training course. There they had learned and practised the new methods of assault, and in doing so had brought discipline and efficiency to a fresh peak of perfection.

Following them came the Royal Armoured Corps with its Centaurs, Cavaliers, armoured cars, Cromwells, Stuarts, jeeps, Crocodiles and Sheridans. Now the manoeuvres were of a different kind, their objective the mastery of the tactical use of tanks in battle. The daily roar of distant barrage was something the little town below had learned to take in its stride, cheerfully accepting the inevitable disruption of the peace it had known for so long. Its citizens could claim with some pride that the whole strategy of the North-African landing had been tried out experimentally there on Bowes Moor. And they could claim, too, that their town had played host in October, 1943, to no fewer than seventy Generals of all the allied nations.

To the east lies the village of Staindrop adjoining Streatlam Castle and the estate of the Earl of Strathmore. Close by is the fourteenth-century fortress of Raby Castle where, over the years, many an assembly of armoured knights had mustered in its Great Hall. Now there was mustering again, and if security regulations had allowed, Teesdale could have boasted of a concentration of modern military training establishments at Stainton, Streatlam, Westwick, Barford, Humbledon and Deerbolt. One of the loveliest areas of the English countryside had become a key point in the overall plan for victory, and Barnard Castle stood at its centre.

Streatlam Camp was the home of the RAC 61st Training Regiment to which my posting had been confirmed. My arrival there early in 1944 was not quite a step into the unknown for I had, at least, known 'Barney' very briefly. At Sandhurst I had been warned that on joining his regiment for the first time a newly-fledged officer could not expect any particular warmth of welcome, even if he were not to be ignored altogether. In all probability, to be fully accepted as a member of Mess would at least take some time. Luckily, my experience was quite the reverse. For the most part my new colleagues were friendly and sociable from the start. A number of them were my contemporaries in age; they, too, were in uniform for the 'duration' and coping as I was with an unfamiliar world.

There were others, some of them less approachable, who were much senior to me both in years and military service. Amongst them were Regular Officers who had served in a peace-time Army for the greater part of their careers, and whose retirement could not now be far away. One or two had barely survived the shock of transition from cavalry to armour, and they made it abundantly clear that they regarded the tank as a very poor, if not altogether unacceptable, substitute for the horse. Their background was India and their dinner-table small-talk betrayed a nostalgic yearning for a life-style long departed and never to return. An overheard comment made one day by a dispirited Captain, wearily mopping his brow after a particularly strenuous day, was entirely characteristic: "If my mother could see me now – working in the afternoons!"

Such attitudes were, of course, exceptional. Overall, the Regiment was a highly efficient machine, with a vast responsibility for training countless men, draft by draft, in all the technical skills required by an armoured corps. We did not know then that we were just six months away from the long awaited invasion of Europe, but no one doubted that it would come, and the growing pressures of preparation for it were already apparent.

I started out as an instructor in the Wireless Wing, initially 'supervising classes'; that was the official phrase. Merely to stand around and listen, which was all it meant, seemed to add up to a very insignificant contribution. A week later, having found that we were sufficiently well-equipped, I ventured to suggest that it might be helpful if we were to make some recordings to demonstrate both correct procedures 'on the air' and the basic principles of security. Surprisingly, it had never been done and the idea was enthusiastically approved. "Go ahead and do it," I was told. For once, I was on firm ground. It was quite like old times to write the little scripts, rehearse them and produce the records.

However far the new technical skills could be developed in the classroom, the results were still mainly theoretical. They had to be tested 'on the ground'. Practical experience in the operation of equipment, wireless procedures, security and especially map-reading was vitally necessary for men whose military service could still only be measured in months. A 'five-day' scheme out on the moors provided it, bringing each new intake in turn face-to-face with some semblance of reality.

My next assignment, shared with one other officer, was to take charge of these tours week by week. Normally, there would be about fifty of us all told, and it was fortunate that our convoys were made up of radio-equipped utility vans, for they were far more comfortable than tanks would have been. We slept mostly in barns where even the rats suffered a war time disturbance, and where I came to terms with camp-bed, sleeping valise, portable wash-basin and other miscellaneous items faintly reminiscent of half-forgotten comforts. The quarter-inch map of Yorkshire's West Riding became thoroughly familiar. It was curious that in general the art of map-reading should have proved to be so elusive. That had been true even at Sandhurst.

I would always remember one afternoon in Salisbury where, during some exercise or other, we had brought a Sherman tank to a temporary halt in one of the city's main streets. Alongside, a large map was spread out on the pavement, and around it knelt four potential officers who, in the war time absence of all sign posts, were entirely at a loss. Simultaneously, on the corner a few yards away, a fifth was asking a helpful passer-by to put us on our way! It was hardly a spectacle which could have enhanced the confidence of our civilian onlookers.

Here on the Yorkshire moors our exercises revealed similar shortcomings all too often. It was positively unnerving to have a dozen vehicles scattered over several hundred square miles with only the pious hope that all the six-figure map references sent to them by radio had been correctly interpreted, and that at the end of the day they would all turn up at the appointed rendezvous. Imagination was haunted by the uncomfortable consequences of a return to the Barnard Castle base minus a utility or two and their crews.

Several factors tended to upset our carefully planned schedules and thereby, in widening the scope of the exercise, added enormously to the value of the practical experience. To learn how to cope with emergencies it was necessary to create them. We knew, therefore, that at some point, usually in the middle of the night, we would receive orders from the base to pack up and move on in the shortest possible time to some other far-distant place – map-reading again, and in the dark. Then there was the weather and the possibility of vehicle breakdown. This was winter, a season which in that part of the world seemed to offer only two alternatives – if not gales and torrential rain, then well-nigh impenetrable blizzards, ice and deep snow. Movement was then very slow, meals out of doors were impossible – though that problem could sometimes be solved by 'borrowing' a cook-house from some nearby Army camp. The breakdowns had to be rounded up; a truck in a ditch could be fifty miles away; broken fan belts had to be replaced; at one moment on a steep gradient no fewer than seven vehicles were stuck in the snow, their wheels spinning uselessly.

We could harbour for the night practically anywhere, though in that weather the comforts of some Home Guard

Drill Hall was appreciated. There was a vicarage somewhere near Bridlington with a vast sitting-room warmed by the most welcoming coal fire we had ever seen. There, I remember, some thirty of us were entertained for an evening with the friendliest courtesy and hospitality. And there was a charming old lady in Kirkby-Moorside who offered me her bathroom for a much needed shave and then shyly presented me with two fresh eggs. I hope she had some hens of her own at the back of the house; otherwise her generous gift must have been her official ration for two weeks.

Such five-day schemes might have repeated themselves to the point of monotonous routine, but I had not reckoned with the extraordinary flexibility of the Regiment in the organisation of its affairs. My sorties across the Yorkshire moors suddenly came to an end when, surprisingly, I was made Assistant Adjutant. No longer would I have to cope with the 'hard lying'; that was the official term for nights spent away from the camp, for each of which I received an extra two shillings. Instead, there would be a comparatively quiet and secluded office, protected from the weather though not from the stresses and strains of administrative necessity. A 'kid-glove job', my colleagues called it, not without a touch of envy. The description, as I was to find out, proved to be far from accurate. The duties, I gathered, would be extremely varied. At one moment I could be playing temporary host to a visiting General, showing him round the camp with just the right blend of warmth and deference; at another I might be taking the Colonel's dog for a walk! The rest lay somewhere between. The immediate effect was to bring me into much closer contact with my colleagues. To some extent, I became administratively involved in their affairs, and knew them more intimately than before. The atmosphere in the Mess clearly changed; even the ATS Sergeant gave me a smile as she poured out the soup.

For the most part, the work itself demanded a good deal of tact and diplomacy, reminiscent of BBC days. It also required a degree of firmness which at first came less easily. In fact, at one point I came in for some criticism from the Adjutant for being 'too polite'. That was a surprise, but by degrees it had to be put right. To see something of the inner workings of the Regiment, its relationship with the outside world in general, and with various other Army centres in particular, was endlessly fascinating.

As the spring came, I found myself with more time in which to listen to music. Amidst the welter of an unaccustomed life, such chances had been few. Now I realised, with sudden shock, how devastating its absence had been. But at last, alone in my room, I could listen to the broadcasts of the BBC Symphony Orchestra and renew my homage to those master-works which had meant so much in the past and were now infinitely more significant. There was an evening in May when the sun streamed through my windows as I looked out on green fields towards the hills in the distance. Music heard in evening sunshine has a very special quality. This was the perfect setting for Schubert's Ninth Symphony; surely it had never before had such eloquence, such tenderness, such festive energy. My thoughts returned to similar moments of enchantment – concert performances at Bristol University, the closing pages of *The Kingdom* in 'Portrait of a Composer', the Summer concerts in the cloisters at Canterbury, Wagner's *Siegfried Idyll,* and Mozart at Glyndebourne.

To the musician, such delight is a personal possession to be cherished, quite apart from his professional obligations, and it is natural that he should feel a powerful impulse to share it more and more widely with those who have yet to be initiated. I have known just one or two colleagues who, curiously, had no wish to do so. They lived in an ivory tower, content to regard music as a private possession of their own. This, they say, is for me, and not for those who would inevitably fail to understand. Any attempt to bring more and more listeners into the fold was not for them. Theirs was a strange philosophy, and fortunately rare.

At Sandhurst, Captain Gordon-Lennox had suggested that I should take charge of some weekly gramophone recitals. It was rewarding, if not even a little surprising, to find that serious music was welcome to so many. Fifty or so cadets attended regularly and were genuinely interested. We worked our way through a great part of the classical repertoire with a lively and encouraging response. I have to admit, however, that one work proved to be the exception. Each movement of the Fifth Symphony by Sibelius held the attention of fewer and fewer listeners until by the end we numbered no more than five or six. Such an unexpected reaction was difficult to account for.

More generally, the impression I acquired during Army service was that a keen interest in music of this kind seemed to be shared much more by the younger generation than by the old. At one time, a good many people regarded the *William Tell* Overture as a typical example of classical music. By the 1940s a change had come about, at least among more youthful listeners, for whom it was then replaced by works such as the *Oberon* Overture and the last three symphonies by Tchaikovsky. Since then, still greater advances have been made on a very broad front. Of that, the enthusiasm of present-day Promenade Concert audiences leaves no shadow of doubt.

IT could not be said that my transition to the office of Assistant Adjutant had brought me to a quiet backwater. In a few weeks, the initial mysteries of Army Administration had largely disappeared, but even then the work was eventful enough to deny the possibility of mere routine. Day by day the rapidly increasing tensions of the build-up towards the invasion of Europe were reflected in our community, distant as it was from the areas of conflict. A crescendo of activity, sudden postings, unexplained cancellations of leave resulting in shorter tempers – these were just some of the factors which contributed to a distinct change of atmosphere and a general conviction that there were great matters afoot.

For me, one or two interruptions brought a temporary change of scene. A course on the interpretation of aerial photographs, for example, took me to Smedley's Hydro in Matlock for a short period. I had no idea what to expect, nor any inkling that it would turn out to be a study of compelling interest. With a direct relevance to the tactics of war it was also of importance at that stage in the course of events. I was fascinated; the immense capacity of stereography to disclose hidden details of enemy positions struck me as little short of miraculous. I only wished that I could have become still more deeply involved, but that was not to be. After another spell as an instructor, passing on some of these new techniques, I was back at my desk again.

To find myself involved in matters of Military Law was another unexpected development. It was part of an Assistant Adjutant's duty to take Summaries of Evidence in those cases of misdemeanour that demanded close investigation. To convert the ramblings of an often incoherent accused and the evidence of witnesses, possibly equally confused, into neatly written statements covering numerous sheets of foolscap paper was a lengthy and challenging task. It could take many hours to bring to order a jumble of unco-ordinated and illogical assertions and to arrive eventually at an honest and accurate account of the facts. Such statements had to be signed by those who had made them, and they formed the basis of a later decision by the Commanding Officer as to whether the case should be referred to a Court Martial or not. It was a responsibility which had to be taken seriously. I was constantly reminded that one of my teenage fantasies, long ago, had pointed waveringly in the direction of a legal career.

Admittedly, this was all at an elementary level but even so I had had no training. To be implicated at any later stage would demand a great deal of preparation, and so a well-thumbed copy of King's Regulations lived with me throughout the day and by my bedside at night. Feverishly I studied in an attempt to learn at least something of the Army's complicated legal procedures. Any mastery was obviously out of the question, but at least I could perhaps aim at a degree of familiarity without which I should be entirely at a loss. The complexities were daunting but I persevered. That King's Regulations, with the benefit of centuries of experience, had made provision for every possible set of circumstances, real or imaginary, was to a layman such as myself enormously impressive. For everything, it seemed, there was a precedent.

When in due course I was ordered to appear at a Court Martial as Prosecuting Officer, I knew that the worst had

154

happened. That was the first of a number of nerve-racking appearances which I was to make, always, as it happened, as a prosecutor and never in defence. This one was a fairly straightforward case of Absence without Leave, though for a period of several months! It went reasonably smoothly and ended, as far as I was concerned, very satisfactorily.

The second, though still successful in the end, was a much less pleasant experience. In the first place, the alleged offence was of a much more complex nature. Secondly, I was unlucky this time to have to face a Judge Advocate whose impatience and irascibility were notorious.

All went well until I sprang to my feet to say, with misguided confidence: "With your permission, sir, I call my first witness." Alas! It was not yet time for that; my grasp of correct procedure was even more inadequate than I suspected and I was out of order. In stentorian tones, the Judge Advocate's words rang round the court. "You may NOT." he roared, and I prayed to be allowed to sink silently through the floorboards. General equilibrium was quickly restored (though mine took rather longer) and the case went forward without further mishap to a conclusion satisfactory to all but the accused. It was one of the worst moments of my life which I cannot look back on without embarrassment. Long afterwards, I derived a morsel of comfort from being told by a lawyer friend that he had committed exactly the same blunder during his military service.

Among the many friends I had by now were two boon companions. Soon after my arrival in Barnard Castle I had met Michael Hansen who was serving in the 61st as an instructor. He had preceded me at Sandhurst and was now a full lieutenant. We quickly discovered that we were kindred spirits, jointly sharing many interests, particularly in music and literature. He it was who introduced me to the works of T.E. Lawrence, and I remember borrowing his copy of *The Seven Pillars of Wisdom* on our first evening together. But our closest bond lay in the music of Mozart for which he had a deep and enduring affection; his knowledge of it was impressive. I envied his relaxed air of detachment from all that surrounded us at that time, though this was deceptive. His approach to the serious issues of life was serious indeed. For all that, his acute sense of humour, his ready laugh and quick eye for the absurd were never far away. It was a friendship to cherish, and so it has continued over the years.

The war had interrupted his studies at University College, Oxford, but when it was all over he returned there to complete them before entering the teaching profession. It was a particular pleasure to me to hear of his later appointment to the staff of my old school at Lancaster where he is now Deputy Headmaster. The Music and Arts Club of that city owed much of its success to his energy and enthusiasm. In 1943 this was all very much in the future.

In due course, we were joined by a new Education Officer who had several training regiments of the district in his care. Willis Grant was a member of my profession, a Doctor of Music of Durham University, organist of Birmingham Cathedral and Lecturer in Music at Sheffield. Further distinction awaited him after the the war when he became Director of Music at King Edward's School, Birmingham, and later still Professor of Music at Bristol University.

His warmth of personality, sense of fun and irrepressible energy added a new dimension to our lives. His lectures at the YMCA, which Mike and I attended whenever we could, were illumined and enlivened by flights of fancy and delightful imagery, products of a uniquely vivid imagination. They must have broadened the horizons of thousands of men for whom Barnard Castle was merely a staging post. We could not have had a more entertaining companion.

Suddenly in 1944 he disappeared. Strict security meant that we knew nothing of his whereabouts until, eventually, I received a postcard signed 'W' which read: 'Grief o'erwhelms me! And now I study Amy Woodford-Finden.' My thoughts went straight to 'Pale hands I love beside the Shalimar', as Willis intended, and the secret was out. The card went on: 'Am on leave till 27th. *Ora pro mio* and send some sunburn ointment. Every cloud has a silver lining, but what if there are no clouds?'

156

Years later, Willis told me the story which lay behind his departure for India. He wrote:

I had an official visit from the Army Bureau of Current Affairs, all Generals from the War Office. In the report I had to give them I gave an account of what was being done for the general troops as a preparation for post-war life as charged by the War Office. I had to mention all the regiments individually. When I had finished one of the generals said: 'You have not mentioned so-and-so battalion' (I forget which). To which I replied: 'It was only last week that the CO said to me: "If we educate these men, where are we going to be when the war is over?" ' This was greeted with amusement by all the others, but I was on the boat for India in a few days, having been told by HQ that the CO and this particular General were bosom pals! However, India proved to be a very rewarding and enjoyable part of my Army service.

Half a lifetime was still to pass before the sad day in 1981 when many of Willis's friends and former students assembled in the church of a Somerset village to pay their last respects at his funeral service. They remembered him in many ways, especially as a perfectionist ever in search of the highest possible standards in performance; as one who, above all else, insisted always on exact intonation. Sombre occasion as it was, an understanding smile lit all faces when the valedictory address came to: "When the Last Trump sounds for Willis, it had better be in tune".

At Barnard Castle Mike, Willis and I spent much of our spare time together, and since we were often joined by Stanley Turnbull, the Director of the YMCA, the trio became a quartet. Not the least of many things we all had in common was our indebtedness to one of the residents of the town. How much we owed to Alan Bean and his family can never be adequately told. As a somewhat bewildered Trooper of the 54th I had known the warmth of his welcome during my first sojourn in Barney. Now, a year or so later, his house in Galgate was again a home from home. We spent many an evening there, happily remembering the past, forgetting for the moment the constraints of the present, and anticipating the future.

I saw already that a very important part of that future would not be mine alone; it belonged also to Jessica. Throughout the years since Bristol our friendship had reached the point at which I knew that I would not be able to do without her. My thoughts ran on ahead. Before very long, we would step out from that homely Galgate house to be married. We would return there to join our friendly well-wishers in its tiny garden, then to board what would inevitably be a crowded troop train for our honeymoon journey.

That is how it all turned out, exactly as I had imagined it. The kindly Beans, who had already met Jessica on one of her previous visits, lent us their house for our little reception, as I guessed they would. I was even right about that train; we had to stand in the guard's van all the way to our destination though that mattered not at all. Such was the pattern of our wartime wedding and the start of a marriage which to this day has brought us great happiness.

But at that moment we could not just yet set up a home together in Barney. That part of my plan had to wait a little before it could be realised. The work Jessica was still doing had been transferred to London and so, for the time being, she had to return there and, to my great concern, brave the hazards of buzz-bombs and rockets, whilst I, with an added dimension to my life, turned again to my military duties.

Demanding as those duties were, they did not preclude all possibility of a pleasant diversion. It was a natural and logical step that Willis and I should join forces in some kind of musical effort. It took the form of a two-piano recital in the outstandingly beautiful Bowes Museum, built in the style of a Second Empire French château on the outskirts of the town. There, we had the pleasure of playing on two really superb Bechsteins. That was a joy. Our programme included two main works: Schumann's Andante and Variations – how persuasive I was about that may be imagined – and the Brahms Variations on a Theme of Haydn – less well-known in its arrangement for two pianos than in its later version for orchestra. There were a number of smaller pieces as well, and for an encore we played Willis's own 'Clog Dance', a witty and attractive little piece which brought the house down. We had not expected that a concert of that kind would arouse much interest, and were truly amazed to see an audience of some five hundred listeners who had been brought from outlying districts by a fleet of buses.

After a hilarious supper at the Beans, we walked back to the camp in pouring rain. Such a detail would not be worthy of mention were it not for the strangely apt coincidence which followed. Back in my room, it was already very late and I had letters to write. But they could wait another day, I decided, and instead I read a few more pages of William Cowper's *Letters* and found, to my great delight, that he had practically done it for me! In September, 1781, he had ended a letter of thanks to Mrs Newton with these lines:

> News have I none that I would deign to write,
> Save that it rain'd prodigiously last night:
> And that ourselves were, at the seventh hour,
> Caught in the first beginning of a shower;
> But walking, running, and with much ado,
> Got home – just time enough to be wet through.
> Yet both are well, and wond'rous to be told,
> Soused as we were, we yet have caught no cold;
> And wishing just the same good hap to you,
> We say, good Madam, and good Sir, Adieu!

SO far, the progress of the war in Europe had brought little relaxation of the administrative pressures. For the duration of the Adjutant's occasional absences, his vast range of responsibilities became mine and gave me some of the most hectic days of my life. Additionally I had acquired two other duties, first as Regimental Security Officer and then as Band President. This latter appointment had been held by one of the Squadron Commanders, who had always disliked it because, he said "I know nothing about it." Attached to the 61st we had the band of the 17th/21st Lancers and the function of the President was to look after its administration and approve all arrangements for its engagements. I did not confess that my knowledge of the Military Band and its music was hardly more extensive than that of its outgoing President. The concealment of my lack of specialised expertise when carrying out the periodical inspection of the instruments and examining the state of their maintenance called for as much diplomacy as I could muster.

All the same, I very much appreciated my close association with such excellent players; it led to my notion of composing a regimental march for the 61st which up to now could not lay claim to one of its own. There was no shortage of splendid examples which could serve as a model, and uppermost in my mind was the one I admired most of all – the RAF March composed by Walford Davies towards the end of the First World War. That, to my mind, was everything that such a March ought to be.

Whilst I could not hope to match it, I did eventually complete my self-imposed task and entitled it 'The Yellow Lanyard', that being the colour of the shoulder decoration worn by the 61st to distinguish it from the other training regiments in the area. If memory is to be relied on, the scoring for military band was done by Bandmaster Hempstead, and I have to confess to feelings of immodest pride and satisfaction when on ceremonial parades it accompanied the march-past of the Squadrons whilst the rest of us stood stiffly to attention.

Later, I made a more elaborate version for orchestra with an additional section in fugal form. That received its one and only performance at a public concert when I had the pleasure of conducting a vastly augmented body of players.

By slow degrees, the end of the war in Europe was coming into sight. Although there was still a long way to go, the Government announced its first demobilisation plans in September, 1944, only a few months after the Normandy invasion; we all rushed off excitedly to calculate what precedence we could expect from those magic numbers to which we were individually entitled. Willis returned from some journey he had made by bus and told us about the overheard conversation of two elderly countrywomen sitting behind him:

1st woman: "Wouldn't it be nice if the war were over?"
2nd woman: "Won't be long now."
1st woman: "So do I."

Throughout the next twenty months, there were great changes at the 61st which would lead eventually to the disbandment of the regiment. It was a very gradual process, imperceptible at first, but as time went on there were fewer and fewer demands to be met, members of the staff disappeared one by one, and what had been an epicentre of ceaseless activity was slowly transformed into a quiet backwater.

There was still work to do, but free time, the most valuable asset of all, was more plentiful. It could not be wasted, and there were many ways in which I wanted to use it. Serious work at the piano had been neglected, of necessity, for longer than I cared to admit. Now it was possible to do something towards putting that right, and by a singular stroke of good fortune there was a passable upright at my disposal. During several of those months I spent as many hours as my duties would allow in persuading my fingers that all in the end would be well, and re-discovering the beauties and the pitfalls of Beethoven's Op. 27, No. 1, and Brahms' Variations and Fugue on a Theme of Handel. It was good to have a positive objective; I had promised to give a final recital in the Bowes Museum and that promise I kept.

There was something else as well. Throughout the war, books had been my mainstay. In reading and re-reading the great classics of English literature I found an escape from what for me always remained an unnatural way of life. At the 61st, for instance, I had read most of Thackeray, invariably looking forward at the end of a busy day to spending more hours in the company of that 'most respectable family', the Newcombes, or with other characters who, through the author's genius had become living human beings. Theirs was yet another world, fully as real, and I had a part in it. Second-hand bookshops, wherever they happened to be, drew me like a magnet, for there I could find older editions, beautifully printed on good paper, often leather-bound. Unlike the current 'utility' volumes, printed in war time on poor paper, they were a joy to possess and so they remain.

How I came to enjoy a much more than casual friendship with the editor of Barnard Castle's local newspaper, the

Teesdale Mercury, I can no longer remember. We saw a great deal of each other and in time he invited me to contribute, first some book reviews and then, more ambitiously, a weekly column on any literary topic of my choice. It was an undertaking after my own heart; the district itself was rich in its association with a number of those who have an assured place among the greatest English writers.

Dotheboys Hall, Mr Wackford Squeers' Academy, was only a few miles away, its schoolroom, as we read in *Nicholas Nickleby* 'a bare and dirty room, with a couple of windows, whereof a tenth part might be of glass, the remainder being stopped up with old copybooks and paper.' Then there was that delightful character, Newman Noggs, the clerk who wrote so pathetic a postscript to his letter: 'If you should go near Barnard Castle, there is good ale at the King's Head.' (I could vouch for that myself). 'Say you know me, and I am sure they will not charge you for it. You may say Mr Noggs there, for I was a gentleman then, I was indeed.'

Even closer was Rokeby, the location chosen by Sir Walter Scott for the poem which followed 'The Lady of the Lake'. In seeking a background sufficiently wild and picturesque for his tale of Cavalier and Roundhead, he must have found something of special appeal in this countryside. His grasp of its local topography was complete:

> Staindrop, who, from her sylvan bowers,
> Salutes proud Raby's battled towers.

His landmarks were familiar to us all. In parenthesis, there is a passage in that poem which sums up, in salutary fashion, my present enterprise:

> '. . . aged men, full loth and slow,
> The varieties of life forego,
> And count their youthful follies o'er
> Till memory lends her light no more.

For my weekly thousand words, there was no shortage of material – Dickens, the man of letters, and Dickens, the crusader, Walter Scott, Smollett and his travels in the

North country, the escapades of Theodore Hook and his 'Lass of Richmond Hill' and, of course, my beloved William Cowper, his poetry touched by a gleam of insight born of genius, his letters nothing less than (in Charles Lamb's words) 'Divine chit-chat'.

These were some of my subjects. I had many others in mind and the series would have continued if a recall to a sterner duty had not intervened.

The Commanding Officer of the 61st was now Lieutenant Colonel R.G. Byron, DSO, of the 4th/7th Dragoon Guards. At the outbreak of war he had been Military Secretary to the Governor of New Zealand. Hurriedly returning, he rejoined his regiment to serve in the British Expeditionary Force and had experienced the horrors of Dunkirk. By D-Day he had taken command of the 4th/7th and won his DSO on the Normandy beachhead. My work had brought me into close contact with him and I admired him enormously for his quiet authority, professional bearing and unfailing courtesy.

It was now 1946 and the preparations for VE-Day were under way. The parade through London was to include a contingent of scout cars, armoured cars, light tanks, Comets, Churchills, Shermans, Crocodiles, flails and bridge-layers. Its commander was to be Colonel Byron and my orders were to join him as Adjutant.

We moved to Sunninghill near Ascot for a series of rehearsals with a number of units drawn from various parts of the country. To begin with, the whole undertaking was beset by unbelievable complications, and until some form of workable organisation was evolved, administrative confusion was the disorder of the day! The problems accumulated from all directions; everything to be done seemed intensely difficult and for several days we made little progress. Eventually, of course, some daylight emerged, and then I derived some comfort from the Colonel's admission that his anxieties had been just as great as mine. Only then was it possible to notice the extraordinary beauties of the Surrey countryside in that wonderful month of May, the fields green and lovely, every cottage garden ablaze with colour. An armoured column on its practice manoeuvres must have seemed an unforgiveable intrusion.

163

The transfer from Sunninghill to our temporary camp in Regent's Park brought me a somewhat daunting assignment, the command of a convoy of thirty-seven tanks on its journey into London. I would have viewed the performance of a late Beethoven sonata with rather less concern. Thanks to the marvellous efficiency of the police escort we negotiated the bottle-neck of Notting Hill Gate, bored our way smoothly through London's traffic and arrived at our destination without serious mishap. It would have been nice to say 'without a single mishap' but I have a strong impression that the track of my leading tank neatly uprooted a kerbstone in Ealing High Street – but only one!

It had been a day of glorious sunshine and that night we slept comfortably under canvas, quite unprepared for the torrential rain to which we awoke. But it did nothing to interfere with our plans; the vehicles squelched their way through the remaining rehearsals which were now crucial. On the Sunday before VE-Day, Reveille was at 3 a.m. and we had London to ourselves. On the day itself, Colonel Byron stood in the turret of a brand-new Comet, resplendent in its spotless green paint. Hidden away below him, I occupied the gunner's seat; at my side was the radio by which the whole contingent could be controlled. That was manned by a Lance-Corporal who in civilian life was a solicitor's clerk. The gunner-mechanic was an eighteen-year-old representative of the new generation of soldiers, and our driver, whose vital job it was to keep the Comet exactly on its scheduled place, was an experienced member of the Royal Tank Regiment who had fought with the 1st Parachute Brigade in Italy.

I saw very little of the scenes of rejoicing on that memorable day. But a restricted view through the periscope enabled me to give the order by radio for the guns of the whole column to be dipped in salute as we passed Buckingham Palace. To have that responsibility was an honour, though I felt that it might well have been given more appropriately to someone whose contribution to the war effort had been far greater than mine.

Almost immediately, I was on Release Leave. With the end of my military service in sight, my thoughts were now

164

concentrated on what might lie ahead in the world I had known so well. It would be the realisation of a wartime dream. Even so, the excitement of anticipation was clouded by shadows of regret. Sadly, I would be saying good-bye to a host of friends and taking my leave of Teesdale and all its beauty – its river of a dozen different moods and never an unlovely vista either upstream or down. That was something I could take with me into a bright, new world along with a host of impressions of Barney itself – the bustling activity of its Wednesday market day when the little town wore a busy air of consequence – and the quiet passage of the hours on Thursday as it rested from its labours and gathered energy for another week. Among many things, I would treasure the sound of boys' voices in the School Chapel as the Royal School of English Church Music held its festival, the evening sun slanting through the windows; above all, I would remember those moments of enchantment as I sat on the edge of the cricket field with a foreground of white-clad players on that marvellous green. Listening to the cawing of the rooks and looking across the greystone houses to the green moorland beyond, it was surely not only in my imagination that the town had seemed to give a little wriggle of content and nestle yet more closely into the gently folding hills. It was in one such moment that I remembered Oliver Wendell Holmes' lines: 'Let a man live in one of these old, quiet places, and the wine of his soul, which is kept thick and turbid by the rattle of busy streets, settles, and, as you hold it up, you may see the sun through it by day, and the stars by night.'

CHAPTER 13

Reprise

FROM the first day to the last, life in the Army had demanded a constant self-adjustment which had never become second nature. For all that, it had been an experience I would not have missed, and for which I could only be grateful. I was returning to civilian life stretched and tested, both mentally and physically, with increased confidence and energy. I could rely upon myself with greater certainty, and above all I now knew the immense value of human companionship. It had taken me a long time to learn that lesson. With these good things to look back on, the future was more firmly in my hands.

My appointment as Assistant Conductor of the BBC Theatre Orchestra brought me immediately within a sphere of stimulating influence. My new chief was Walter Goehr who had just taken over the orchestra. We had not met previously but very quickly I came to appreciate my close association with him, both for his broadening of my musical horizons and his faith in me.

In the years which had passed since his arrival in this country from Germany he had earned much distinction in the field of light music. His Orchestra Raymonde, which played his own brilliant arrangements, was greatly admired for the outstanding success of its radio programme and for its gramophone recordings. He had also made his name in London's theatre world – I recalled a highly successful West End production of *The Gipsy Baron* under his direction. More importantly, he had much to offer to serious music, to which his gifts and aspirations belonged. It is not without significance that at this time, towards the end of the 1940s, he had a profound knowledge of the Mahler symphonies which were then little known in England. Later in this chapter I shall return to his contribution to the cause of contemporary music.

His energy was inexhaustible; one could sense the vibrations of a power-house. I have rarely known anyone who could work so hard without becoming completely oblivious of the world about him, and that could never be said of Walter Goehr. Small wonder that his secretary found it impossibly exhausting to work for a boss who could dictate several letters in one breath whilst dealing simultaneously with two or three telephone callers. Then, at the end of a long day, he would say, as vigorously as ever: "Now, what else must we do?" His was the kind of energy which depressingly reveals the frailties of those who witness it, and there were times when I shared their despair. Those pressures were Goehr's natural element; his mental range was enormous and his grasp of detail impressive.

His creative gifts were invariably sustained by impeccably good taste, superb craftsmanship and the liveliest of imaginations. Vying with Ravel, he had made his own orchestration of Mussorgsky's *Pictures from an Exhibition*; in several performances of his edition of Monteverdi's Vespers I had the pleasure of playing the harpsichord; in yet another field, he was known to a wider public for the lyrical score he had composed for the film, *Great Expectations*.

In the early days of my association with him, it was his expertise in rehearsal which impressed me so much; sometimes, I have to admit, to a greater extent than did the subsequent performance. For the preparation of a work he could call upon two invaluable assets – the ability to convey his ideas with the utmost clarity and an excellent command of English. Still vividly in my memory is a session in which he worked with chorus and orchestra on one of Bach's Church Cantatas. His insistence on such matters as phrasing, nuance, distribution of accent and subtleties of many kinds brought that score to unimagined life.

He could be exasperating, even unreasonable, and on occasion his comments were sarcastic and hurtful. But somehow, they left no continuing resentment and were quickly forgotten.

With an orchestra of fifty to sixty players and our own Theatre Chorus we could draw upon a vast repertoire; the symphonic works of the masters, both past and present, opera and operetta, and musical comedy all offered limitless scope. Our brief also included some emphasis on 'popular' music which, when attractively presented, could win the interest and the confidence of new listeners. For this, some significant difference of approach, however small, was needed and so we adopted the idea of a 'non-stop' sequence of musical items, uninterrupted by announcements. It was a simple but highly effective device which contributed quite largely to the success of the *Fantasia* series.

To put together an hour-long programme for each week was a challenging and by no means easy task. Subtle changes of mood and interesting key relationships were only two of the factors to be taken into account if a smoothly-running continuity were to be achieved. We had some introductory music specially written and on occasion one or two necessary linking passages would be composed and orchestrated even during rehearsal, perhaps only an hour or so before going on the air. For the items themselves, the choice was wide. There was often a movement from a much-loved concerto, and excerpt from opera or ballet, and some unexpected juxtaposition of styles. The flexibility of *Fantasia* also allowed the use of a connecting theme, now and again; I remember 'The English Waltz', 'Music of Childhood' and 'The Story of Sadler's Wells' coming into this category.

Perhaps not surprisingly, this new but very simple format provoked some wider consideration of the whole art of programme building. One much-respected critic commented: 'This non-stop method is surely a wise way of creeping into the confidence of the simpler sort of listener. We musicians might well be much more subtle, whenever we set out to do people good – and even when we have not such deadly design. I've pleaded for subtler approaches all my life.'

Thirty years ago a policy clearly designed to entice as many listeners as possible into the musical fold was wholly acceptable and we certainly did not think of it as a 'deadly design'. Today the planned segregation of broadcast programmes reflects a change of attitude. The propagandist is much less in evidence although he is no less essential to our musical life than he was then. How difficult it would be to imagine a contemporary commentator using such phrases as 'the simpler sort of listener' or 'whenever we set out to do people good.'

Apart from *Fantasia* and several other series on similar lines, there were other broadcasts such as *Concert Hour*, *Music of the Masters* and *The Friday Concert* which invited more conventional planning. Here we could include symphonies and concertos in their entirety and draw upon the greater part of the vast orchestral repertoire. Rehearsal time was usually ample and in the leader of the orchestra, Alfred Barker, we had a tower of strength. As a youthful prodigy, Barker had proved his outstanding talent as a pupil of Adolph Brodsky and could already look back on a career of distinction.

A large proportion of our output was devoted to studio opera. Two series ran for a long time under the titles of *Ring up the Curtain* and *Come to the Opera*. They brought to the microphone a number of famous opera stars from abroad. It was exciting and immensely valuable to meet and work with such artists as Ljuba Welitsch, Jennie Tourel, Margherita Grandi, Silveri, Tito Gobbi and Mariano Stabile. But there were also many fine singers of our own. Among my own contribution to these programmes I have the happiest memories of *Faust* with Heddle Nash and Owen Brannigan, *Madame Butterfly* and *La Bohème* with Victoria Sladen, *La Favourita* with Marjorie Thomas, and a thrilling *Il Travatore* with Joan Hammond. These were our 'Stars by Night' and their names will remind a new generation of music-lovers that yesterday also had its glories.

In addition to our normal contributions to the broadcast schedules, occasional opportunities to collaborate with other departments, particularly Drama, added a new dimension to the work of the Theatre Orchestra. Of these, the production by Val Gielgud of Edward Sackville-West's melodrama *The Rescue* was one of the most notable. Based on Homer's

169

Odyssey and freely written in both verse and prose, songs and orchestral music formed an integral part of its dramatic structure. The music score was composed by Benjamin Britten whose collaboration with the author resulted in a startling development of sound-radio technique, so skilfully were speech and music integrated, so unprecedented was the device of associating single instruments of the orchestra with particular characters in the play. I recall the saxophone for Penelope, the trumpet for Athene, the strings for Odysseus.

An earlier broadcast of *The Rescue* in 1943 had been hailed as a landmark in radio creation. That successful experiment was now to be done again with a star-studded cast headed by Clifford Evans, Rachel Gurney, Leslie French and Leon Quartermaine. On the musical side I was glad to become actively involved in the very lengthy advance preparation, and although Walter Goehr conducted the final performance, I took charge of the combined rehearsals when the intricacies of co-ordination were being met for the first time. They were formidable; to be associated with that production was a magical experience, and not merely because of the technical complications. Britten's music, in characterisation, in scene-setting or the representation of action, above all for its extraordinarily evocative quality, was masterly.

Not all drama productions were as elaborate as *The Rescue*, but it was always rewarding to take charge of the often more straightforward incidental music for Shakepeare's plays. Frequently, it was specially composed for the occasion, not usually for full orchestra but a smaller group of players. A performance of *Love's Labour's Lost*, with Pauline Letts and Paul Scofield gave me the pleasure of meeting a composer whose work I have always liked immensely. Gerald Finzi had written the music which included his settings of the poems for spring and winter, 'When Daisies Pied' and 'When icicles hang by the wall'. He came to the studio to supervise its first performance. I found him very shy and reserved on that particular afternoon, obviously concerned that all would go well. But this, I felt, was only a passing tension, a temporary disturbance of that serenity of spirit which was as much a part of his personal nature as it was of his music. I wished so much that I could have known him better, but at least I could treasure the charming letter of thanks he wrote to me a few days later.

One of our most exciting visitors was Percy Grainger who came to conduct the Theatre Orchestra in a programme of his own works. I was delighted to come into contact with a composer whose outlook on music was so individual, to find on meeting him that his work exactly reflected his infectious love of life. His warm personality radiated an air of physical well-being. He was then in his middle sixties and that boundless energy which was a legend throughout our profession was still unimpaired. He had apparently listened with approval to some of my own performances of his music and on his departure for Sweden he kindly sent me an interesting photograph of himself 'in memory of our nice times'.

Association with Percy Grainger, brief as it was, further confirmed my conviction that vigour and an unwearying stamina were the essential prerequisites for achievement of any kind. I was surrounded by the evidence. Water Goehr's capacity, for example, was not at all monopolised by the heavy demands of our department; beyond the studios of the BBC he had many other interests. An important one, to which he devoted a great deal of concentrated energy, was his association with Michael Tippett and the enterprising Morley College Concerts Society. It was inevitable that I should become involved as well, and I very much welcomed the chance to help in various ways, either as a member of the orchestra for some piano obbligato part or as accompanist for some of their chorus rehearsals. The Society's programmes were always interesting. Among many other things, they provided me with a first practical acquaintance with Richard Strauss's marvellous Suite, *Le Bourgeois Gentilhomme* and the pleasure of playing the harpsichord in a memorable performance of Vivaldi's 'Four Seasons' with Campoli as soloist. I also remember the splendour of Kathleen Ferrier's voice throughout the rehearsals for Vaughan Williams' *Riders to the Sea*.

Contemporary music formed an important part of the work at Morley College and in 1947 an oratorio by the Swiss composer, Frank Martin, was proposed for the forthcoming season. This was *Le Vin Herbé* which had been first heard in Zurich some years previously. Martin had based it on three chapters of *Le Roman de Tristan et Iseut* by one of the foremost French mediaeval scholars, Joseph Bédier. In this version of the tragic Tristan story there are departures from the more familiar one used by Wagner; here there are two Isoldes, Isolde the Fair and Isolde of the White Hands, and their conflict had inspired Martin to music of great power and eloquence. Of the work as a whole he later wrote: 'If I had to name a high point in my work, I think I would name *Le Vin Herbé* which is perhaps the first of my works in which I succeeded in forging a personal idiom.' He achieved tremendous effects using only slender resources – a choir of twelve voices which includes both soloists and chorus, two violins, two violas, two 'cellos, one double bass and piano.

That no English translation existed was the one problem which stood in the way of the Morley College project. How it came about that Walter Goehr asked me to make one, I cannot now recall, but after some initial hesitation it was an assignment I gladly accepted. To meet the all-important necessity of devising an English text within the restrictions imposed both by the original French and the rhythms of Martin's music was a stimulating and rewarding challenge. The possibility that, in the reading, my translation would fail to convey the quality of Bédier's style was worrying, but to have attempted that might well have proved to be a mistake. My concern was eased, to some extent, by the undeniable fact that in the end music imposes its own character and colouring.

Goehr's first performance was exciting and it aroused a good deal of interest. He had an excellent group of singers and instrumentalists – the string players, incidentally, included four young men who had just recently left their student days behind and would very shortly come together to form the Amadeus Quartet.

Le Vin Herbé, hailed by many, if not universally, as a landmark in the history of modern music, was performed and broadcast several times in England. Later, in 1961, it was given in New York and a gramophone recording, made in Lausanne with the composer himself at the piano, was issued under the Westminster label.

At that time I had just discovered Thomas Mann, and was enthralled by work of an author who had won so undisputed a place among contemporary figures in German literature. First, I read *The Magic Mountain* and then the recently published *Doctor Faustus*. Here was a novel of outstanding appeal to a musician; I returned to it in every available moment, astounded by Mann's intellectual grasp of the theories of Schönberg and deeply impressed by his tragic history of the composer, Adrian Leverkühn. So vivid and compelling was his detailed description of Leverkühn's *Apocalypse* that I found it more and more difficult to convince myself that the work was wholly fictitious. It had existed with astonishing clarity in the mind of the author and the power of his written word had brought imagined music to the brink of reality.

It happened that one evening I was idly turning the dial of a radio and picked up from some foreign source the performance of a work for chorus and orchestra. It was quite unknown to me but its character was arresting and held my close attention. Reception was not good, but I continued to listen, more and more intently as the work proceeded. Soon, I was convinced that this music was the *Apocalypse* by Adrian Leverkühn; it seemed to conform so precisely with what I remembered of the details minutely outlined by Thomas Mann. It was an illusion, of course, and a foolish one, but if, at the end an announcement had confirmed my flight of fancy, I would not have been surprised. Unfortunately, I heard no announcement; at the crucial moment the transmission was lost in a welter of interference. It was an uncanny experience; if not *Apocalypse*, then by what music had I been deceived? The answer to that question came shortly afterwards, quite by chance, when I attended a Morley College performance of *Ulysses* by Matyas Seiber. That was the unknown music I had heard – and the link was there for Seiber, I knew, had studied with Schönberg.

In the studio the Theatre Orchestra had a very full commitment, and since it happened on occasion that the demands exceeded its availability it was necessary to engage other players. It thus came about that for a number of concerts which needed smaller resources I found myself conducting the Boyd Neel Orchestra. It was a pleasure to work with such talented, friendly and co-operative players, and to experience at close quarters that distinctive quality of sound which was itself a tribute to their founder who had created it. Without exception, every member clearly showed his personal interest in seeking the highest possible standard. Rehearsals were a joy, and characterised by a democratic approach such as I had never met before. The double-bass would have a suggestion; "How would it be if...?"; a second violin would say "Wouldn't it be a good idea if...?"; and there could be some contribution from any quarter. With vigilant co-ordination by the leader, Maurice Clare, flexibility still ensured that the conductor would have the last word, and as a result, that last word was a much better one. It would not have worked with a large orchestra, but here a chamber music ambience was brought to the orchestral scene, with unique results.

When Walter had a series of Opera Proms at the Royal Albert Hall with the London Symphony Orchestra he drew me in, to help in various ways. Cuts in the orchestral parts had to be made, cue sheets prepared, programme notes written – there were numberless details to see to, and my presence was necessary at all rehearsals and performances. I resented this not at all – it was valuable experience and I enjoyed it. But Walter could never realise how draining his demands could be; never, that is, until Hermann Scherchen came to us for a few days as guest conductor. In character, personality and intense concern for a thousand details, some serious, some trivial, Scherchen was Walter's exact counterpart. It was Walter who now found himself rushing here and there at Scherchen's command. The tables were turned, and he took it not at all well. "This is terrible," he told me. "It cannot go on – I haven't a minute to myself!" It would have been charitable to resist saying "Now you know what it is like," but it was too good a chance to miss.

For the most part, the Theatre Orchestra's usual studio was the beautifully restored Camden Theatre, inseparably associated with the name of Ellen Terry. The glow of those golden cherubs, acrobatically poised around its proscenium arch, was a hardly necessary reminder of the lustre which that legendary actress had brought to the London stage. The theatre still breathed her spirit although its role was changed – not Shakespeare now, but music, infinitely varied. It was an ideal studio for us, and now and again there could be an invited audience.

Another guest conductor who came to the Camden was Sir Thomas Beecham; it was my duty to 'look after' him, whatever that might mean. The rehearsals were memorable; everything was there, the wit and humour, the unhurried drawl, the extraordinary command of word and phrase, picked casually from the air. Was this last attribute born of vanity, I wondered? More seriously, I watched him intently at work, marvelling at his moulding of a phrase – and I believed I had fathomed the secret of those electrifying sforzandos which were his alone – for each one a flash of the baton came early, almost half a beat early, producing the accent with sudden, forceful and startled shock.

Twenty minutes before the concert was due to begin, I was with him in the Artists' Room. He was in quite serious mood, commenting on features of the orchestra in complimentary terms. Then suddenly he said "Helliwell, come with me – I want to speak to the audience!" I was taken aback; it was unusual, to say the least, but I followed him dutifully. In the corridor on the way, he picked up a large copper bucket which served as an outsize ashtray. His appearance was no small surprise to the audience, but he now addressed them in that inimitable voice, still holding the bucket, and spoke with evident and sincere warmth of his profound sympathy with Covent Garden Opera in its present plight. (Financially, Covent Garden had just been taken over by the Arts Council, and was being supported by public funds for the first time in its history). Tongue in cheek, Sir Thomas suggested that any small donation which

175

a member of the audience might be moved to make would be most gratefully received. Solemnly, he walked forward, moving along the first rows, appealingly offering the bucket. For a moment, the general mood was sober, but very quickly turned to all-round laughter as the joke went home.

That virtuoso command of the unexpected phrase never failed him. We went together one dank November evening to the Royal Albert Hall where he was due to rehearse the *Mass of Life* by Delius. (My presence was merely to provide any assistance which might be necessary with the off-stage chorus). It was bitterly cold, and he clearly did not relish the prospect. As we mounted the steps, he turned and said: "We are now upon the threshold of the great imperial ice-house of the Empire."

It is remarkable that, apart from Delius, Sir Thomas could find so little sympathetic response to English music. I had heard him conduct what was, in my view, a thoroughly disappointing performance of Elgar's A flat Symphony – and his quarrel with the composer over the severe and wanton 'cuts' he had made in that work was well known. His reaction to Vaughan Williams was much the same. Happily, Neville Cardus has left an account of one of Beecham's performances of the 'Pastoral' Symphony. At the end, in the silence which follows the quiet, final notes of the solo soprano, he had turned to give a commanding down-beat to the violins. "There's nothing else to play," whispered the leader. Sir Thomas's "Thank God!" was clearly audible. That story is well known, but there is another, much less known, in which I had some personal involvement.

A year or so after the Camden concert, I was playing the celesta with the BBC Symphony Orchestra in a broadcast conducted by Sir Thomas in the large Maida Vale studio. The inclusion of the 'Pastoral' Symphony in that programme was obviously unwelcome to him. When we came to it at each rehearsal, he would say, "Now, gentlemen, we will take the mangle-wurzel symphony!" At the performance, my celesta was placed very close to the conductor's rostrum. I was his nearest neighbour, about three feet away. The symphony reached its closing bars, the sound of the orchestra died away leaving only the final soprano cadence, beautifully sung by Dorothy Bond, to recede gradually into the distance. In the silence which followed, and long before the announcer could speak, Sir Thomas leaned over in my direction. Quite audibly, and with a firm note of satisfaction, he said: "A city life for me!"

Towards the end of the 1940s, and for some years to come, the music of one composer dominated public orchestral concerts. For the success of his commercial enterprise, the sponsor's faith rested on Tchaikovsky who, it was believed, could be relied upon to attract the largest audiences. The concert agents vied with each other in their efforts to devise the most tempting selection of his works for their programmes, drawing upon the symphonies (the last three), concert overtures, concertos, ballet suites and the well-known operatic arias. The public knew what it liked and that was what would bring them in. For the 'one-composer' programme, Tchaikovsky was the man. It was a blinkered philosophy, reasonable enough in some eyes, which to some limited extent is still with us to this day.

In December 1948 I was invited to conduct one of these programmes myself with the Philharmonia Orchestra in the Royal Albert Hall, and how proud I was to have my mother, for once, in the audience. The B flat minor Piano Concerto was, of course, essential, and for this we had the Viennese pianist Arminski, whose genuine musicality tended to be overshadowed by a dazzling virtuosity. His technical skill tempted him to despatch the Finale in what must surely have been record time, and, as might be expected, one could have wished for more warmth. But it was an exciting performance. In the Violin Concerto we had the young Hungarian Gabriella Lengyel, the winner of a number of international awards who had not previously appeared in England. Here was beautiful tone, infectious rhythm and lyrical response to a work which can reveal fresh subtleties however often it is played. Not content with two concertos, the programme also included arias from *Eugen Onegin* and *Pique Dame*, sung by Andrea Bielecki from the San Carlo Opera in Naples. To complete the commitment there were the two orchestral Suites from *Swan Lake* and *Casse-Noisette*. Admittedly all these works have a permanent place in the standard repertoire of a professional orchestra but, even so, very careful organisation is essential if a single rehearsal is to suffice. A conductor who wishes to achieve something more than a merely routine performance must plan those three hours in the minutest detail. He must have a clear view of priorities and he must also remember that no orchestra takes kindly to the misuse of time.

CHAPTER 14

At the Piano

A NOTABLE feature of our musical life towards the end of the 1940s was a revival of interest in opera. Naturally enough, the public had been deprived of this colourful and spectacular form of music-making throughout the years of the war, and, at least in our provincial cities, the opportunities were few and far between. In the years ahead the advent of the touring opera companies would change the situation but, with one or two exceptions that development was still to come. In the meantime, there was a gap to be filled, a demand which did not go unnoticed by those concert agents who could offer, not staged opera but the operatic highlights, the much loved arias, the well-known scenes and ensembles – with piano accompaniment! A far from adequate substitute for the real thing it might be said, and yet the decision of one agent to present something on those lines proved to be very well judged. Perhaps the chosen title *Opera in Miniature* owed something to the long-running and very popular BBC series, *Music in Miniature*, produced by Basil Douglas, but it was precise and to the point, and it played its part in attracting an enthusiastic response.

I was grateful for the BBC's permission to allow me to accept an invitation to accompany these concerts and to help in other ways. The planning of the programmes was not without its problems; much depended on the availability of suitable artists of calibre and it was essential that the selection of items should have balance and cohesion. The pattern which eventually emerged allowed for excerpts from three operas to be performed by a quartet of singers. It

179

was fortunate that the project could count on the support of various bodies such as local authorities and the press; our first concerts in Leeds and Harrogate were sponsored by the *Yorkshire Evening Post.* Here, in excerpts from *Rigoletto, Carmen* and *La Bohème,* were two greatly admired British singers, Constance Shacklock of Covent Garden and Redvers Llewellyn from Sadler's Wells. (Because of another commitment, the latter was replaced at Harrogate by another representative of Sadler's Wells, Roderick Jones). To Yorkshire these concerts introduced Christina Carroll, a young soprano of promise who had achieved success at the Metropolitan Opera in New York and had already appeared with the Glyndebourne Opera Company at the Edinburgh Festival. There was also the young Italian tenor, Luigi Infantino, fresh from his triumphs in Milan, Paris, London and New York. His meteoric success dated from the end of the war years, and the reasons for it were not far to seek. The voice was enchanting and the technique impeccable, even if the subtleties of artistry sometimes took second place. Above all, he knew how to win the hearts and minds of his audience, taking the fullest advantage of an extrovert personality. I had never before accompanied a singer whose Latin fervour prompted him to throw farewell flowers to the audience, nor had I ever met an artist whose regard for the necessities of rehearsal was so casual. Spontaneity in performance is one thing, unpredictability quite another; to accompany him demanded at first an abnormal degree of speculation on my part although after several concerts and some gentle insistence from me we did eventually achieve a measure of understanding.

For the accompanist who is replacing an orchestra there are a number of problems. An obvious one is the need to convey, at the top of the tonal scale, some impression of the full orchestral resonance, its range and sustained weight; how often he finds that the keyboard reduction has had to fall back on that most unpianistic device, the tremolo. It can be well done and its inadequacy concealed, but only by dint of prolonged practice, by acute listening and sometimes the subtle modification of the chord distribution. More generally, the accompanist must have the widest possible variety of tone at his command, and nothing is more helpful than a close acquaintance with the tone colouring of the original instruments of the orchestra.

In accompanying these excerpts in *Opera in Miniature* it was of particular interest to me to discover that the partner-relationship between singer and piano differed quite fundamentally from that which would have been the case in a *lieder* recital. This was music which my singers were accustomed to perform with orchestra under the baton of the conductor. In his absence, it was very clear that at times they looked to the accompanist for a similar measure of authority and direction, most noticeably, of course, in the ensembles. The need for some positive leadership at the piano became very obvious when we rehearsed, for example, the quartet from *Rigoletto* and the closing scene from Act III of *La Bohème*.

We all needed a great deal of stamina, and I was hardly surprised by the admission of all four singers that they found the programmes far more exhausting than the complete stage performance of any one of the operas would have been. The sequence of 'highlights' kept them tuned to concert pitch throughout the evening and deprived them of those periods of comparative relaxation which, in a full opera, separate the peaks of intensity. Nothing could have more clearly demonstrated the skill and understanding with which Verdi, Bizet and Puccini had planned and created the works in their complete form.

But these considerations were not for the audiences. They were hearing exactly what they wanted to hear and the enthusiasm was undeniable. Only a few weeks later we were in Yorkshire again. Apart from the welcome reappearance of Constance Shacklock there were now three changes in the quartet of soloists. Martin Lawrence from the New London Opera Company was masterly in the 'Slander' song from *The Barber of Seville*; there were scenes of wild enthusiasm when Margherita Grandi sang 'Vissi d'Arte'; and the limpid tones of the Greek lyric tenor, Tano Ferandinos, won all hearts.

On that peaceful Sunday afternoon there were poignant memories of the dark days of war for two of those artists.

Until the arrival of the Allied troops in Italy, to whom she would later sing in their thousands, the Nazis had forbidden Margherita Grandi to sing at all because of her Italian-Irish parentage. For Ferandinos, recent history was more tragic. His family has been persistent in their activities in helping Allied prisoners of war to escape from the Germans in Athens. As a result, his sister had been executed and he himself imprisoned.

On a lighter note, the miscellaneous character of the second half of that concert prompted Ernest Bradbury of the *Yorkshire Post* to write: 'Operatic concerts, like cricket matches, have a character all their own. One cannot say beforehand how they will turn out . . . just as a spectacular boundary catch can sometimes eclipse the significance of a carefully made century, so here; the joy, warmth and thrills of the afternoon were to be found in that "etc." '

From then on, over quite a lengthy period, *Opera in Miniature* was given in many provincial cities throughout the British Isles.

For me, it was all a foretaste of things to come, for at the BBC there were changes afoot. In 1949 a reorganisation brought the life of the Theatre Orchestra to an end. Under a new dispensation it was destined to become the Opera Orchestra and I was happy to find that the way was clear for me to return to my first love as a staff accompanist. It was a prospect I eagerly welcomed for now I would be able to develop a single-minded intimacy with the piano in a way which had not been possible for a long time.

The change-over brought no decrease in activity. My colleagues were Ernest Lush, Frederick Stone and Josephine Lee and so extensive were the demands in those days that even the four of us needed supplementary assistance from time to time. Our duties were extremely varied. In every week we each had three or four live broadcasts or recordings with their respective rehearsals, Schools Broadcasts, the Overseas and Transcription programmes all of which required the help of an accompanist. Today, when each service has acquired a character of its own, the pattern of broadcasting has changed fundamentally, but thirty years ago music played a large part in all transmissions – the

182

'Home' and 'Light' Programmes and, most important of all from our point of view, the 'Third'.

One of my early assignments was to accompany a series of recitals devoted to the songs of Peter Warlock, not all of which I had met before. I was now playing many of them for the first time, enchanted by their originality, their subtle harmonies, the beauty of their melodic lines, above all by the extraordinary skill with which Warlock had captured in a modern idiom the echoes of a bygone age. Even at that time some were out of print and though there have been some important recent publications I suspect that quite a number remain comparatively unknown.

It would appear from a close study of the songs that Warlock was not always consciously aware of the range of voice for which he was writing, and for a singer who finds the published key unsuitable the question of transposition arises. Here there can be a problem. His accompaniments are marvellously laid out for the piano and often very difficult to play. Sometimes he contrives chords of many notes, including perhaps two adjacent white notes to be played by the thumb. But in a transposed key one of those is likely to become a black one and the passage can therefore no longer be played with accuracy. In these recitals I was confronted by several copies of the songs carefully written out in an unmanageable key; it was not at all easy to convince my soloists that, strictly speaking, an insoluble technical problem had been created.

Warlock himself must have played the piano superbly. To my great regret I never met him. His tragic death came in 1930, 'apparently' say some biographers, 'by his own hand'. But his close friend, the conductor Anthony Bernard, whom I knew well, was far from convinced that this was the case. He gave me a graphic account of his visit to see Warlock in his room at Earls Court on the afternoon before the tragedy. Whilst there he saw the kitten, to which Warlock was devoted, jump on to the divan by the fireplace and in doing so turn on the tap for the gas fire which was very loose and easily disturbed. Bernard was naturally alarmed and quick to point out the potential danger. But Warlock merely laughed and said that it happened quite frequently.

Only a few hours later he died in that gas-filled room and we had lost a composer whose influence upon British music can never be fully estimated.

Those Third Programme recitals marked the beginning of my long and continuing devotion to Warlock's music. I remember them with affection and delight.

Despite the many day-to-day pressures, the Corporation was very willing to grant permission to the four of us to accept 'outside' engagements which did not conflict with our commitments. It was a policy much to be appreciated and it meant that I could continue my participation in *Opera in Miniature*, accompany recitals in venues such as the Wigmore Hall, and conduct several concerts with the Lancaster Orchestral Society in that city's Ashton Hall. This was a particular pleasure, for here I was on my home ground; in this same hall I had first appeared as a schoolboy, playing what I seem now to remember as a not particularly attractive Polonaise by Scharwenka. But these concerts, marked by the zest and vigour of an amateur orchestra which had attained remarkably high standards, were a joy. There was Heddle Nash to sing in one of them and naturally he chose the lovely Serenade from *The Fair Maid of Perth* which he had made so much his own. "Still a golden voice, isn't it?" he whispered modestly in my ear as we walked off the platform. There was Owen Brannigan to sing Mozart in another; and in a third the highlight was Michal Hambourg's performance of the Grieg Piano Concerto.

Towards the end of 1949 an engagement to accompany Infantino in a 'Celebrity Concert' took me yet again to Leeds Town Hall. The programme had aroused a good deal of anticipatory interest for in addition to Infantino, who by now had Yorkshire in the hollow of his hand, it presented the blind Greek pianist, Georges Themeli and accompanied by her mother, a fourteen-year old coloratura soprano whose name was Julie Andrews. With a neat pink sash on her sleeveless white dress and her white ankle socks, and captivating her audience by her charm and graceful curtseys, she sang, astonishingly, nothing less than 'Ah, fors' e lui' from *La Traviata* and followed that

184

by other arias, both Italian and French. It would have been unreasonable to expect maturity from one so young but the technique was well-founded, the intonation flawless, and the tone in the middle register a sheer delight – here was a truly formidable talent which was to be recognised fully by the Press notices. One of them added: 'It was a pity she sang mere ditties at her final appearance...but perhaps it was nearly bedtime!'

I have one other recollection of that concert. For an unrehearsed encore Infantino thrust several tattered sheets of music into my hand as we returned to the platform. I spread them out on the music-rest of the piano and was about to play the first bar when, by good fortune, I happened to notice that the page on the left was numbered 19, the one on the right 43. They were completely unrelated. I offered a heartfelt prayer of thanks for having been prevented from playing that first chord. There was a little platform comedy whilst Infantino found what he wanted and we were then able to proceed without the disaster which would certainly have overtaken us. The accompanist's hazards are many!

Day by day in the studios I was joining singers and instrumentalists in their quest for the ideal performance, attempting in every case to establish a participation which in style and conception would support my soloists in reaching that goal. For the accompanist it is a responsibility which demands much flexibility for, on occasion, he may be required to view a work through a window very different from his own. At such times, whilst not negating his own musical personality nor assuming a purely subordinate function, he must be prepared to modify his ideas in the interests of an ultimate performance of apparently definitive character.

Here lies one of the most fascinating aspects of the accompanist's art for no two performances are ever identical. On separate occasions within the space of a few days I partnered two violinists in the Debussy Violin Sonata. Between the two there were several significant differences of approach to this most beautiful work, but perhaps the most notable was that in one case the duration of the whole work was eleven minutes, in the other, fourteen. There

185

was much to admire in both interpretations, each in its own way emphasising certain characteristic elements, but the disparity between them can be imagined. My hope is that no listener to either was led to suspect that my own preference lay somewhere between the two.

The greatest and most experienced performers, I have invariably found, present the accompanist with the fewest problems. They have come close to the fullest possible understanding of the composer's thought, and therein lies their greatness. Their study of every minute detail has not obscured the broad conception and nothing stands in the way of that intimate relationship on which so much depends; and to the final performance there will be added that spontaneous and indefinable quality of projection which can not only weave a spell for the audience but inspire an accompanist to play better than ever before.

According to the personality of the artist, attitudes to rehearsals can vary enormously. There are some who will leave nothing to chance, even in the standard repertoire; they will discuss every nuance in detail, dot every 'i' and cross every 't' leaving little room for that unstudied and magical moment which will illuminate and make memorable the performance to come. It is entirely understandable. Not all artists are equally trustful and in an imperfect world not all accompanists are equally trustworthy, as they may well have discovered. In contrast, there are those who like to limit rehearsal to the essential minimum, having satisfied themselves after perhaps only a few bars that they have a partner who is on the right wavelength.

The ability to listen to the quality of sound lies at the heart of every successful performance. The singer and the instrumentalist is acutely aware of the sound he produces. I hope it would not be unjust to suggest that for the pianist it is a consideration which tends, to some extent, to take second place. But his ear, too, must be finely tuned if a diversity of colour and its infinite graduation are to be at his command. Under his fingers, as Anton Rubinstein so vividly said, lies not one instrument, but a hundred.

For the accompanist, such listening is just as vital, and even more complex. His is a double responsibility calling for a response to the tonal qualities and rhythmic subtleties of his soloist and at the same time to the sound he produces himself which, if it is to blend and support as it should, will be constantly varied in colouring and dynamic gradation. A study of the score will have shown him that his contribution will often be of a rapidly changing nature. At one point he will take the lead, both tonally and rhythmically, and his partner will expect him to do so; at another he will provide a background of sound, precisely judged in strength of tone, and perhaps a bar or so later play out in a more positive way to contribute a musical point which is his alone.

I counted myself fortunate, as all accompanists must, that I could collaborate in performances of the classic song cycles and the vast legacy of nineteenth century German *lieder,* often with varied concepts of interpretation yielding fresh subtleties. How greatly I valued the opportunity to partner Hans Hotter in the *Dichterliebe,* Hermann Prey in the *Magelone* songs of Brahms, and Hilde Guden in her recital of songs by Richard Strauss. These are just three of the many great singers to whom I remain immeasurably indebted.

With the less experienced soloist the accompanist can have extended responsibilities. Lacking confidence and conviction, the young performer may look to him for a measure of leadership. At the piano, he can help to ensure that the lengthy phrase remains comfortably within the limits of breath control, he can raise the emotional temperature and, perhaps most valuably of all, judge an overall tempo. How often a nervous singer has said "You won't let me get too slow, will you?" There are so many ways in which an accompanist can be helpful – and there are some significant psychological considerations. Discretion and tact are among his essential assets. He must conceal any nervousness which he may feel himself and whilst never forgetting that humility is the hallmark of every great artist he must leave his soloist in no doubt of his strength and purpose. For those occasions he must have diplomacy, above all.

There will be times, of course, when some request may tax his creative impulse beyond reasonable limits. I remember a rehearsal of *Dichterliebe,*and sitting at the piano ready to play those first four bars which establish the springtime mood of the introductory song, 'In Wunderschönen Monat Mai'. Before I could begin the singer suggested that he would like those few opening notes to convey a hint of the tragic end of the cycle, sixteen songs later. With an unsettled harmonic scheme, hovering between F sharp and F sharp minor, Schumann has certainly implied the doubts and uncertainties of love, but at this point tragedy is still far away. How could it be done, I wondered – I doubted that it could be done at all. But it was hardly the moment for analytical discussion and so I accepted his suggestion and proceeded to play the opening bars as expressively as I could, but with no thought of tragedy. My soloist was perfectly content and said, gratefully: "That is exactly as I had imagined it!" I privately wondered if he had heard something that I had not heard.

There can be few accompanists for whom technical considerations do not loom large. Many accompaniments present a formidable challenge and the mastery of their complicated passage work demands nothing less than the meticulous and organised approach required by the solo repertoire. Furthermore, a flawless reliability proves to be marginally more elusive when in partnership with another performer. Every week I was spending many hours in study of this kind, always careful to ensure, after one disconcerting experience, that I was preparing a song in the right key. (I had attended a rehearsal with the difficult 'Love's Philosophy' by Delius reliably in my fingers, only to find that my singer had changed her mind and now proposed to sing it a tone down. Technically it was a different song altogether.)

For me, the songs of Schubert are the embodiment of all beauty, but many are difficult to play. Schubert himself found them so, we are told. Their accompaniments lie under the fingers much less comfortably than those of Schumann, for instance, and for every performance they have to be practised and re-practised. Probably the most difficult of all, technically, is 'The Erl King' because of the stamina demanded by those long stretches of rapidly repeated octave triplets. Here, perhaps through some fortunate knack. I have been lucky to have few problems, although I was invariably grateful for that moment of blissful relief when, after a page or two, the pattern changes and the octave repetition temporarily disappears. Though I had never attempted it myself, I remembered Claud Biggs' marvellous playing of Liszt's 'Erl King' transcription. The intricate fingering he had devised for it seemed to me to be quite beyond the bounds of possibility.

There was one occasion when the 'Erl King' brought me close to utter exhaustion. A broadcast for schools made a feature of the song, explaining Goethe's narrative verses, and illustrating its various sections with numerous repetitions. It meant that I was playing almost continually up to the point towards the end of the half-hour when a complete and uninterrupted performance of the song brought the programme to an end. I left the studio in a state closely akin to that which I had felt on the assault course at Barney, praying that rapidly repeated octave triplets would not come my way again for a very long time.

Many instrumentalists visiting London from abroad were engaged to record recitals for future use; more often than not, their programme included duo-sonatas. In their own countries these artists would naturally have their own piano-partners in such works; as visitors a temporary collaboration was necessary, and this added a new dimension to the work of the four staff accompanists.

These were commitments to be welcomed, and how satisfactory it was to find, as the years went by, that so many of these masters works, the Mozart, Beethoven and Brahms sonatas, for example, belonged to one's repertoire and were no longer being practised, rehearsed and performed for the first time.

Naturally, there were other duo-sonatas of more recent date. A recital with the Hungarian violinist, Tibor Varga, brought me into what was at that time less familiar territory. Those strange keyboard textures of the Second Violin Sonata by Bartok remained stubbornly elusive during my preliminary work though in the end they yielded, as they must, to slow practice. But the composer's metronome marks were puzzling, especially in one 'vivo' section where the indicated speed was unbelievably fast. It still eluded me when I went to meet Varga for our first rehearsal. I admitted this before we started and was immensely relieved by what he had to tell me.

"Don't worry," he said. "I played it with the composer and he couldn't manage it himself at that speed! His printed instruction was designed to ensure that the passage would be played as fast as possible."

With that, I could enjoy every moment of our rehearsal and the subsequent performance of a truly magnificent work which I would play many more times in the years to come.

Television, no longer in its infancy, was making greater and greater impact. In 1955 I went to the studios in Lime Grove for the first time to accompany the Polish soprano, Renata Bogdanska, and also to play some piano solos. It seemed very strange to make music in such unusual surroundings, to find the studio, huge as it was, crowded by so many people, all of whom had some vital function to perform, to have a camera at such close quarters, peering over my shoulder at one moment, moving silently away at another. Strangest of all was to be separated from my singer by practically the full length of the studio. She was so far away that I could no longer hear her at all, and the answer to that little problem was to wear headphones! But that meant that someone had to whisk them away whenever the camera turned in my direction. At Miss Bogdanska's end of the studio she had a little tent into which she disappeared to change her costume whilst I played the Backhaus transcription of the *Don Giovanni* Serenade. It was all very intriguing and by today's standards somewhat primitive.

In subsequent television appearances, when pre-recording had become the order of the day, there were no longer such problems. Conditions were more normal and in recitals with Johanna Martzy, Pierre Fournier and Nathan Milstein complete concentration on the work in hand, with far fewer problems, was much more possible.

Milstein holds pride of place as the most exacting artist I have accompanied. Apart from coping with a wonderful rubato which kept me possibly more alert than ever before, that recital produced a new and unexpected hazard. We were playing, amongst other works, the D major Sonata of Handel, in my view the most magnificent of the set, and Milstein's performance was masterly. During our rehearsals it was soon clear that his interest, at least for the time being, lay more in the piano part than his own, so anxious was he to ensure that the keyboard texture should achieve the utmost clarity and match that transparent elegance which one would associate with the harpsichord. The Handel sonatas exist in a number of editions, all of which vary considerably in their 'realisation' of Handel's figured bass. Milstein had not found one entirely to his liking and had therefore made his own by pasting little pieces of manuscript on to a printed score. They were not too easy to read, but the ideas were splendid and I could see the point of every suggested alteration. Unfortunately, that score, having been used already by many accompanists in many parts of the world, had become very tattered; some of those added bits of paper were even coming adrift. Clearly, I would have to learn this version note be note, and that I did before the next rehearsal. But worse was to come! So lively was Milstein's creative imagination that, as we worked on, further improvements to the keyboard part occurred to him, and so now the alterations were being altered. I had the impression that this situation must have happened many times in the past. In the end, all was well, and to partner such violin playing was an inspiring, if somewhat anxious task.

Of all the performances in which I shared at that time it is not the most spectacular, or the most demanding, which remains most strongly in my memory. There was a Sunday evening song recital given by the American bass-baritone, Norman Foster, who had come to London during a break in his opera commitments in Vienna. To accompany him in the Negro spiritual, 'Lord, what a morning' – which must surely be the most moving of them all – was for me an unforgettable experience, so overwhelming was his powerful declamation of faith within the space of a few simple and unpretentious bars of music. If proof were needed that simplicity lies at the heart of the greatest artistry, here it was – and I remember it as though it were yesterday.

A few days later, Norman Foster and I came together again to pre-record the *Sieben Lieder aus letzte Zeit* by Mahler, a very different assignment in which his singing was equally impressive.

Our work as stafff accompanists offered infinite variety. We were not constantly at concert pitch for the demands upon us were subject to abrupt contrasts of tension. From the peak of concentration required by some important recital we would move on to something very different, perhaps to accompany a chorus rehearsal or a series of auditions, perhaps to play in that ever-intriguing *Music and Movement* for Schools, a programme which owed everything to the incomparable improvisations of Marjorie Eele. To be asked here to "Play something which sounds like an elephant", was not at all unusual.

We were often involved in preliminary rehearsals for some forthcoming orchestral concert. I remember being asked one afternoon to be ready the following morning to play through Mahler's *Das Lied von der Erde* with two very distinguished singers and the conductor, Issy Dobrowen. This was a tall order, for I had never yet met that huge work. Despite the burning of much midnight oil the keyboard reduction of its orchestral score stubbornly refused to lie comfortably under my fingers in that short time. I attended the rehearsal in some trepidation and to Mr Dobrowen I apologised in advance for the shortcomings which I had no doubt would soon be apparent. A little smile, kindly and sympathetic, crossed his face. "You have come to play Mahler all by yourself?" he asked. "In my country, for this, we always have *two* pianists!" My burden was lifted, and all went well.

In the preliminary rehearsals for a little-known opera which was to be broadcast in the Third Programme I joined forces with Leo Wurmser whose experience in this field, both in his native Germany and in this country, was a byword in our profession. He was known to us all, not only for his expertise but for his gloomy and lugubrious outlook on life. That, too, was a byword. Rarely did I ever see him smile; his inbuilt pessimism and an absence of faith in anything at all seemed to be symbolised by the umbrella without which he was never seen, even on the hottest summer day.

The opera was to be sung in English in a translation made for the occasion by Professor E.J. Dent who attended one of those rehearsals. As he stood by the piano that afternoon, surrounded by the cast, his dignity was impressive. His world-wide reputation as a musicologist filled the studio, and he dominated the assembly with unquestionable authority. I had the impression that here was a man whose path could never be crossed, nor even approached. The rehearsal proceeded smoothly enough until the moment when Wurmser, as dispirited as ever, took issue with the Professor, insisting that at one point the translation failed to do justice to the original text. Could there have been anything more suicidally reckless? There was an awesome silence, charged with impending doom. Time stood still until at last the Professor spoke. "Mr Wurmser," he said, "you have the advantage of me. You have studied English; I merely picked it up!"

At this period the Third Programme's weekly series of 'Invitation Concerts', given before an invited audience in the Concert Hall of Broadcasting House, provided an important platform for contemporary music. To those of us who were involved, in my case as an accompanist or as a member of a chamber music group, they were irreverently known as the 'Irritation Concerts'. Naturally, the works were of an experimental nature, being performed for the first time and mostly in manuscript. Happily, the scores were usually available sufficiently far in advance to allow the extensive study needed for the grasp of new musical language. Sometimes, the result was clearly rewarding; on the other hand, the style and purpose of a new work could remain persistently elusive, far removed from the immediate understanding of both performers and listeners. What strange things could be found in those scores! There was one, I recall, which began with a single note for the piano, the highest white note on the keyboard, marked to be played *fppp!* If I could only have guessed how to deal with that flight from reality!

193

For the chamber works a group of us would meet after individual preparation for numerous ensemble rehearsals, achieving each time some further degree of security. And sometimes, as the performance drew nearer, we would just begin to feel some vague impression of the composer's purpose and say to each other: "Perhaps there *is* something in this, after all". But, we thought, if those hours of study can bring professional musicians only this far, what possibility of contact can there be for the ordinary listener? Was there ever a time in music's history, I wondered, when the contemporary composer was so remote from his audience?

This is not to say that his work should not be performed. The 'Invitation Concerts' were important and most valuable of all to the composers whose work they presented. Creative art cannot stand still; the innovators must continue to explore uncharted territory, accepting their comparative loneliness; and in the years to come posterity will establish which of those solitary journeys were fruitful.

The process is continuous. Claud Biggs, I remember, merely 'tolerated' Stravinsky; that was his word. Yet for me, less than a generation later, Stravinsky was a master whose music I revered. Nothing had given me greater pleasure than participation in performances of *Les Noces,* especially under the leadership of the inspiring conductor, Bruno Maderna. His grasp of that complicated score enabled him to direct from memory not only the performances but the rehearsals as well. That was a profoundly impressive experience which marked the beginning of my lasting admiration and affection for Stravinsky. Just as important was the music of Frank Martin, pointing still further forward. My introduction had been *Le Vin Herbé;* now came the preparation of his magnificent *Ballade* for 'cello and piano with Henri Honegger, and at about the same time the Petite Symphonie Concertante for harp, harpsichord and piano with the BBC Orchestra under Jean Martinon. The study of these two works alone was enough to bring me to a realisation of his genius, and I looked forward eagerly to the repeat performances to which I was committed.

Unhappily, they were not to materialise as far as I was concerned. On Christmas Eve, 1957, I was admitted to St George's Hospital where from my solitary room a unique view of Hyde Park Gate was as unwelcome as it was unexpected. Something was badly wrong. For too long, some particularly virulent form of influenza had stubbornly resisted treatment of any kind, and by now my weight had been reduced to little more than eight stone. It was time now for the experts to carry out their tests; they were determined to unravel the mystery and I was in very good hands. But Christmas, which in the normal way ought to be the happiest day of the year, dawned very bleakly. My spirits were at a low ebb; faced by the unknown an unfettered imagination can find room for every imaginable calamity, and mine did not fail! At intervals throughout the day there were sympathetic voices on the telephone at my bedside, and there was a note of good wishes from Henri Honegger with some heartwarming comments on our recent recital. That was cheering, and so was another from Frank Martin who wrote: *pour le pianiste que j'ai remplacé aujourdhui dans le Ballade avec mes meilleurs voeux de prompte guérison.'*

The diagnosis was not long delayed. The TB suspected from the beginning was confirmed beyond any doubt. There was a hole in the lung "about the size of a golf ball", they said. To Jessica, this news came as a great relief for she had been told, though I had not, that there were two possibilities. This was one of them; the other would have been infinitely worse. Even so, it was staggering for both of us – something beyond the wildest imagining, for I had known so little ill-health over the years. We were given all kinds of assurances that all would be well in the end, but no one could deny that it would take a long time.

Not yet had I realised the impact on Jessica of this disaster. It was the most cheerless, and the most anxious, Christmas of her life. She was with me on the afternoon of Boxing Day, and together we tried to find the answers to a host of questions. How could it have happened? Was this the outcome of all the pressures of the past ten years or so? Could I blame those countless, studio-secluded hours spent far removed from the bright light of day? There were no satisfactory answers, though we had plenty of time now

195

to think about all that had been, and to wonder about what might be. For me, the greatest shock of all was to have come to so sudden a stop; to accept a complete cessation of all normal activity demanded a far greater adjustment than I could have imagined. Now I saw clearly that for Jessica too adjustment would be equally dramatic. She was facing an unknown period of uncertainty, an onset of responsibilities which she would have to cope with on her own. None of this was mentioned that day; her strength was greater than mine.

The King Edward Sanatorium at Midhurst in Sussex to which I was transferred only a day or so later was warm, comfortable and welcoming. Its atmosphere filled me with confidence; anxieties largely disappeared, at least for the time being. Tranquillity and an essential peace of mind were within reach. The staff gave me the impression that they were concentrating their energies on me alone.

"We'll get you fixed up all right," said one of the senior doctors within minutes of our first meeting. I hardly ever saw him without his much-loved pipe. He told me with some satisfaction that he smoked seven ounces of tobacco every week. Eventually the day would come when I was allowed to return to mine, and what bliss that was! I guessed that he would not delay that any longer than necessary. But in the meantime, there was a long way to go. I was put to bed, initially for three months, I was told. Outside my window, winter passed by in a pageant of inconstant moods. The snow and rain, the wintry sunshine, the gales and fog – all this was merely hearsay, belonging not at all to my world. By the time I could take a closer look the primroses were in bloom.

It can be imagined how much, from now on, Jessica's visits meant to me. Throughout my stay, which in the end amounted to eight long months, and however capricious the weather, she made the journey from Wimbledon to Midhurst twice weekly, driving our none-too-reliable Morris car without the benefit of a heater. She allowed nothing whatever to interrupt that faithful routine.

Later on, when no longer confined to my room, I was able to make many friends among my fellow-patients.

One of them was the actress-daughter of the composer, Dr Herbert Howells, whose performances we had so often admired in the past – a delightful companion who was as interested as I was in the daily arrival of the nuthatches and woodpeckers which came in a flurry to the nut feeders outside our windows. Occasionally, Ursula's parents and Jessica came together, either by bus, or sharing the inadequacies of that little car.

Curiously enough, even within a week or so of my arrival at Midhurst, I began to feel terribly well. No one was in the least surprised. Bed-rest, they told me, was the most wonderful panacea for all ills, although the most expensive and the most difficult to organise for patients in their own homes. Naturally, that was not all. The new drugs, and especially the daily injections, were working well and the sequence of X-ray photographs confirmed that the healing process had started. How lucky I was not to have had this setback some ten years earlier when the outcome could have been very different.

But the possibility of lung surgery, foreseen at the beginning, had not receded. It hung over me like a black cloud; not to brood on that would have needed far more will-power than I could command. Of course I ought not to have worried, nor dreaded it so much. I was in marvellously expert hands and receiving what was probably the finest treatment available anywhere in the country. But to have known the worst, to have had some assurance during those long weeks, one way or the other, would have made all the difference. The question mark remained. Three or four months passed before it was finally resolved. That was when I brought my uncertainties out into the open and put my query to the Medical Superintendent, Sir Geoffrey Todd. "Oh," he said, "I don't think we had thought of that for you!" He could not have known the relief which I felt at that moment. The black cloud had suddenly passed over and the sunlight from behind it chased away the shadows which for so long had darkened my hopes. Not that I was yet out of the wood. The setbacks, disappointments and a heart-sickening deferment of the long-awaited day of freedom for yet another six weeks were all still to come.

Meanwhile, by very gradual stages, I acquired more independence. I could take meals in the dining-room, walk in the grounds and meet my fellow patients, to share with them the one concern we all had in common – how much longer would we be there? That was the question which took precedence over all others. It was even uppermost in the mind of one new arrival who was well enough to drive his car to Midhurst and present himself for admission. He had parked his car in the drive, walked over to the front door to speak to someone who happened to be standing there.

"You look very well," said the new patient. "How long have you been here?"

"I've been here seventeen years – who are you?" was the reply, for the 'someone' was none other than Sir Geoffrey Todd! Punch would have added: 'Collapse of far-from-stout party!'

It was a strange, abnormal way of life, a state of suspended animation which seemed to be shared even by the calendar, for time passed so slowly. Separated as I was from the sights and sounds of the world I had known, how easy it would be, I thought, to lose one's identity altogether. There was one afternoon when I actually tried to bring that figment of imagination to reality. I was with a group of patients in the therapy room, attempting with only indifferent success to master the intricacies of basket-weaving, when a visitor arrived on a conducted tour of the building. To my horror, it was Val Gielgud; I recognised him immediately. Had we met he would have been kindness itself, of course, but I shrank from any contact. At that moment there was nothing in the world I wanted more than to remain anonymous. I sat quietly in my corner, made no movement, did not look up; eventually, he went away and I breathed again. It was all very puzzling; I had no explanation for that curious and quite unjustifiable sense of humiliation which had taken hold of me for those few moments. It was not only puzzling; it was entirely irrational.

Within a few more weeks I was seeing things from quite another viewpoint. Comforting reassurances had raised my spirits and the world to which I belonged was coming into clearer focus. To be well on the way to recovery was a blessing for which I could be devoutly thankful, and so I was. With a new sense of perspective I cherished the thought that one day I would be able to look back on Midhurst and see it merely as an interlude in life. At the same time my thoughts went out in sorrow and compassion for those of my new companions who had been so much less fortunate, and for whom stern destiny had denied any bright future. I would not forget them. The time was to come when one of Thomas Hardy's verses (still more beautiful in Gerald Finzi's musical setting) would persuade me to remember them rather differently:

> They ride their diurnal round
> Each day-span's sum of hours
> In peerless ease, without jolt or bound
> Or ache like ours.

I LEFT Midhurst after some eight months, to find that the world moved around far more restlessly than I remembered; the streets were busier, the pavements narrower and the traffic more dangerous. These were superficial impressions and they soon passed. My one objective was to get back to the piano after the long separation. It was an emotional as well as a practical necessity. At Midhurst I had played for only a few hours all told, although on one very happy day towards the end my friend, Wilfred Brown, had found time amidst his busy professional life to come down to Sussex to give a song recital. For the patients and staff it was a memorable occasion; for me, as his accompanist, it was of still greater consequence – a reminder of past joys and a promise of what could still lie ahead. For the rest there had been only impersonal contact with music through the radio, which had also occasionally provided the doubtful pleasure of listening to one of my own recordings.

Now it was possible to get down to some serious work and happily there was plenty of time. With generous consideration the BBC had arranged no firm commitment for me until the autumn, and even then there was to be only a gradual return to a full schedule.

To discover what had been lost I began very slowly. There were, indeed, discoveries to be made. The sound of the piano and its infinite variety of tonal colour was a sheer delight. I found myself listening with a perception which seemed to me to be far more acute than in the past; I fell in love with single notes, each one the precious product of human thought, and I marvelled afresh at the exceptional dynamic range of the instrument. I put those single notes together, delighting in their harmonic juxtaposition and finding subtle and unsuspected possibilities. This close examination of sound, as though through some aural magnifying glass, the whole process slowed down in time, was the direct outcome of a lengthy severance from the instrument I had known all my life. It was invaluable. My debt to Midhurst was incalculable in more ways than one.

When it came to the somewhat more obvious question of technical facility, there were discoveries of a similar kind. I was a student again, faced by the exercises of my youth. To practise them now, with the experience of half a lifetime behind me, was revealing. I saw them quite differently; I could see their objectives so much more easily and relate their demands to my own shortcomings with far greater clarity. They were torture no longer and they yielded their benefits far less reluctantly.

Those weeks of preparation were intensive, enjoyable and immensely rewarding. As I worked on I came to realise that what had seemed, at the beginning of the year, to be so disastrous a stroke of fate had been transformed into a blessing of inestimable value. By an accident of chance I had been allowed to make a new beginning with deeper insight and fresh understanding.

When at last the long interruption came to an end my first assignment was to accompany a performance of Brahms' *Four Serious Songs,* But on this special occasion with its very personal significance, those 'little songs' as Brahms so oddly described them, took on still greater stature. Nothing could have matched my mood more exactly than the cycle's wonderful transition from the doubts and uncertainties of the Apochrypha to the final, incomparable affirmation of St Paul. As the work came to its eloquent and majestic close

I dared to feel that now, perhaps, I might claim to be able to see just a little further; that, at least, was my hope.

The music of Brahms was much on my mind at this time for I was also re-studying the three violin and piano sonatas in readiness for some forthcoming recitals. It seemed a little more than just a passing coincidence that the original and possibly unpublished photograph of the master, should now come into my possession.

The very limited amount of teaching which I had been able to undertake in London had brought me the friendship of Mrs Miri Zwillinger whose lifelong devotion to the piano was directed particularly towards the music of her native city, Vienna.

In 1950 she had spent a holiday in the South Tirol, and in her Merano hotel she had made the brief acquaintance of a fellow guest from Vienna with whom she could share her musical interests and enthusiasm. Captain Eugen Müller von Aichholz was a member of the family which had been very closely and hospitably associated with Brahms during his last years. He still lived in the house to which the composer had been a constant visitor and which had been the regular meeting-place of the Brahms circle. He was now an old man, but in his youth he had been a keen amateur photographer, never failing to pursue his hobby whenever Brahms was present, either in Vienna or at the family's beautiful house in Gmunden, near Ischl. He promised to send to Mrs Zwillinger some of the intimate snapshots of the composer taken during those years, and was as good as his word, for eventually the prints arrived in London.

I was quite overwhelmed by Mrs Zwillinger's insistence that I should have one of them as a token of our friendship, and I have cherished it over the years. It was yet another link with the past to be treasured. My thoughts went back to the College in Manchester and I saw again the dumpy figure of Adolph Brodsky, another close friend of Brahms, as he walked slowly across the Hall. After thirty years, the fearful anxieties of the afternoons in his studio were as yesterday.

That in all those years the opportunities for me to re-visit the College had been so rare was something I

201

deeply regretted. Then, out of the blue, came a letter from the Principal, Frederic Cox, inviting me on behalf of the Council and the Board of Professors to become a Fellow of the College. It was a very unexpected honour which I accepted with the greatest pleasure and no little pride. To be unable to attend the Annual General Meeting at which the Fellowship was to be conferred was a great disappointment, but on that same day I was committed to that already-mentioned recording of the *Dichterliebe*, an engagement which could not be altered. Nevertheless, to be allowed *in absentia* to join the ranks of so many distinguished predecessors on the Roll of Fellows was something to be deeply appreciated.

Memories of Midhurst were rapidly fading, and many concerts followed. There were a number of Wigmore Hall recitals and the Third Programme was insatiable. It gave me particular pleasure to join forces with the outstanding players of the Quintette à Vent Francais in one of the Sunday concerts at Kenwood House. It was June, and the audience were supposed to sit in the open and enjoy the evening sunshine as well as the music. But it was also an English June and the rain poured in torrents! We played to a closely crowded and somewhat bedraggled audience huddled for shelter in a very confined space. Even so, it was still a joy to partner the superb flautist, Jean Pierre Rampal in a Bach sonata, and to accompany the equally elegant clarinettist, Jacques Lancelot. With artistry of that order the elements were of little account.

Then came my first meeting with Henryk Szeryng, whose standing among the world's greatest violinists was rapidly becoming recognised. We came together initially for a solo recital on television and I was immediately enchanted by the wide-ranging beauty of his tone. Here, too, was not only complete technical authority but a subtlety of rubato which for perfect ensemble demanded considerably flexibility and anticipation in accompaniment, especially in the lighter pieces he had chosen for this first programme. They included, I remember, a little Mexican folk song of tender and evocative charm which he had arranged himself.

202

In all the much more serious recitals which followed Szeryng proved to be one of the most interesting artists with whom I had ever worked. I have played with many violinists whose view of the work in hand was solely in terms of their own instrument. Szeryng was different, always acutely aware of the significance of the piano part and its contribution to the whole. This was the case even in his accompanied solo items, quite apart from the duo-sonatas. Of these we played Mozart, Beethoven, Brahms, Debussy, Prokofiev, and he invariably insisted on my role as a 'co-partner' – that was his word. And in the performance of earlier music, in Corelli and Leclair for example, a rare sense of freedom could initiate spontaneous and unrehearsed nuances. If, as sometimes happened, I made some slip or other in rehearsal and a repeat of the passage was necessary, he would stop, not to point it out but to tune his violin! That, I thought, was the height of courtesy.

To work with him was fascinating; in the Brahms D minor, to quote just one example, he had some interesting and valuable views on the dynamic markings. Some, he believed, had been added by Joachim, clearly for the benefit of the violin, though with some disregard for the work as a whole. Those were very logical theories. In performance his authority was awe-inspiring, and I look back on my association with him as one of the most rewarding and musically fulfilling episodes of my life.

CHAPTER 15

A wheelbarrow on Booth Street

THE two years which followed my return from Midhurst were stirring and eventful. The work I was doing was exactly what I wanted to do, and for that I could count myself fortunate; no one could ask for more. I could also expect it to continue, for the date when I would have to retire from the BBC was still six years ahead. No possibility of any change crossed my mind.

For some little time I had been travelling to Manchester on a free day in alternate weeks to take charge of an Accompaniment Class at the College. It was work which I loved and happily it had brought me into close touch once more with Claud Biggs. Shortly after my student days he had been appointed senior piano professor at the Royal Irish Academy in Dublin, but he had returned to Manchester in 1947 to command once more the respect and affection of a vast number of piano students. Among them, a little later, was John Ogdon. Now in 1961 Claud was approaching his eighties and still teaching, though retirement was inevitably imminent. It came in that year which also saw, coincidentally, the departure of several other members of the piano staff.

Eight years earlier, the appointment of Frederic Cox as Principal had brought a fresh and powerful impetus to the work of the College. His name was already then a byword in the sphere of vocal training, and it was to be expected that his energies would be specially directed towards opera. That proved to be the case, though not by any means to the disadvantage of other disciplines. His interest in the development of the piano department, for example, and his pride in its past achievements, were very soon to be recognised. Under his wise guidance and many-sided influence, the traditions of the College were to be fully maintained and its high reputation still further advanced.

His proposal that I should consider a full-time position on the staff came as a great surprise. No such possibility had occurred to me and, at that moment, the idea of turning away from London and the work I was doing was quite unacceptable. But the offer was very tangible; there was even something flattering in the suggestion that I should take over responsibility for the students whom Claud would leave behind. The Principal also had in mind the creation of a new 'Accompaniment and Recital' department which would seek to develop a further emphasis on performance. Such scope and opportunities were very attractive, though it was difficult to imagine myself removed from the BBC background which I had known for so long. Even so, the six years which remained to me gradually began to look very limited in comparison with a new activity in Manchester which could extend much further into the future.

Eventually, the days of indecision came to an end when, much to the surprise of my colleagues, I resigned from the BBC. It was a big step to take, but one that I have never regretted. It was also a logical one for it seemed somehow appropriate that my life in music should shape itself in accordance with the honourable pattern of sonata form, my student days in Manchester as the exposition, the years of music-making as the development, and now the recapitulation. A fanciful notion perhaps, but we are all inheritors of the past, and if that development had taught me anything at all it was not a bad thing that I should now try to pass on something of that experience to a new generation. A few months later I took up my new post at the beginning of the academic year.

The College was very much as it had been in my day. Apart from a building extension which had provided a few more studios it had not moved with the times in any material sense, nor indeed was that necessary; its concern remained, rightly, with the unchanging verities. (The Bechstein, at least, was in fine shape, and it made no difference to Beethoven if the door handle of my studio fell off occasionally during the day!)

The students were more numerous than they had been, but for the most part they shared the same hopes and ambitions of their predecessors. My impression was that their approach to a career in music was more business-like, more forward-looking than ours had been. They looked more to the future and rather less to the past; theirs was naturally a modern world and they were more than ready to enlist the help of its technology. I was considerably taken aback one day when one of them told me that he had made a tape recording of some recent broadcast of mine, and had since been listening to it at half speed in order to check the accuracy of my piano part!

The piano lessons were absorbing, so varied were the natural talents and personal characteristics of the twenty or so pupils who came into my charge. Among them were those with heaven-sent gifts, good hands and innate musical insight, qualities which in some cases, alas, were sadly unsupported by patience, application and the will to achieve. To bring about some realistic appreciation of the many-sided assets the performer needs was an anxious and difficult task, the outcome of which could never be certain. There were others, very different, who worked unstintingly, sparing no painstaking effort to reach a goal which, in the absence of a so far undeveloped artistic impulse, might in the end be denied to them altogether. They were the ones who presented the most interesting problems, and commanded my sympathies and respect.

The search for the most helpful ways in which to guide a group of young people, so diverse in talent, character and temperament, was of never-ending fascination.

I was determined to teach, not only piano playing, but music – to cultivate a personal initiative which would lead to good taste and musical perception within the framework of each individual personality. Teaching should never be dictatorial, in my view. Within certain limits there is scope for the approach to interpretation to be infinitely variable; any attempt by a teacher to turn a gifted pupil into a carbon copy of himself I would regard as a positive disservice. It ought surely to be his aim to make himself eventually dispensable, for the student will one day be on his own with no mentor to tell him what to do. Let the student be presented with various options, encouraged to think for himself, and persuasively steered away from that which is less acceptable. I could still hear Claud Biggs saying "There's much to be said for . . . "

I am thinking, of course, of the fairly advanced pupil, and I have to admit that there will be occasions when such procedure will not work. There was one young lady who came to me towards the end of her studies on the course which was run jointly by the College and the University. Amongst the works she had in hand was a Mozart sonata which she played quite dreadfully. It was not inaccurate, for she had a certain facility, but the erratic and wilful distortion of its phrases made them practically unrecognisable. Nothing further from a Mozartian grace and elegance could be imagined. I sat at the piano and played some parts of that movement, in particular the initial subject statements, as expressively as I could, and asked her if she did not think that a simpler and more straightforward treatment of those beautiful phrases would come nearer to the truth. She replied, quite firmly: "I prefer mine!" She was with me for only a brief period in which, I fear, we made little progress.

This was an exceptional case. For the most part my students joined willingly and co-operatively in the search for artistic integrity and I like to think that we did not always seek in vain. Between teacher and pupil the pursuit of an ideal creates a very special relationship, a bond of intimacy and a warmth of friendship. For that I have been more than grateful; at the same time it would be churlish if I failed to acknowledge how very much I have learned from my students. The exchange of our ideas was never one-way.

It cannot be denied that in our present-day institutions for advanced musical studies all students have a very heavy schedule of commitments. Apart from their obligations to a principal study, which in itself could well dominate their waking hours, they must cope with a multitude of ancillary subjects, all time-consuming yet all essential if the well-rounded musician is ultimately to develop. They have a work load which puts at risk those vital and crucially important hours which, if justice is to be done, must be spent on private practice.

It is an enormous and well recognised problem to which a solution has not yet been found despite the most strenuous efforts. The pianists are fortunate to be somewhat less affected than their fellows – they do not sing in a chorus nor play in an orchestra. But when they came to me as a group for the weekly classes in accompaniment and chamber music, there was always some difficulty in ensuring that their vocal and instrumental partners would be available. Even the most careful and time-consuming organisation could fail to solve the problem completely.

For all that, some good work was done. The method of collective study of the great song-cycles and the duo-sonatas was invaluable. Listening to each other, sometimes competing with each other, the students could make comparisons for themselves and so develop powers of selection and an all-essential critical sense. For some, the opportunity to hear works which they had not so far played themselves provided an extension of repertoire knowledge. That, too, was of great importance for student days are comparatively brief and there is much to learn. I was never free of the conviction that for the pianist so much would be inevitably left undone, however much of his enormous territory we explored.

Not everyone took a practical part in that class; there were students who joined us from other departments merely to listen. There was one charming young lady, a novice from a neighbouring convent, who attended with great regularity. As a pianist she ought to have made the most of the opportunities open to her, but she resolutely resisted all my efforts to draw her in and I never heard her play. Each week she would sit quietly in a corner with a huge exercise book on her knee, and in that she conscientiously noted my every suggestion and comment on the works being played. Such painstaking industry was laudable but also somewhat embarrassing, for out of context those words of mine could have made little sense. Her one shy approach came when she asked me one day if she might leave a little early. "You see," she explained, "I very much want to go to the Hallé concert tonight, but before that I have so many prayers to say that I really don't know how I can get them all in."

Through advancing technical security, the growth of stylistic understanding and increasing co-operative flexibility, our objective was to reach an acceptable, if still interim, standard of performance. Then the performers were recommended for inclusion in one of the Students' Concerts. That was the acid test which would reveal their ability to rise to the occasion, to project, to maintain control and a quiet mind at the moment when it mattered most of all. Those who feel immediately at home when playing in public are the lucky ones, but they are, on the whole, the exceptions. The majority of young performers find it very difficult to be oblivious of their surroundings. For them it is question of mental attitude and this needs some probing of the subconscious self if the psychological stresses which put calm confidence at risk are to be overcome. The dictum of that wonderfully wise counsellor, Nadia Boulanger, was stern. In her philosophy there was no place at all for stage-fright. When the performer cares more for the music than himself, she maintained, all fears will disappear. She was right, of course, but the advice is not easy to follow.

In the early years of the 1960s, concerts in Manchester were far less plentiful than they are today. Apart from the Hallé Orchestra and the Manchester Chamber Concerts Society, the College itself could claim with some justification to be one of the city's prominent venues for the music-loving public. There were, of course, the operas which, through the inspiration of the Principal and in defiance of untold difficulties, brought fresh lustre to the College's reputation. The enterprising productions of works as diverse as Bellini's *Capuletti ed i Monteichi* and Debussy's *Pelléas and Mélisande* (to mention only two) drew capacity audiences and favourable critical comment from far afield. Incidentally, they also provided a stage for many young singers whose names are now closely associated with the world's greatest opera companies.

The concerts in the Hall of the College were not limited to student performers. There were other recitals in which the staff frequently participated, and in one of these, shortly after my arrival, I collaborated with the senior violin Professor, Endre Wolf. We had actually met once before in London, very briefly, for a rehearsal with Basil Cameron of a concerto which he was to play with the BBC Symphony Orchestra, though neither of us remembered the occasion very clearly. Now, in this Manchester concert, arranged in honour of Aaron Copland by the Institute of Contemporary Arts, we joined forces in the Piano Quartet and the lyrical Violin Sonata. It was the beginning of what was to be not only a lengthy and very happy musical association, but a valued, personal friendship which has continued over the years.

I found in Endre Wolf a musician of rare sensibility. Apart from supreme technical authority he had at his command a tone of great beauty, rich in diversity of nuance, and a power of expression which was invariably at the service of deep musical insight. Whatever the work, this was fastidious playing, its hallmark good taste and a sure sense of style. In the past I had had the good fortune to become familiar with the work of many very great violinists, but never until now had I heard the unaccompanied Partitas of Bach to glow with such human warmth.

Over the next few years we established a repertoire of the duo-sonatas ranging from Mozart and Beethoven to Stravinsky and other modern masters. In the two Bartok Sonatas, Endre's violin spoke with an authentic voice, for this was music which was his birthright; and in his solo work the brilliance of his playing of Ravel's Tzigane echoed the spirit of Jelly d'Aranyi for whom it was written and whose performance of it I could never forget.

We played together many times – in the College, for the BBC, at the Wigmore Hall, for many societies, for the radio in Stockholm and so on. On one little tour the Brahms G major took us to Border Television where, influenced culturally by the producer, Maurice Lindsay, the programmes at that time had a place for music of that kind. A recital in Carlisle Cathedral that same evening I remember chiefly for the freezing temperature in which we had to cope with the hazards of the César Franck Sonata.

Endre and I shared many interests beyond music. Although I could never hope to match his surprisingly detailed knowledge of many and varied scientific developments, we were on common ground when it came to photography. In that field our efforts to reach the highest possible standards amounted to something like an obsession. For him, only the best would do and I have had every reason to be grateful for his persuasive insistence that a Leicaflex would bring me nearest to the heart's desire.

He had been teaching at the College since 1954, at the same time taking charge of special violin and chamber music courses in Stockholm arranged by the Swedish Broadcasting Corporation. In addition to that heavy schedule he was much in demand as a soloist in concertos with many European orchestras. He always took his camera with him and from a lengthy tour with the Israel Philharmonic he brought back a series of stunning photographs. Unfortunately for me, there were changes afoot. In 1964 he decided to relinquish his Manchester appointment and make a permanent home in Sweden. It was a move which, to my great regret, brought our partnership to an end as far as music was concerned. Happily, it has done nothing to impair our friendship.

Nevertheless, I retained a pleasing number of performing engagements, widely varied in character and often involving participation with visiting violinists, Zvi Zeitlin, Leon Spierer and Ruggiero Ricci among them. Before very long, the arrival of two new members of the College staff, the 'cellist Raphael Sommer and the violinist Yossi Zivoni, created fresh opportunities for chamber music performance. We played together in trios and sonatas on many occasions, not only in England but further afield in Belgium, France, Switzerland and Italy. Recitals with Zivoni in Pescara and Verona introduced me for the first time to the demonstrative excitability of Italian audiences, so unlike any others I had known – a heartening if somewhat intimidating experience.

None of these activities (which were not as time-consuming as might by expected) put my students at any disadvantage. The hopes and fears of those young people, their problems and their onward progress towards a fully professional life in music, remained infinitely rewarding and the energies I could call upon were constantly supplemented by their own infectious vitality, the freshness of their outlook and boundless faith in a future still unknown.

In the busy life of every performer there lurks an inherent danger. By the nature of his work, by his awareness that he will be judged only on the quality of his latest performance, he must, of necessity, look inwards. He must continually examine every detail of his art and technique, every aspect of his personality, and reassess his reactions to a composer's thought and intentions. But, Narcissus-like, he can over-do it. In that case, his vision narrows, perspective and proportion are at risk and his world diminishes. The remedy is at hand. To work with those for whom maturity is still to come is, in my view, the perfect antidote.

In due course, I became a member of the Board of Professors and joined there a group of congenial colleagues among whom were two of my old fellow-students, Gordon Green and Clifford Knowles, and a new friend, Derrick Wyndham of the piano department. Naturally, the Board's concern was with academic matters but there were other pressing problems which looked larger day by day. By now the College building was in a sad state of disrepair and the battle with the ravages of time, if not lost, was certainly not being won. The accommodation was woefully inadequate; the basement, the attics, every hole and corner, every nook and cranny was being put to use. When, eventually, I became involved in administrative matters as Assistant to the Principal, I could see the problem at close quarters. Not all the staff attended every day, and so the pressures varied. Even so, to ensure that some space, however undesirable, could be found for every class before the day could begin was a constant anxiety. Happily, our tutors were understanding, patient and undefeated.

At one period, I remember, there were road works in progress just outside the front door, elegantly supplemented by a smart little hut for the night watchmen. It stood invitingly empty throughout the day and it would have been no surprise to find that it had been appropriated for some academic purpose, perhaps a tiny harmony class though not a quartet of trombones!

These difficulties, and many others of a much more serious nature, were for consideration by the Council of the College on which, under the chairmanship of the Vice-Chancellor of the University of Manchester, I was in time privileged to serve. But the Council's hands were tied in very many ways; it was already too late, for there were great and far-reaching changes on the way.

Throughout these years it was widely known that the life of the Royal Manchester College of Music would come to an end before very long. As early as 1955 Frederic Cox had been involved in the discussion of a number of alternative possibilities for its future, some of which involved co-operation between the College and the Northern School of Music. In the two years which followed, the exploration of various avenues of approach pointed towards the advisability of some form of amalgamation between the two institutions, however fiercely independent in spirit they both were. In 1957 Lancashire Education Committee called a meeting of the two Councils together with representatives of the three local Education Committees most closely concerned – those of Manchester, Salford and Cheshire. Three years were to pass before these bodies reached a full agreement to establish a new college by amalgamation, but the first step towards the formation of the Northern College of Music had been taken.

This is not the place for a detailed history of the lengthy and protracted birthpangs of what was to become the first purpose-designed conservatoire of music built in Britain in modern times. That story has still to be written though part of it has been meticulously told by Michael Kennedy in his *History of the RMCM* (Manchester University Press, 1971). It is not for me to attempt to follow in his footsteps: from 1961 I merely stood on the fringe of epoch-making events. Occasionally, however, I represented the Principal at one of his innumerable meetings, and in 1966 I was one of the signatories of the document which confirmed formal agreement and set up a Joint Committee as an Interim Governing Body.

That committee, chaired successively by the late County Alderman, Mrs Fletcher, the late Alderman Sir Maurice Pariser and Alderman Dame Kathleen Ollerenshaw, was charged with the responsibility for the establishment of a College, which, sited on the corner of Oxford Road and Booth Street West, would form part of the City's project to create on that area a huge education campus. 'The Manchester education precinct,' said its planners, 'represents one of the great challenges of urban development at this time. The opportunities that exist are perhaps unequalled in any city in Europe; here there can be created a fine group of buildings and inter-related spaces worthy of a great educational centre in a great city.'

One of those buildings would be the new College, a concept unique in its dual function – firstly to provide the best possible facilities for the training of musicians; secondly, to make a significant contribution to Manchester's musical life as a centre for professional performances available to the general public. The plans already embraced an opera theatre and a concert hall.

The financial basis of the whole project lies well beyond the scope of these reminiscences of mine, and so does much of what happened during those heady years. It was a time for progress and for intermittent setbacks, for failure as well as success. It was also a time for sacrifice for it could be clearly seen that in this merger of the Royal Manchester College of Music and the Northern School of Music, both would lose their individual indentities. It says much for the vision and good will of the two Principals, Frederic Cox and Ida Carroll, that in the end they were able to put such considerations aside and share their confidence that the College-to-be would be nourished by the fine traditions of the two earlier institutions.

Patience, too, was a virtue in those years. A series of financial freezes and economic restraints upset all timing schedules, and in the end delayed the building programme until November, 1969. In that month, I walked down the road to the corner of Booth Street West to find that the

214

presence of a solitary wheelbarrow on the site revealed the first sign of activity. The new College was on its way.

But under whose direction would it be? That was the question and as yet, no appointment of its Principal had been made. For reasons of age, neither Frederic Cox nor Ida Carroll were under consideration for the post. For a lengthy period which in fact was to last for yet another year, that question remained unanswered.

In the meantime, at a meeting of the RMCM Council held early in 1970, from which our Principal was absent through illness, it was my sad duty to read on his behalf a statement he had prepared. It announced his intention to resign, a decision which he had made against a background of ill-health, personal circumstances and a burden of uncertainties. Subsequent attempts by dismayed members of the Council to dissuade him were all unsuccessful and in September of that year Frederic Cox, now Principal Emeritus, stepped down.

For eighteen years at the helm he had steered the fortunes of the College through both calm and tumultuous seas. With leadership which had never become obtrusive he had assured its honoured place among the world's great centres of musical learning – and he had brought it to the end of an era. The Royal Manchester College of Music would soon be no more, but for what remained of its life our Warden, Dr John Wray, became its Acting Principal.

The last years were as active as ever. We still had a full complement of students though their numbers decreased year by year as their various courses were completed. Happily, my administrative duties diminished, and I could devote more energies to teaching, at least for the time being.

This was the year of the Beethoven bicentenary, an important event which was to be fittingly observed. Our celebration took the form of a series of recitals to include the thirty-two Piano Sonatas, played by David Wilde, the ten Violin and Piano Sonatas, and the entire works for 'cello and piano. Additionally, in association with the Manchester Chamber Concerts Society, there were performances of the 'Archduke' and 'Ghost' Trios given by the Trio di

215

Trieste. These fifteen concerts were given over a period of several months starting in September, 1970, and they brought me the long-coveted opportunity of collaboration in the complete violin and 'cello works; my partners were John Brown, Yossi Zivoni and Raphael Sommer. I had, of course, played many of them previously, but it was a joy to perform the cycles in their entirety and to come, thereby, to an inevitably wider grasp and perspective.

Meanwhile, the solitary wheelbarrow down the road had been replaced by massive operations and a forest of scaffolding. Building was going apace and in April, 1971, an impressive ceremony marked the laying of the Foundation Stone by Ida Carroll and Frederic Cox. By this time, the long-awaited announcement of the new College's Principal-Designate had been made.

The news of John Manduell's appointment gave me particular pleasure. We had known each other for a long time, our friendship dating back to 1956 when he joined the Music staff of the BBC. For four or five years we met frequently in the studio for the broadcast recitals which he devised and produced. Then, with his departure to become BBC Head of Music for the Midlands and East Anglia, and mine for Manchester, we went our separate ways. Not that we lost touch, for he was good enough to engage me for a number of interesting chamber music concerts in his new area of the country. One of those – a performances of the Elgar Piano Quintet in the wonderfully appropriate setting of the Chapter House at Worcester – I still remember with delight.

But for John Manduell that post served only as a stepping-stone to the still greater responsibilities which he accepted in 1964 when taking charge of the newly-inaugurated BBC Music Programmes – to shape the policy of the Third Programme and to organise its output. It was a task for which he had the most admirable and the most essential qualities – vast knowledge, an unwavering insistence on the highest possible standards, boundless energy and enthusiasm, a critical faculty of the first order and an administrative expertise. Such assets stood him in good stead when four years later he became the University of

Lancaster's first Music Director with a mandate to establish its Department of Music. Now he had taken up the challenge of the new College. I had no doubt whatever that under his direction it would set out on its long journey in the right spirit and with the brightest of ideals.

CHAPTER 16

Fovet musica omnes

TO find myself still in the North after ten years was something of a surprise. I had not expected to stay so long, but I had not foreseen the long delay in the establishment of the new College, and in that I had not anticipated any participation at all. But by now I was very much involved, not only in the winding up of RMCM but in concert engagements and other commitments of a more academic nature.

Invitations to examine took me to the Royal Academy in London and the Royal Scottish Academy in Glasgow; there were lectures for a number of societies and opportunities for adjudication at Music Festivals, of which there were many in the area. This last was a new departure for me and proved to be a heartening experience; with it came the realisation of how much our profession and the cause of music owes to the Competitive Festival movement for the way in which it has implanted a love of music so widely, and for its strengthening of our national tradition, especially in choral music. In every aspect of musical performance the standards reached in these competitions can be astonishingly high. On one of my visits to the famous 'Feis' in Dublin I shared a Concerto Class with the late Harry Isaacs, Piano Professor of the Royal Academy, and I recall the extraordinary difficulty we had in selecting a winner from among no fewer than nine outstanding performances of the Mozart D minor. That that music, after four or five hours of repetition, could remain as fresh as ever says much for Mozart and even something for the staying power of both audience and adjudicators!

I was about to become still more deeply immersed in the music of Mozart for a series of programmes on Radio Manchester. At that time, the Station Manager of the local radio service was Raphael Gonley whom I had known in the BBC and whose many-sided musical gifts went far beyond the vocal studies which he had later pursued enthusiastically as a mature student at the College. (In a production of *Die Meistersinger* at the University Theatre he had given a memorable performance, remarkable for its shrewd characterisation, in the exacting role of Beckmesser.)

Raph's lively enterprise lay behind many projects for Radio Manchester and amongst them was his idea for a sequence of ten half-hour programmes on the life and works of Mozart. They were to be illustrated by gramophone recordings and bore the general title *Hats off, Gentlemen*. I was delighted to accept his suggestion that I should write and present them. From my earliest days in broadcasting I had been fascinated by the potential of a combination of music and the spoken word. Here, in the story of the Salzburg miracle, was a chance to discover yet more of the possibilities the medium could offer. Moreover, it occurred to me, there could be a place for some of the earlier works – the *singspiel*, *Bastien und Bastienne*, the opera, *La Finta Giardiniera*, for example – music far less well-known but pointing surely to the master works to come.

It was marvellous to have a producer of Raph's experience. We discussed it all in great detail and in the studio a workable procedure emerged, the recording of each programme taking some two hours. No doubt it could have been argued that this was not really suitable material for a local radio audience, but in the event Raph's faith was justified. A favourable response encouraged a quite lengthy extension of the series. Over a period of a year or so Brahms, Mendelssohn, Debussy and Dvorak became in turn the subjects for similar treatment – in all, there were sixty-four programmes, most of the series being acquired by a number of other local radio organisations for re-broadcasting.

Having been appointed Principal of the new College in 1971, one of John Manduell's first moves was to establish a Steering Committee of which I became a member, joining forces under his chairmanship with Ida Carroll, John Wray and Percy Welton, a senior member of the Northern School. At a later date we were joined by the newly-appointed Dean of Development, Terence Greaves and the new Secretary, Air Commodore M.C.M. Vaughan.

Our concern as an instrument of planning was with a host of matters which were now pressing. The new building was rapidly taking shape; not yet finished, nor yet free of scaffolding, it was still surrounded by the builders' fencing, but its distinctive character, its superb proportions and near severity of outline were already attracting attention. We shared the Principal's determination to 'make the new College an exciting and significant place, a place where it is a privilege to work, a place where the highest standards are sought after, a place where the only criterion is quality.'

Although academic considerations did not yet loom large, since the first months of the new College's life would be devoted to the completion of the founding institutions' still existing courses, the Steering Committee was faced by a task of considerable proportions if the right decisions were to be made and a sound basis for development established. With a concert hall, an opera theatre, recital room, library, lecture rooms, to say nothing of nearly one hundred teaching and practice rooms, even merely basic organisation raised complex questions of which the all-important matter of staffing was just one. Our meetings were numerous and lengthy, sometimes extending into the small hours; underlying those discussions, however serious and purposeful they were, was an inescapable sense of excitement. From any standpoint the creation of the first purpose-built conservatoire of music in the country could only be seen as an event of far-reaching significance. It was now coming very close.

John Manuell's decision to divide the College into six separate schools of study – Composition and Performance, Keyboard, Strings, Wind and Percussion, Vocal, Theory and Humanities – each enjoying a large measure of autonomy, was an imaginative departure from accepted practice. From the beginning, it proved to be highly successful, each student being admitted to his appropriate School which claimed his immediate allegiance and encouraged, at the earliest stage, a valuable community of spirit.

In September, 1972, my appointment as Head of the Keyboard School – it was the first of the six to come into existence – effectively dispelled any ideas which lingered still in my mind of a quiet retirement to the peace of a Cotswold village. That dream had been with me for quite some time. Now it was gone, and I saw it disappear without any regret. There were better things to do.

Before the College could open its doors, three months remained. For me they were occupied by a major concern of a purely practical nature. The work of the Keyboard School would embrace the study of Organ, Harpsichord, Piano and Accompaniment; it was obviously of the greatest importance that we should be adequately equipped instrumentally.

For the moment I had no worries about the Organ department. We were more than fortunate to have the magnificent Hradetsky which had been specially built in Austria, for the College, and was now nearing completion in the Concert Hall. There were also two tutorial organs to come from the founding institutions.

Pianos were a different matter; our requirements were enormous for in addition to those for the large number of teaching and practice studios, many others of the right type were needed throughout the building. The acquisition of no fewer than forty-eight new Steinway grands had been proposed at an earlier stage, but that, unfortunately, over-stretched the available financial resourcess; in the end, the purchase of half that number, together with some new uprights, was agreed. From the two older institutions there would be rather more than a hundred instruments, though included among them were quite a number which had already reached the end of their useful life. To assess their suitability and allocate both old and new pianos throughout the building was no mean task. Without the expert advice and assistance of John Hoffmann, a highly respected technician who had faithfully served the old College for a generation, and whose expertise was widely recognised, I would have found it impossible.

221

We considered it highly important that the training of potential performers should be sufficiently comprehensive to provide experience of playing on more than one make of instrument. In their future career they would find beyond doubt that concert pianos of different families offer a range of individual characteristics. For this reason the Recital Room was to be equipped with a Bösendorfer Imperial. In the middle of this whole exercise, which seemed to grow in complexity each day, I hurried off to the factory in Vienna to select it, returning just in time to attend a conference which the Principal had arranged at Giggleswick School. Those three days were of great value, for now the teaching and administrative staff of the old College and the Northern School came together for the first time. That was the start of a fundamental transformation which would not be accomplished overnight; the respective loyalties which we had all owed for years past were not to be abandoned lightly. It would take time, and if for the moment those present looked at each other a little warily, jealously guarding their heritage, that was not surprising. But even now new friendships were being formed and a first positive step towards a spirit of joint allegiance had been taken.

On a Monday morning, January 8th, 1973, quietly and unobtrusively, teaching at the Northern College began. (The Royal Charter was still to come). Ida Carroll was Dean of Management, the Dean of Studies was John Wray, who also took charge of Theory and Humanities; the Schools of Composition and Performance, Strings and Vocal Studies, were headed respectively by the Principal and Dean of Development, Cecil Aronowitz and Alexander Young. The creation of the School of Keyboard Studies could now begin in earnest. With some forty keyboard tutors from the earlier institutions, the department was large; for the time being its major task was to complete the previous courses on which our students were already embarked. As yet the new College had no students of its own. It was a somewhat complicated situation, which would continue for a year or so, for those older courses varied in structure and content, and they led, naturally, to different Diplomas.

222

Simultaneously, we continued in the Academic Board meetings to hammer out the details of RNCM's own four-year Diploma Course which was to be divided into two parts. The first two years were to be devoted to intensive application to the principal study together with a wide range of ancillary subjects; the pattern of Part Two would 'point towards that branch of the profession indicated by the student's aptitude'. We also set great store by the proposed award of a Performer's Laureate for 'composers and executants whose ability places them on the threshold of an international career.'

In the spring we came to the first of the annual series of auditions which were met by a vigorous response from aspiring candidates both from Britain and abroad. We set the standards high and the assessment procedures were thorough and penetrating. The outcome was a comparatively small intake, representing a success rate of some fifteen per cent, but we were reasonably confident that those who had been selected would reach the level of achievement which we had so clearly and firmly in mind. The advent of the new academic year would mark the start of a four-year period which would test the validity of our decisions and the soundness of all our planning.

In later years it was noticeable that quite a number of enquiries and applications came to us from the Far East. Among them was one from a young man in Hong Kong who made, very charmingly, the most astonishing claims. He was already one of the elect, apparently, perhaps the most brilliant young pianist in the world, certainly the best we would ever have! That was not all; he was also the world's greatest poet, comparing his own work with that of Shakespeare and one or two other writers of similar calibre in terms which were not at all to their advantage. His letter provided every reason for us to doubt his sanity. For all that, my reply was as courteous and as helpful as I could make it. This, he must have felt, merited some appreciation which he expressed by addressing his next letter to Mr C. Heavenlywell! Our correspondence bore no fruitful outcome but he kept in touch and wrote some time later to tell me that he had become a member of

MENSA, which he hastened to explain was an International Association of Geniuses.

In spite of all the general teething troubles, which were naturally to be expected, we rejoiced in the splendid facilities which the new building had to offer. The tutorial areas were on the top floor and in many of the studios of the Keyboard School there were two grand pianos. They were a little cramped, perhaps, but this was an invaluable, even essential, advantage for advanced teaching. It was mandatory for every student, whatever his discipline, to study the piano as a subsidiary instrument – the piano, after all, has a special place as the most versatile of all instruments – and for that we had ample room. The ground floor, with its Concert Hall, adjacent Opera Theatre, the Recital Room and the spacious foyer, was the public area, very soon to be crowded night after night by audiences who were drawn there by a sequence of varied events.

In the planning of the new curriculum we had never lost sight of the need for an emphasis on performance – by visiting artists, by members of our own community and by students at all stages of their development, either potential executants or teachers. On the one hand, the College had its role as an Arts Centre; on the other it was a centre for learning and could within that framework provide realistic opportunities for performing experience. We therefore established a progressive pattern of weekly internal concerts at lunchtime and in the late afternoon. The first of these provided a platform for those who had never before played in public. These were the nursery slopes where dangers unforeseen lay in wait for apprentice fingers. But these concerts were of great value both to the participants and their tutors. They led logically to a more demanding second stage to be followed in turn, when successful, by public appearances arranged by the College in association with external promoters. Overall, the scheme represented a comprehensive gradation of opportunity.

This emphasis on performance pervaded the life of the College; a year or so later it was extended still further by the organisation of London recitals. From 1975 onwards our most advanced students could be selected to appear

224

in that holy of holies, the Wigmore Hall or, if organists, in St George's, Hanover Square.

In seeking to establish an individual character and a sense of entity for the School of Keyboard Studies, I had a special interest in our young organists who in the future could be called upon to play a leading part in the musical life of their respective communities. Remembering my own student days and the situation as I had seen it in more recent years I had the impression that this particular study had often remained very much behind the scenes, attracting little general attention, its objectives unrecognised and its achievements unsung. It had never been possible, for instance, for organists to participate in internal concerts, simply because the instrument itself was unsuitably placed. This alone must have contributed in no small measure to a noticeable lack of integration within the life of a College.

Now at RNCM that problem no longer existed for there in the Concert Hall was the Hradetsky and in the Recital Room, somewhat later, a beautiful early English organ, the gift of a generous donor.

Bearing in mind their ultimate responsibilities, the training of these young organists would have to embrace not only a mastery of the instrument itself in its many forms, but a breadth of knowledge and experience in a variety of associated skills such as church music, choir training and conducting. We planned accordingly. Much of this had been done in the past, of course, but what was perhaps a new departure was the provision of a workshop. The organist needs a working knowledge of his instrument's structure, if only to be able to deal with an unwelcome cipher; the repeated dismantling and assembly of the old organ we placed in that extra room served to reveal at least some of its secrets and appealed especially to the more mechanically-minded.

As an added impetus to the tutorial work of the department, which was in excellent hands, I was extremely happy to succeed in persuading Gillian Weir to visit us at intervals for two or three days of seminars and individual teaching. With a busy schedule of engagements and frequent tours abroad, her time-table resembled the most complicated jigsaw puzzle; even so, she agreed. From the moment of her first arrival she has continued to capture the imagination of successive generations of organ students with her warmth and generous nature, her scholarship and unquestionable authority in so many aspects of the repertoire.

There were equally exciting developments in other directions. The inception of the fortnightly classes in Style and Interpretation under the direction of Sir William Glock, now retired after thirteen years as the BBC's Controller of Music, was a milestone in the life of the College. This was an important step, for there can be little doubt that in the performance of any work a genuine grasp of style persistently remains the most elusive feature. The organisation of these classes fell to me. They brought together selected students (in groups or individually) and they represented a valuable extension of work in other departments. Glock's erudition, insight and judgement, the products of his vast experience, have created a sphere of influence which has brought very many young performers to an increasing awareness and deeper understanding.

On one of the happy and often strenuous weekends spent with John and Renna Manduell at their home in the glorious countryside of North Yorkshire a fellow guest was the pianist, Vlado Perlemuter, whom I had not previously met, although I had known and admired his playing for many years.

The sun shone brilliantly on that Sunday afternoon as the three of us walked in the garden. We talked of many things, mostly musical, of course, and as always the College was uppermost in our minds. Out of that discussion there gradually emerged a project which was to be another landmark in the evolution of the School of Keyboard Studies. From his home in Paris, Perlemuter would be happy to come to Manchester two or three times a year to give master classes.

Naturally, I was overjoyed, for here was authority in another sphere and a precious link with the past. Throughout a distinguished career of very many years, Perlemuter's playing had commanded universal acclaim; in particular, he was intimately associated with the music of the French masters. Even as this thought crossed my mind he was recalling his lessons with Ravel, and the many hidden details of the composer's intention which he had had at first-hand and which were not to be found in the scores.

A few months later his first class was arranged for the day before a public recital he was to give in the Concert Hall of the College, playing amongst other works the B flat minor Sonata by Chopin. The students who had been selected to play in the preceding class had looked forward to the occasion with some eager excitement, but also with a degree of trepidation. After all, Perlemuter was an unknown quantity; how difficult would he be?

By coincidence, the first player presented the B flat minor Sonata! It must have been comforting to him to be told, before he began to play: "Now don't worry about the wrong notes. I'm going to play all those tomorrow!" An all-round sigh of relief from the large assembly of listeners was almost audible.

Perlemuter, always pale and fragile in appearance, was by nature kindly and sympathetic, ever ready to be helpful and with an innate understanding of the pianist's problems. But if he detected even a hint of carelessness his patience could be very limited; he would not and could not tolerate any suggestion of slipshod work. At such moments, and happily they were rare, his tone of voice, no long persuasive, would take on a harsher note, and when his comments were prefaced by a peremptory "Monsieur!" or "Mademoiselle!" it was easy to see that there were some uncomfortable moments lying ahead. He could also be gently roguish. Much later that same afternoon we came to the 'Miroirs' of Ravel. Tongue in cheek, Perlemuter turned to the apprehensive student who was to play the work. "Now," he said, "I'm going to be very fierce with you about this – because Ravel was very fierce with me!" As it turned out, there was no need for him to be fierce at all, for in that young player he found all the intelligent co-operation he could wish for.

The master classes were safely launched. In supplementing the sterling work of the resident tutors they have continued over the years to make a vital contribution to studies in piano repertoire.

Naturally enough, the training of accompanists occupied much of my thinking. It was immediately clear that the division of the Graduate Course into two parts offered an admirable framework. Following the first two years of what we hoped would be positive development in technique and musicianship there could be specialisation in the third and fourth for those whose skill, disposition and personality pointed in that direction. This was the broad basis of a scheme which would bring selected students at the appropriate time to concentration on a modified repertoire, leading to a growing mastery of ensemble, grasp of style, tonal blend and ability to share in the performance of a work clearly seen as a partnership – the duo-sonatas of Beethoven, for example, rather than the thirty-two solo sonatas. So it worked out.

The formidable extent of the accompanist's repertoire remained ever present and inescapable, but here at hand was ample scope for collaboration with the work of instrumental and vocal tutors. The opportunities of the *lieder* classes were invaluable and the general day-to-day activity of the College, including that of the Opera Unit for the oncoming *répétiteurs*, offered ever-widening experience. When the first four-year cycle came to an end it was heartening to see the first fully-fledged accompanists emerge from these studies.

To begin with there were not many students of the harpsichord. That was natural enough and it was not to be expected that they would ever be very numerous. Nevertheless, with the enterprise of Robert Elliott, my expert colleague of many years, we had high hopes for that aspect of our keyboard work. The day for specialised work in that field of early music was not far off and we were going to be well equipped. A first class Goble harpsichord and a spinet were already available, soon to be joined by one of Tom Goff's beautiful clavichords. We also looked forward to the restoration of a truly magnificent Schudi-Broadwood harpischord of 1792 which we had had the good fortune to inherit. There was some unavoidable delay before that could be done but the Schudi eventually took its place among the College's most treasured possessions to serve as an inspiration to a growing number of dedicated students.

One of our early initiatives in this specialist field was a master-class by the French harpsichordist, Huguette Dreyfus, whose elegant playing and captivating personality attracted a surprising measure of interest. The impact of her teaching paved the way for much of what was to come. Recitals and classes given later by the American, Alexander Kipnis, marked a further step forward, offering fresh impetus to those students who were by now revealing a special aptitude for the harpsichord. They would remain comparatively few in number, but for those who pursued a successful major study of the instrument and its repertoire, there could well be a significant place in tomorrow's musical world.

In all aspects of our keyboard studies we owed much to the external stimulus of our distinguished visitors. But much more was owed to the dedication of our permanent tutors who bore the heat and burden of the day, and withstood the pressures of continuing responsibility. Whilst the College as a whole was rapidly acquiring a corporate identity, the Keyboard School was becoming a family within a family. To have avoided altogether the stresses and strains inseparable from domesticity would have been too much to expect, but set against our shared objective of reaching the highest possible standards, they were of little significance. That the paths to that goal should vary so widely was not surprising. Musicians, first and foremost, are individualists who see the way for themselves. It did not really matter. What mattered much more was the growth of that community of spirit for which I had so earnestly hoped. It was more and more in evidence from day to day.

From the beginning the College has deeply appreciated the gracious support of its President, Her Royal Highness, the Duchess of Kent. Her close and detailed interest in every facet of the College's life, of which her frequent visits to Manchester are just one indication, has been a source of strength and immense encouragement. Each year we held our Congregation for the conferment of awards over which she presided with great warmth and dignity and in

1976 the Duchess herself accepted conferment as the first Companion of the College. These were great occasions, days to be remembered for a lifetime by those students who had successfully completed their course, and could now for the first time don the coveted cap and gown.

The conferment of the honorary award of Fellowship of the College, in recognition of distinguished service to our profession, also formed part of these ceremonies. In 1974 I was privileged to act as Presenter of the Principal. In preparing the citation I had a welcome opportunity to refer not only to his gifts as a composer and the impact of his influence in many musical fields, but also to the challenge of his new task. He had shown us the international role which the College could play and he had given us a glimpse of the future.

A year later I was honoured myself by admission to the Fellowship. In that exalted moment as the President took my hand I believed that there was nothing in the whole world which I could not do, if only I set my mind to it. That treacherous flight of imagination lasted some sixty seconds – and I could not even claim the foolishness of youth as an excuse for it.

Among the many state occasions graced by the presence of the Duchess, one of particular significance came in 1978 with the presentation of the Grant of Armorial Bearings. That colourful ceremony, which transported us briefly from the twentieth century to the Middle Ages, led us towards the unknown region of heraldic mysteries. Even if we fell short of complete understanding, when all was explained, we came away knowing at least that the shield, quartered in red and blue, symbolised a northern musical establishment and acknowledged the four areas on which it was based. We knew also that the crest specified the College's origin and the Royal title which Her Majesty the Queen had previously been graciously pleased to command. The motto was to be *Fovet musica omnes* – Music enriches everyone. That was aptly chosen, for nothing could have justified our purpose more precisely.

As I look back on those first six years in the history of the College I recapture the eager spirit of those intensely active days. An undercurrent of excitement to which none of us, it seemed, could be indifferent, easily outweighed the frustrations and disappointments inseparable from creative endeavour.

Beyond the scope of these reminiscences of mine, centred as they are on the area with which I had the closest concern, lies the story of the striking advances and impressive success in other departments. One day it will certainly be told.

I have the happiest memories. My visit to Israel in 1974 to attend the first Artur Rubinstein International Piano Master Competition ranks high among them. The opportunity of hearing some thirty or forty of the world's most promising young pianists, representing many countries, afforded a valuable indication of international standards. It left me with the impression that we could go ahead in Manchester with heart and mind, and without any sense of discouragement. In that year I witnessed the triumph of Emmanuel Ax, had the very great pleasure of a chat with Rubinstein, who remembered Manchester with much affection, and at the final reception was honoured to be presented to the President of the State of Israel, Ephraim Katzir. And to visit Jerusalem, the golden city quite unlike any other in the world, was an experience to be treasured.

Then in 1977, with the sponsorship of the British Council, a series of lectures on the training of accompanists coupled with a survey of contemporary British piano and vocal music, took me to Scandinavia. These were topics close to my heart and to be able to talk to the students of the conservatoires of Copenhagen, Stockholm, Oslo and Bergen was more than welcome. It was winter and bitterly cold, but that was quite offset by the warmth of interest and enthusiasm shown by those young people and the cordiality of many new friends. Our own music, I found, was much admired and respected in Scandinavia. But known and largely familiar as it was, its popularity could not match that of British football. In Bergen the local knowledge of every intimate detail relating to Manchester United was astonishing; in fact, I gathered that the televising of any football at all on a Saturday afternoon brought Norway virtually to a standstill.

By now I was coming very close to the end of my term of office. The date of my retirement had been deferred a number of times; at the end of the Summer term in 1978 it became a reality, marking the close of my official life in music. I viewed the prospect with some equanimity, well aware that musicians rarely fail to find some outlet for their energies. No doubt there would still be a contribution I could make, and it would be very pleasant to accept commitments from choice rather than necessity.

For the onward progress of the School of Keyboard Studies much remained to be done; that would always be the case. But I could claim, perhaps, that by now it had assumed a character and a spirit of its own. It was a going concern and I was delighted to know that its future would be guided by Robert Elliott who was to take my place. No decision could have given me greater confidence or satisfaction, for I knew that the bright hopes which had been mine were also his.

IN setting out to record some account of a life in music, my primary purpose has been to acknowledge the good things which that life has had to offer. I come to the end of the task with a deep sense of gratitude. There have been blessings in plenty, and much happiness, perhaps more than my share, has come my way. And I have learned to see happiness in its proper perspective and not to regard it as a constantly essential ingredient of life. I have no recriminations; the only regrets I feel are for my own inadequacies. I could well have done better if, from time to time, I had been less aware of them. Sorrows and misfortunes I have certainly known – they are the birthright of us all – but if those darker shadows have merited only passing reference in these pages, that in itself is a measure of their comparative unimportance.

Memories are precious; as one grows older there are fewer, alas, with whom they can be shared. They bring with them a temptation to live in the past, but that is a danger which I resist with might and main. For me the present is as quickening and alive as ever it was, and so I trust it will remain. I know nothing of that natural melancholy which is supposed to be the companion of old age. Let it never be said that only memories are left to those who look back. Nevertheless, to be able to relive and celebrate once again the events of yesterday is a freedom to be guarded and cherished in a world where, in the totalitarian states of today, the mind is circumscribed and the very act of forgetting is imposed.

We live now in a new world, a world very different from that of my youth. In my lifetime there have been more striking advances than history has ever recorded in the past. A new, undreamed-of technology lies at the heart of things, (and my current preoccupation with a recently acquired micro-computer indicates my determination not to be left behind!). In music, the impact of that technology has been tremendous – recording techniques, the means of reproduction and the use of the synthesiser – the list could go on. Even the career of the performer has been revolutionised. He can exercise his art in half a dozen different countries in the space of a week.

And what of the new music? Immersed as our composers are in ceaseless experiment, I cannot yet see that the way ahead is at all clear. At this stage, perhaps it is understandable that composers should be tempted to write for each other, leaving a wider audience behind. That phase will pass, and let us hope that ultimately the heart, as well as the cerebral artifice and electronic wizardry, will be a source of inspiration.

We are all inheritors; we cannot shed the past, nor should we wish to do so. The works of Bach, Beethoven and a hundred others immeasurably enrich our lives as they have for generations long gone, and as they will for generations to come. For the brief space of a lifetime, we have the privilege of that legacy, the right to rejoice in those treasures and to study their message. And when we, as mortals, are crumbled into dust, they will still be there. They do not die. They belong equally to the unborn, among whom will be those who will pass again and again through the portals of learning to encounter afresh the Forty-eight Preludes and Fugues, and to attempt, as we did, to unlock the secrets of Beethoven's visionary world.

233

We come – and we go; and for what lies beyond there is faith. But the pattern of life is clear and recognisable, even as it was to Homer so long ago: 'Even as are the generations of leaves, so are those of men; the wind scatters the leaves on the earth and the forest buds put forth more when the Spring comes round; so of the generations of men one puts forth and the other ceases.'